30 DAYS TO THE GRE

Rajiv N. Rimal, Ph.D.
and
Peter Z Orton, Ph.D.

Macmillan • USA

First Edition

Macmillan General Reference
A Simon & Schuster Macmillan Company
1633 Broadway
New York, NY 10019-6785

An Arco Book

Manufactured in the United States of America

10 9 8 7 6 5 4 3 2 1

ISBN: 0-02-861261-2

Design by: Rachael McBrearty

Introduction

This book is designed to help you master the GRE in 30 days. You will learn about important test strategies, and you will be introduced to dozens of specific verbal, math, and analytical strategies designed to make you a smart test-taker. You will also find two full-length tests in this book—tests that have been modeled after the real thing. To get the most out of this book, we suggest that you follow the *30-Day* program closely. Depending on your schedule and how quickly you work, you will need to set aside 30 to 60 minutes each day.

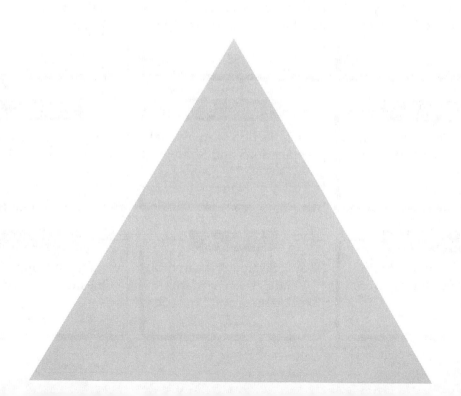

THE 30-DAY PROGRAM

About the Authors

Rajiv N. Rimal, Ph.D., and Peter Z Orton, Ph.D., have a combined twenty years experience teaching SAT preparation programs for the California State Universities. Together they wrote and produced "TEAM SAT," a multimedia, interactive CD-ROM program (Zelos Digital Learning) which was awarded the "Best of Show" prize at the International Interactive Computer Society's 1995 Summit Awards and the Gold Prize in Interactive Education at the 1995 CINDY Awards.

Dr. Rimal is an Assistant Professor of Speech Communication at Texas A&M University, where he writes, teaches, and conducts research on health and communication.

Dr. Orton is a producer of new media at Harvard Business School Publishing and co-author of fourteen test-preparation textbooks.

**Test Structure
and Strategies**

Day 1

Get to Know the GRE

Assignments for Today:

1. Learn the structure of the GRE.
2. Learn how the GRE is scored.
3. Call the schools you want to apply to.
4. Learn about the computerized version of the GRE.

THE STRUCTURE OF THE GRE

Sections of the Test

The GRE consists of six sections that count toward your score and one "equating section" that does not count toward your score. The sections are as follows:

1.	Math	30 minutes
2.	Math	30 minutes
3.	Verbal	30 minutes
4.	Verbal	30 minutes
5.	Analytical	30 minutes
6.	Analytical	30 minutes
7.	Equating section	30 minutes

NOTE: These seven sections can be in any order, not necessarily the one shown above.

The "equating section" can be a math section, a verbal section, or an analytical section. It is 30 minutes long, and it can come at any point in the test. The "equating section" is used by the testmakers to check their own test questions. However, you will not know which 30-minute section is the one that doesn't count toward your score.

During the time alloted for a section, you can work in only that section. You are not permitted to move from section to section, even if you finish a section before time is called. You can go to the next section only when told to do so, and you can never return to a previous section. But you can move around within the one section you are working in.

TYPES OF QUESTIONS ON THE TEST

Verbal (approximately 76 questions)

There are four types of verbal questions:

1. **Reading Comprehension:** Read a passage and answer questions.

   Total questions = 22

2. **Sentence Completion:** Read a sentence that has one or more blanks, and choose the word or words that fit the meaning of the sentence.

   Total questions = 14

3. **Analogy:** Figure out the relationship between two words, and select the choice that has the same relationship.

   Total questions = 18

4. **Antonym:** Find the word most opposite in meaning to the given word.

   Total questions = 22

Math (approximately 60 questions)

There are three types of math questions:

1. **Problem Solving:** Standard multiple-choice math questions, with five answer choices.

   Total questions = 20

2. **Quantitative Comparison:** Compare two quantities and determine which is greater, or if they are equal, or if there's no way to determine the relationship. Quantitative Comparison questions have only four answer choices.

   Total questions = 30

3. **Data Interpretation:** Answer questions based on a chart or charts given in the problem.

   Total questions = 10

Analytical (50 questions)

There are two types of analytical questions:

1. **Analytical Reasoning:** Given a set of fictional conditions, answer a group of questions.

   Total questions = 40

2. **Logical Reasoning:** Answer questions based on a short passage, usually a paragraph in length.

   Total questions = 10

SCORING OF THE GRE

You will get three separate scores, one for math, one for verbal, and one for the analytical section. Each score ranges from 200 (no questions answered correctly) to 800 (all, or nearly all, questions answered correctly). 500 is the "median" score, meaning that about half the students taking the test will score higher than 500, and half will score lower than 500.

You'll get your scores in the mail 4 to 6 weeks after you take the test.

CALL YOUR SCHOOLS

You probably have a number of schools that you want to apply to. Call them today and find out how much you need to score on the GRE to be admitted or to qualify for fellowships. Schools can often give you the average GRE scores of their incoming students. You can use this information to set your own personal GRE goals.

THE COMPUTERIZED VERSION OF THE GRE

As you probably know, you can now take the GRE on the computer. If you know for sure that you will be taking the traditional, paper-and-pencil version of the test, skip this section of this book. If you're not sure, or if you know for a fact that you will be taking your test on the computer, read this section carefully.

The computerized version of the test is different from the paper-and-pencil version in some very important ways. The question types will be the same: reading comprehension, antonyms, analogies, sentence completion, quantitative comparison, and so on. But the two tests are set up differently, and how they are scored is very different.

How the Test Is Set Up

On the paper-and-pencil test, if you are having trouble with any question, you can take a guess and come back to work on it later (as long as the time for that particular section hasn't run out). If you want to change an answer later, you can always do so. And if you want to do the questions in a section in a different order, that's up to you, too.

But on the computerized test, if you want to skip a question, you can't. If you want to change a previous answer, you can't. If you want to work the questions in a different order, you can't. You must register a final answer to each question in the order in which the questions are presented. Even if you're uncertain, you must register a final answer before you can see any other question.

What else is different? On the paper-and-pencil test, you can do your scratch work right on the test booklet, which is great because you can mark a diagram, highlight words, or cross out incorrect answer choices. But on the computerized test, you can't mark on any diagrams, unless you redraw them on the scratch paper that is provided. This obviously takes extra time and effort.

And you can't mark important words or cross out wrong choices, unless you write those on your scratch paper, which of course uses up still more precious time.

Another big difference is the order of the questions. On the paper-and-pencil test, in the verbal section, all the questions of one type are together, and the first ones are easy whereas the later ones get progressively more difficult. So on the paper-and-pencil test, you immediately know which questions are easy and which ones are tricky and require more thought. But on the computerized test, several different things happen.

First, say, on the verbal section, a few antonym questions are followed by some analogy questions, which are followed by a reading comprehension passage with a few questions, which is followed by a couple of sentence completion questions, which are followed by more antonym questions, and so on. So it's difficult to keep focused on the type of question that's being asked and the strategies that work for that particular question type. And the same mixed-up order is true for the other sections of the test—the math and analytical sections.

How the Test Is Scored

On the paper-and-pencil test, each of the questions is worth the same: You get the same amount of points for answering an easy question correctly as you do for a tough question. Your score is the number of questions you answer correctly. And there's no penalty for incorrect answers.

On the computerized test, your first question is of moderate difficulty. If you answer the question correctly, you will be given another question of equal or greater difficulty. If you answer it correctly, your score will start to grow. And the next question will be equal or greater in difficulty than the last. As you continue to answer questions correctly, the level of difficulty of each question will increase and so will your score. This happens with each section of the GRE: the math, verbal, and analytical sections.

But suppose you don't answer all the questions correctly? What happens then? If you answer the first question incorrectly, your score begins to decrease. And your next question will either be of equal or lesser difficulty than the previous question. If you answer it incorrectly, it will be followed by an easier question. But if you answer these easier questions correctly, your score doesn't rise as quickly as if you had answered a tough question correctly.

If you answer the easy questions correctly, the computer test eventually moves you back into more difficult questions. Eventually, the computer test will determine the level of difficulty where you have the most success, and assign you a score for that level. So the computer test is said to "adapt" to your highest level of difficulty and then assign you a score.

Advantages of the Computerized GRE

If you decide to take the computerized GRE, you'll have all the time you need before the test to practice and get comfortable using the computer. And you'll get to use as much scratch paper as you'll need.

Also, you can get your score immediately after you take the test, which is why many people take the computerized test. You may even have fewer questions than on the paper-and-pencil test.

Disadvantages of the Computerized GRE

The disadvantage of taking the computer GRE may far outweigh its advantages. These are the disadvantages:

> It costs you more.
>
> You can't skip questions.
>
> You can't mark on diagrams.
>
> You can't cross off incorrect choices.
>
> You can't mark reading passages.
>
> You have to scroll through the reading passages because you cannot see the entire passage at one time.

You won't be able to use the position of a question to determine whether that question is easy or difficult, and whether solving it will require a lot of thinking or just a little.

So the decision is yours. Our recommendation is that you take the computerized version of the GRE only if you have to—if you need your score right away and you don't have enough time to wait for the next paper-and-pencil test date.

Whichever version of the GRE you decide to take, good luck!

General Strategies

Assignment for Today:

Learn seven important test-taking strategies.

TEST STRATEGY 1.
Don't Get Stuck

The most important thing to know for your test is this: Don't get stuck. You're not expected to get all the questions right on the test. In fact, if you can answer just *half* the questions right, you'll get an above-average score! That means that when you hit a question that's a killer, just guess and move on.

Find the questions that you can do or have a shot at. For the others, just guess and move on. So remember:

- If a question's doable, work it. Circle the answer in your test booklet, and then darken the proper space on your answer sheet.

- As soon as you realize a question's a killer, put a question mark beside the question and fill in a guess answer.

- If a question will take a lot of time, even if you can do it, mark it, take a guess, and come back to it later if you have time.

TEST STRATEGY 2.
Zap the Losers

Do you know what the directions on your test say? They ask you to choose not the right answer, but the best answer. Why "best"? Because the "right" answer may not even be in the choices. So sometimes you've got to settle for the best of what they offer, and the best may not be great.

Suppose you read a passage, and it's all about how to improve your social life in college. One question might go something like this:

Which of the following is the most appropriate title for this passage?

Now you're thinking the title ought to be something like "How to improve a college social life," or "How college students can improve their social life," or "How a college social life can be improved," or some arrangement of those words.

But on the GRE, there's a good chance that none of these will be among the choices.

Let's look at the choices:

(A) Improving your high school social life
(B) Improving your social life in school
(C) Improving your test scores in college
(D) Improving quality of life in college
(E) How to publish in graduate school

Choice (A) has two key words wrong: high school. The passage was about the social life of college students, so the words "high school" make this choice off-topic and wrong. At this point, take your pencil and "zap (A)"—cross it off in your test booklet.

Now to choice (B). This says, "Improving your social life in school." For it to be perfect, it should read "Improving your social life in college." Just the word "school," by itself, is too general. But so far, it's better than choice (A), and it might be the best answer of all. So quickly draw a question mark and keep going.

Choice (C) is highly commendable, but off topic. Zap it.

Choice (D), "Improving the quality of life in college" is also not perfect. You'd like it to read "Improving the quality of social life in college." Here you have "college" but you don't have "social" life. So what do you do? It's too general, but it's possible, so consider it. Put a question mark beside it.

Choice (E) would certainly improve your college academic life, but it's off topic. Zap it!

So now you're down to two possible answers.

Compare choice (B) against choice (D) to find the better one, but even if you can't find the one winner, you've narrowed five choices down to just two, so take your best guess and move on.

Zapping wrong choices not only saves time, but also helps you get more questions right.

So remember: zap the losers and come out a winner.

TEST STRATEGY 3.
Always Guess

What if you can't do a problem? Should you leave it blank, or should you take a guess? There is no penalty on the GRE for wrong answers, so the golden rule is: Never leave an answer blank. Even if you don't have any clue about the problem, take a guess. That way you have at least some chance of getting credit.

And if you can knock out even one answer choice and guess from the other choices, you'll have a better chance of getting a question right. So at least take a guess. Never leave a blank.

Here's another reason why you should not leave a question unanswered. If you skip questions and leave blanks on your answer sheet, there's a chance that you'll darken the wrong answer spaces. Keeping track of where the answers go is a headache. And it's confusing. But if you fill in an answer for every question, even with guess answers, you won't make this serious error. And you can always erase an answer if you need to.

TEST STRATEGY 4.
Answer What's Asked

One way people lose points on the GRE is that they know how to work a problem, but they don't read the question correctly. This should never happen to you. Take a look at this question.

If $3n - 7 = 2$, what is $5n$?

(A) 3
(B) 6
(C) 9
(D) 12
(E) 15

You might answer this question this way:

$$3n = 2 + 7$$
$$3n = 9$$
$$n = \frac{9}{3}$$
$$n = 3$$

At this point, you might think (A) is your answer, because *n* equals 3. But the answer is NOT 3 because the question asks for the value of $5n$, not *n*. You have to take the value of *n* (3) and multiply by 5 to get choice (E), 15.

This might look simple enough, but imagine you're taking your test. You're under time pressure, you've been working for several hours under severe stress, your concentration's starting to flag, and the person sitting behind you is tapping his pencil and sniffling.

Under such conditions it's easy to misread the question and answer the wrong thing. So what can you do?

Here's something that can help.

As you read a problem, identify what you finally have to solve for, and circle it! Circling helps you focus on your final goal. And it helps you avoid the common misreading errors built into the test.

You should also use this circling strategy on the reading questions of your test. What would you circle in this typical reading question: "With which of the following would the author disagree?"

"Disagree" or "author disagree" is really the heart of the question. You're looking for an answer that's *opposite* to the author's point of view. If you circle "author disagree," you will avoid misreading the question.

Circling your "goal" is a super strategy to make sure you answer what's asked. The worst thing to happen on your test is to know how to work a problem, spend time working it, and yet get it wrong because you answered the wrong thing. Circling your "goal" helps you get those questions right.

TEST STRATEGY 5.
Know Where the Question Lives

Most question sets on the test start easy and get harder. Why is this important to know? And how can it help you?

The first few questions in each set are very easy, almost obvious, and the rest are of medium difficulty, except for the last two or three which are very difficult, if not downright tricky.

So what do you do? On the first few questions, you're probably safe choosing the obvious answer. But on a question near the end, you should be wary of the fast answer because it is probably wrong.

Here's how this works. Suppose the last math question in a section goes like this:

On a thermometer, R is 7 degrees away from P, and P is at 5 degrees. What is the reading at R?

(A) $12°$

(B) $7°$

(C) $-2°$

(D) $-2°$ or $12°$

(E) None of these

Remember, this is a question at the end of the math section. So what is the correct answer?

The fast answer here is (A), $12°$. But (A) is only partially correct. Yes, R could be at $12°$, since 12 is 7 degrees higher than 5. But what if R is 7 degrees lower than P? R could be at either 12 degrees or -2 degrees. So the more thoughtful—and correct—answer is (D).

Use this strategy on all math questions and on the sentence completion and analogy questions. The first few of each will be easy, and the last few will be very tricky.

But don't use this strategy for the reading questions, because these questions are scrambled in difficulty.

Remember, knowing where questions live can be important to you when you take the test.

TEST STRATEGY 6.
Know the I-II-III Strategy

A few questions on your test may use Roman numerals. These questions look something like this:

XXXXXXXXXXXX XXXXXXXXXXXXXXX
XXXXX XXXXXXX XXXXXXX XXXXXXXX
XXXXX XXXXXXXXXXX XXXXXXXXX?

   I. XXXXX

  II. XXXXX

 III. XXXXX

(A) I only

(B) II only

(C) III only

(D) I and II only

(E) I, II, and III

Believe it or not, these are easier than the regular questions—the ones without Roman numerals. Let's look at an example.

Sal, Pat and Chris run in a race with ten other people. Sal finished somewhere ahead of Chris. Which of the following must be true?

  I. Sal did not finish in last place.

  II. Chris finished in first place.

  III. Pat finished in second place.

(A) I only

(B) II only

(C) III only

(D) I & II only

(E) I, II, & III

Which do you think is the right answer? The question asks "what is true?" We know that Sal finished somewhere ahead of Chris. So let's see which of the Roman numerals are true.

Since Sal finished ahead of Chris, Roman numeral I is true: Sal did not finish in last place. This tells you that the correct answer has to have numeral I in it. At this point, you can knock out choices (B) and (C) because they do not include numeral I. With your pencil, strike out (B) and (C).

Now numeral II: Chris finished in first place. Since Sal finished ahead of Chris, we know Chris could not have finished first. This Roman numeral is false. So you should take your pencil and strike out all remaining answer choices that include numeral II. This means you can knock out choices (D) and (E).

Immediately you can see that only one choice remains—choice (A)—and so that has to be the right answer. Notice that you didn't even have to try the third Roman numeral. You will not always be this lucky, but you can see how this strategy helps you beat the test.

TEST STRATEGY 7.
Don't Read the Directions

Here's a quick tip that will save you time, and because it saves you time it will help you get a few more questions right: Do not waste time reading directions on your test. The more time you spend reading the directions, the less time you have to answer questions. So what should you do? Work through this program. By the time you finish, you'll know the directions for every question type inside and out. And you'll also know which strategies and tips to use for which questions.

So when your test day comes and the proctor says open your test booklet and begin section one, you can go directly to the questions because you will already know the directions.

Here's a quick list of question types for your review:

Verbal Section

1. Reading comprehension—Read the passage and answer questions based on what's stated or implied in the passage.

2. Sentence completion—Select the word or words that best complete the sentence from the list of choices.

3. Analogies—Find the relationship between the two words in the question and look for the answer choice that has the same relationship.

4. Antonyms—Find the word that is most opposite in meaning to the given word.

Math Section

1. Problem solving—Solve the problem and find the answer from among the five choices given.

2. Quantitative comparison—Compare the two columns and choose:

    (A) if Column A is greater than Column B

    (B) if Column B is greater than Column A

(C) if Column A is equal to Column B

(D) if the relationship cannot be determined based on the information given.

Do not choose (E). There is no such choice in this question type.

3. Data interpretation—Answer questions based on one or more charts given in the problem.

Analytical Section

1. Analytical reasoning—Read a fictional scenario, then answer questions based on it (the questions come in groups of three or more).

2. Logical reasoning—Read a short passage, then answer the question asked.

Instant Replay: Test Strategies

1. Don't get stuck.

2. Zap the losers.

3. Always guess.

4. Answer what's asked.

5. Know where the question lives.

6. Know the I-II-III strategy.

7. Don't read the directions.

Day 3

Verbal Strategies: Reading and Analogies

Assignments for Today:

1. Learn reading comprehension strategies and question types.
2. Learn analogy strategies and question types.

READING COMPREHENSION QUESTIONS

The reading part of the verbal section takes a lot of time. You've got to read some long passages and answer questions based on them. It's best to leave the reading questions for the end of that section.

What else should you know about the reading parts? Here are some good tips.

READING STRATEGY 1.

Read the Interesting Passages First

One passage may be more interesting to you. If so, start with the one you find more interesting. You will have a better chance of getting more questions right. But if you read passages out of order, be sure to put your answers in the right places on your answer sheet.

READING STRATEGY 2.

Use Only What You Read

The reading questions test only what's *in* the passage, so don't bring in any outside information. Use only what's stated or implied in the passage, even if you know a lot about the topic.

READING STRATEGY 3.

Let the Paragraphs Help

A reading passage can seem really long. But the author has already broken it down for you into manageable pieces—the paragraphs. Don't try to rush through from the first word to the last word. That's not the best way to read. Instead, read paragraph by paragraph. After reading the first paragraph, take a quick mental breath and think to yourself, "What, briefly, was that paragraph about?" Then read the next paragraph and do that again. And then do the same for the one after that. When you finish the passage, what have you done? You've summarized all the important ideas in the passage.

READING STRATEGY 4.
Read and Mark

Use your pencil and mark the passage as you read. If you think something's important, circle it. If something's unusual or troublesome, mark that too. But don't mark so much that you can't find anything. And don't let your marking slow you down. Keep moving ahead, like a shark.

READING STRATEGY 5.
Make a Movie in Your Head

What if you're reading a passage and nothing is sinking in? The clock's ticking and you have no idea of what you just read. This happens to all of us. If it happens to you, the best thing to do is to "make a movie" in your head. Believe it or not, you understand better if you visualize what you read. Don't memorize, just visualize. As you read the passage, form interesting pictures in your head.

READING STRATEGY 6.
Know the Different Types of Reading Questions

Here are the most common types of reading questions. Familiarize yourself with these question types so that when you see them on the test, you'll know what they are asking you to do.

Type 1: Main Idea

For each passage you'll be asked to determine the main idea. Sometimes the question says just that: "What is the main idea of the passage?" Or it can use other words, such as, "What is the most appropriate title of the passage?" or, "What is the author's central argument?" or, "The passage is primarily concerned with the subject of . . ." Each of these questions asks the same thing: What is the main theme of the passage? The correct answer to a "main idea" question isn't necessarily found in the first

sentence or the last. These may, or may not, express the "main idea." But the main idea is *always* a theme that runs through most, if not all, of the paragraphs.

Type 2: Vocabulary

Some questions ask you to define words or phrases from the passage. To do this, you'll have to look back to where the word or phrase was used and see what it means as it's used in that particular sentence. For example, the question might say, "The word 'estate' in line 46 most nearly means . . ." Depending on the sentence, "estate" could mean someone's property, someone's status, a piece of land, or even an inheritance. To figure out which sense is meant, start from a little before line 46, and read through that line and past it. You'll then have a handle on what the author meant by that term. Then answer the question.

Type 3: Specific Information

Some questions ask about specific information from the passage. For example, the question might say, "The passage mentions which of the following as important to the success of a feature film?" or, "The author discusses the hobbies of which Presidents?" or, "The incident in lines 21–35 describes which of the following?" If you can answer these from what you remember having read in the passage, great! Otherwise, simply go back to the paragraph, find that part, and re-read enough to find the answer.

Type 4: Author's Point-of-View

Another type of question asks you to determine the author's tone or point of view. For example, the question might say, "The author's attitude toward large dogs is . . .," or, "The author believes strongly that . . .," or, "The author would most likely agree with which of the following?" As you read, small details should help you become aware of how the author of the passage feels about the topic presented. Is the author in favor . . . or opposed . . . or neutral . . . or sarcastic . . . or doubtful . . . or excited?

Type 5: Reasoning

And finally, questions also ask you to apply or interpret what you just read. For example, the question might say, "The author most likely describes the traffic on the highway in order to . . . ," or, "The reference to loud chewing is inappropriate as an argument for gum control because . . . ," or, "The description of George Washington's cow serves to . . . ." Reasoning questions are usually the toughest because the answers won't be stated directly in the passage. You have to read beneath the surface. But you still can't bring in your own information. You can use only what the author implies. It's tough, but with practice you can do it.

ANALOGY QUESTIONS

Another of the verbal question types on your test is analogies. Analogies look like this:

STEM:WORDS::

(A) first pair

(B) second pair

(C) third pair

(D) fourth pair

(E) fifth pair

ANALOGY STRATEGY 1.
Figure Out the Relationship Between the Stem Words

The analogy questions on your test follow a simple rule. First you find the relationship between the stem words, and then you find that same relationship in one of the choices. Let's try one.

SKYSCRAPER:SHACK::

(A) elevator:escalator

(B) house:building

(C) village:town

(D) jetliner:biplane

(E) chimney:fireplace

The stem words are *skyscraper* and *shack*. What's the relationship between skyscraper and shack? A skyscraper is a large, modern structure. A shack is a small structure. So the relationship is: the first word is a large, modern version of the second word.

ANALOGY STRATEGY 2.
Find the Same Relationship Between the Words in One of the Answer Choices

Once you know how the stem words are related, your next job is to find the one answer choice that best matches this relationship. Let's try the answer choices above one at a time.

Choice (A): Is the first word, *elevator*, a large, modern version of the second word, *escalator*? Obviously not. So knock this choice out.

Choice (B): Is a *house* a large, modern version of a *building*? Not at all. So cross out this choice.

Choice (C): Is a *village* a large, modern version of a *town*? Of course not. So eliminate this choice.

Choice (D): Is a *jetliner* a large, modern version of a *biplane*? Yes. A jetliner is a large, modern aircraft. A biplane is one of those small double-wing planes with two seats. So the relationship in this choice matches the relationship of the stem words. The first word is a large, modern version of the second word. Looks like you have a winner. Mark it, but let's look at the remaining choice, just in case.

Choice (E): Is a *chimney* a large, modern version of a *fireplace*? Well, a chimney is a part of a fireplace, not a modern version of it. Even though this choice has something to do with buildings, its relationship doesn't match, so knock it out.

Did you notice something? The stem words are about buildings, but the correct answer has nothing to do with buildings. You're looking for same relationships, not same categories. The first word was a-modern-and-big "whatever the second word was."

ANALOGY STRATEGY 3.
Consider Starting with the Second Stem Word

Sometimes it's easier to define the relationship between the stem words if you start with the second word in the pair instead of the first one. Let's look at another analogy question to see how this strategy works.

SPORT:SOCCER::

(A) fish:river

(B) volleyball:net

(C) field:fun

(D) stadium:game

(E) literature:sonnet

Here it's easier to say, "Soccer is a kind of sport." The second word is a specific type of the first word. Can you find the choice where the second word is a specific type of the first word?

The correct answer is choice (E). A sonnet is a type of literature. Remember: Whatever order you choose to use in the stem words must be the same order you use in the choices.

ANALOGY STRATEGY 4.
Use the Answer Choices to Determine the Part of Speech of the Stem Words

Sometimes you need to know the part of speech of the stem words in order to determine their meaning and figure out how they are related. For example, suppose you have this question:

SPRING:RAIN::

(A) suitor:gifts

(B) pollen:bee

(C) farm:tractor

(D) automobile:traffic

(E) requirement:limitation

The stem words are puzzling. Is *spring* the action verb meaning *jump* or *bounce*? Or is spring a *thing*, the noun that means the season? Or is it the noun that means the coiled piece of metal that you find in mattresses and watches? One way to find out is to look at the answer choices. Are the first words in the answer choices verbs or nouns?

Farm can be either a verb or a noun, but the other first words are nouns. So from that you know that all the first words are nouns, including *spring* and *farm*. We don't know what the second words are yet. But now that you know the stem word *spring* is a noun—not the verb that means to jump—can you find the answer to this question?

Choice (A) is the right answer. Spring, the season, brings rain, in the same way that a suitor brings gifts.

Questions like that one can be tricky if a word has more than one meaning. If you try one meaning and have no luck, try another meaning and see if that one works. But once you know a word is, say, a noun, try only different *noun* meanings, not meanings of verbs or adjectives.

ANALOGY STRATEGY 5.
Make Sure You Know the Most Common Analogy Relationships

Here are the 11 most common GRE analogy relationships:

1. Type of.

SOCCER:SPORT:: You saw one like this before, remember? Soccer is a type of sport. Here's another example: JAYWALK:MISDEMEANOR:: Jaywalk is a type of misdemeanor, or minor crime.

2. Definition.

PROCRASTINATOR:DELAY:: A procrastinator is someone who delays. Or you could say that delay is what a procrastinator does. Whatever order you use for the stem words is the order you must use for each of the choices.

3. Opposites.

STARVATION:BINGING:: Starvation is the opposite of binging.

4. Lack of.

PAUPER:MONEY:: A pauper lacks money. The first word lacks the second word.

5. Same.

PERSUASIVE:CONVINCING:: Someone who is persuasive is also convincing; the two words are synonyms.

6. Extremes.

HOT:SCALDING:: The second word is the extreme of the first word.

7. Part-to-whole.

PLATOON:SOLDIER:: The second word is part of the first word.

8. Use.

GILLS:BREATHING:: Gills are used for breathing. The first word is used for the purpose of the second word.

9. Place.

DESERT:OASIS:: The second word is located in the first word.

10. Sign of.

SNARL:ANGER:: The first word is a sign of the second word.

11. Job-related pairs.

Analogies that have to do with jobs or work also appear on your test. For example:

  a) SURGERY:INCISION:: An incision is performed in surgery. The second word is something that is done during the first word.

  b) SCALPEL:SURGERY:: A scalpel—which is a doctor's cutting tool—is used in surgery. The first word is a tool used for doing the second word.

  c) CONSTRUCTION:CARPENTER:: The second word is someone who performs the first word.

ANALOGY STRATEGY 6.
Practice With Lots of Analogy Questions

The best thing you can do to improve your analogy score is to practice answering analogy questions. That way, you can learn the many types of analogies, practice using the strategies, and learn meanings of new words. There are many analogy questions in this book. Make sure you do them all.

Instant Replay: Reading Comprehension and Analogies

Reading Comprehension

1. Read the interesting passages first.

2. Use only what you read.

3. Let the paragraphs help.

4. Read and mark.

5. Make a movie in your head.

6. Know the different types of reading questions.

Analogies

1. Figure out the relationship between the stem words.

2. Find the same relationship in one of the answer pairs.

3. Consider starting with the second stem word.

4. Use the answer choices to determine the part of speech of the stem word.

5. Make sure you know the most common analogy relationships.

6. Practice with lots of analogy questions.

Verbal Strategies: Sentence Completion and Antonyms

Assignments for Today:

1. Learn important sentence completion strategies.
2. Learn important antonym strategies.

SENTENCE COMPLETION QUESTIONS

In this section of your test, all you do is fill in the blanks. But, you've got to find the choice that makes the most sense. Here's an example.

Although my uncle is usually a generous person, yesterday he gave _____ to a woman soliciting for a popular charity.

(A) money
(B) advice
(C) thanks
(D) nothing
(E) food

SENTENCE COMPLETION STRATEGY 1.
Use Your Own Word

What word best fits the blank in the sentence above? The correct answer is choice (D), *nothing*. Although my uncle is usually a generous person, yesterday he gave *nothing* to a woman soliciting for a popular charity.

Were you able to guess what word fit the blank even before looking at the choices? If you could, that was a great way to answer the question. But that's something you can do only on the easiest sentence completion questions. So here's another strategy you can try.

SENTENCE COMPLETION STRATEGY 2.
Look for Flag Words

Certain words—called flag words—give important information about the direction of a sentence. For example, here the flag word is "although," because "although" changed the direction of the sentence. "*Although* my uncle is usually a generous person, yesterday he gave *nothing* . . . " The first part of the sentence describes the guy as generous. But in the the second part he isn't generous at all. The word, "although" reversed the direction of the sentence, signaling that the correct completion will be the opposite of *generous*.

Now suppose instead of *although*, the flag word is "since." Now try completing the sentence . . . *Since* my uncle is usually a generous person,

19

yesterday he gave _____ to a woman soliciting for a popular charity. Now the word "money" fits.

The word "since" continues the direction of the sentence. The first part says that uncle is generous, and the second part continues that thought. "*Since my uncle is usually a generous person, yesterday he gave money to a woman soliciting for a popular charity.*"

So there are two kinds of flags:

- **Opposite flags.** These are words and phrases that reverse the direction of a sentence Opposite flags include: *although, despite, but, even though, instead of, nevertheless, contrary to, rather than, in spite of,* and *however*.

- **Same flags.** These are words that continue the direction of a sentence. Same flags include words like *since, thus, therefore, as, hence, because, for, for instance, and, moreover, so, due to,* and, check this out, a semicolon (;), which also continues the thought of the sentence.

Let's look at this example:

Julia had spent the entire previous week studying; on her final examination, she encountered _____ difficulties.

(A) myriad

(B) frequent

(C) formidable

(D) few

(E) remarkable

This sentence contains a semicolon, which is a same flag. It continues the same feeling or thought throughout the entire sentence. In the first part of the sentence, you learned that Julia spent quite some time studying and so the idea is that she's preparing well for the test. Now continue this thought. She was prepared, so what did she encounter on the test? *Lots* of difficulty? No. Continue the thought: Julia will find almost *no* difficulty on the test. The choice that gives that meaning is "few."

SENTENCE COMPLETION STRATEGY 3.
Try the Second Blank First

Quite a few GRE sentence completion questions have two blanks instead of one. Sometimes the second blank is easier to fill in than the first blank. Look at this example:

Even though he had not eaten all day and had ____ money in his pocket, David ____ the offer of a free meal.

(A) considerable..refused

(B) various..accepted

(C) extra..renegotiated

(D) little..declined

(E) enough..applauded

The flag words "even though" tell you that the direction of the sentence will reverse. The first part of the sentence tells you that David hasn't eaten all day so he must be hungry. The flags "even though" tell you that in the second part of the sentence David will do the opposite of what his hunger would cause him to do. The two choices that work for the second blank are (A) refused, and (D) declined. So knock out choices (B), (C) and (E). Now try each of the remaining choices.

First try (A). "Even though he had not eaten all day and had considerable money in his pocket, David refused the offer of a free meal." The second blank works fine, but the first word, "considerable," doesn't make much sense. Remember that the flag "even though" tells you that the direction should change. If David had considerable money, he *could* refuse a free meal—nothing surprising about that. There's no change of direction.

So try choice (D). "Even though he had not eaten all day and had little money in his pocket, David declined the offer of a free meal." The second blank works as before, but now the first blank also works. Even though he had little money and was hungry, David said "no" to a free meal. With little money we would have expected him to jump at the chance for a free meal. But the flag words "even though" told you that the direction of the sentence will reverse and the opposite will happen. And so it did!

SENTENCE COMPLETION STRATEGY 4.
Try All the Choices

In the question above, you had to read only two choices to find the winner. But for some questions you may have to read all five choices. That happens when there are no flag words, or when the sentence is very long, or when it's just plain tough. Here is an example:

> The team members had few, if any, _____ about postponing those long, arduous practice sessions that tended only to deflate their enthusiasm, _____ their coach's frustration at their inconsistent execution.
>
> (A) desires..undermining
> (B) misgivings..increasing
> (C) hesitations..embracing
> (D) qualifications..ceasing
> (E) ideas..reducing

It's hard to tell what's going on. On your test it may be better to come back to a question like this and do it at the end, since it's probably going to take a lot of time. But when you do come back to it, try reading in each choice to see which makes the most sense.

Let's try choice (A): "The team members had few, if any, *desires* about postponing those long, arduous practice sessions that tended only to deflate their enthusiasm, *undermining* their coach's frustration . . . ." Long practice sessions that deflate enthusiasm wouldn't *undermine* (or lessen) their coach's frustration; they would increase it. Forget this choice.

Choice (B): "The team members had few, if any, *misgivings* about postponing those long, arduous practice sessions that tended only to deflate their enthusiasm, *increasing* their coach's frustration at their inconsistent execution." This works. The team had no problem with postponing the dreaded practices,

and these practices not only deflated the team's enthusiasm but also increased their coach's frustration at the team's lousy work. This is a winner, so mark it.

But try the others, just in case one of them is better than (B). Choice (C): "The team members had few if any *hesitations* about postponing those long, arduous practice sessions that tended only to deflate their enthusiasm, *embracing* their coach's frustration at their inconsistent execution." "Embracing their coach's frustration" doesn't make much sense in the context of this sentence, and besides, it's not anywhere as good as (B). Strike it and keep going.

Choice (D): "The team members had few if any *qualifications* about postponing those long, arduous practice sessions that tended only to deflate their enthusiasm, *ceasing* their coach's frustration at their inconsistent execution." Here, too, the last phrase, "ceasing their coach's frustration" just doesn't make sense in this sentence. Strike this one and check the last one.

Choice (E): "The team members had few if any *ideas* about postponing those long, arduous practice sessions that tended only to deflate their enthusiasm, *reducing* their coach's frustration at their inconsistent execution." This also doesn't make much sense with the entire sentence. The team had no ideas about postponing a practice, and the tough practice reduced the coach's frustration at the team's lousy play? It just doesn't fit right. And certainly it doesn't make the kind of sense that choice (B) does.

Reading in each choice and checking for its meaning is time-consuming. But it's a last-ditch strategy that you'll probably need to use from time to time.

SENTENCE COMPLETION STRATEGY 5.
Read in Your Answer Choice

Even if you don't read all the answer choices into the original sentence, you should at least read in the one you picked as the correct answer. That will help you make sure it fits in the meaning of the sentence.

ANTONYM QUESTIONS

The antonym questions in the verbal section test your vocabulary. You have to know the meaning of a word, and then select the choice that's *opposite* in meaning to that word. Here's an easy example:

ROUGH:

    (A) large

    (B) round

    (C) smooth

    (D) reliable

    (E) friendly

ANTONYM STRATEGY 1.
Define the Word

The first strategy for attacking antonym questions is to read the stem word (the word in capital letters at the top) and define that word. Do your best to determine its meaning. In this case, you probably have a picture in your mind of "rough" being something that's jagged, bumpy, or bristly.

ANTONYM STRATEGY 2.
Come up with Your Own Opposite Word

Once you have defined the stem word, think of a word that you consider to be its opposite. In the case of *rough*, you might think of the word *smooth* as its opposite. Now look for your word among the answer choices. If it's there, that's great—you've solved the problem. If it's not, your word will give you a clue to the kind of word you're looking for. In the case of *rough*, if *smooth* isn't among the answer choices, you know you're looking for a word like *smooth* that's also an opposite of *rough*. Looking at the answers, one of the choices might be *sleek*. *Sleek* means the same as *smooth* and is another opposite of *rough*, so it is the correct answer.

If the antonym questions on the GRE were this easy, then these two strategies—define the stem word and then come up with your own opposite— would be all you'd need. Unfortunately, all the questions aren't this easy, which is why you'll need more strategies.

ANTONYM STRATEGY 3.
Put the Word in Context

Sometimes when you're faced with a difficult stem word in an antonym question, you'll realize you've heard the word used before but you can't pin down its exact definition. But if you can place the word in a familiar phrase or sentence, you can help yourself remember what it means and choose the correct answer. For example, consider the following antonym question:

VETO:

    (A) refuse

    (B) reject

    (C) disengage

    (D) allow

    (E) vote

You've no doubt heard the word *veto* before, but you may have trouble defining it precisely. Do you remember how you heard it used? Perhaps you heard a news report that "the president vetoed the bill." What does that mean? It means that the president cancelled the bill and stopped it from becoming law. Now what's the opposite of *stop*? That's right, *allow*.

What we've just done was to put the stem word "in context."

Whenever you can't immediately pinpoint the stem word's meaning, try putting it in context.

ANTONYM STRATEGY 4.
Identify the Word's Emotional Charge

Sometimes you won't know the exact definition of the stem word of an antonym question, and you won't be able to use it in any particular context. But even if you don't know the word's exact meaning, you may have a good sense of its "emotional charge." What's an emotional charge?

Many words will have either a positive or negative feeling to them. Take this word: *virulent*. How does it sound to you? Positive or negative? *Virulent* means poisonous or deadly. But even if you didn't know its exact meaning, if you felt it sounded negatively charged, you could look for its opposite—a positively charged word—as the correct answer.

Let's look at the choices.

VIRULENT:

(A) deadly

(B) malignant

(C) benign

(D) bacterial

(E) yellow

Choices (A) and (B) are extremely negative. In fact, these are good definitions of the word *virulent*. Since you are looking for an opposite, something positive, eliminate (A) and (B). Choice (C) looks possible. *Benign* means gentle or kind. Since it's positive, you should consider it. Choice (D), *bacterial*, sounds like bacteria, which feels negative. Eliminate it. Finally, choice (E) is neutral. Since you're looking for a positive word, eliminate it. Even if you didn't know the meaning of the word *virulent*, you could have used its negative emotional charge to help you select its opposite, a positive word.

ANTONYM STRATEGY 5.
Look for Clues in Word Parts

Word roots, prefixes, and suffixes can offer important clues to help you solve GRE antonym questions. Let's look at an example. Suppose an antonym question looked like this:

MORIBUND:

(A) contentious

(B) malignant

(C) pretentious

(D) detestable

(E) vital

You may not know the meaning of the word *moribund*, but you may know that the word part *mor-*

signifies death, as in the word *mortal*. So its opposite would be a word that in some way signifies life or good health. The correct answer is choice (E), *vital*.

Whereas memorizing extensive word lists is probably a waste of time, knowing prefixes, suffixes and roots can be extremely helpful for this question type.

As you practice the many antonymn questions in the test section of this book, pay careful attention to prefixes, suffixes and roots, and learn them as you work problems. You will probably see them again when you take the real exam.

ANTONYM STRATEGY 6.
Look for Clues in Parts of Speech

Sometimes an antonym question will be difficult because you aren't certain which of the several meanings of the stem word is meant. For example, you might see this question:

FREQUENT

(A) mean

(B) content

(C) disturb

(D) evade

(E) reserve

Frequent has several meanings depending on its part of speech. As a verb, *to frequent* means *to visit*. "I used to frequent the casino until I lost all my money." But as an adjective, *frequent* means many or repeated. "The hospital made frequent requests for blood." Which meaning works in this question—the verb or the adjective?

One way to find out is to look at the answer choices. Each antonym question will use only one part of speech. That means that if the stem word is a verb, all the choices in that question are verbs. If the stem word is a noun, all the choices in that question are nouns.

So you can sometimes get a big hint by checking the part of speech of the answer choices. In the question above, choices (A) and (B) can be both verbs and adjectives, so they aren't much help. But choices (C), *disturb*, and (D), *evade*, can be only verbs—so all the choices must therefore be considered as verbs, and the stem word too must be a verb. Now you know that the stem word is the verb *to frequent*, meaning to visit. And you can solve the problem by choosing the opposite of *to frequent*, which is choice (D), *evade*.

So remember, knowing parts of speech can be extremely helpful when you're working antonym questions.

ANTONYM STRATEGY 7.
Consider Alternate Meanings

Difficult analogy questions sometimes use a stem word that has several meanings, all of which are the same part of speech. For instance, try this one:

ORDER:

(A) menu

(B) list

(C) chaos

(D) summons

(E) paper

Notice that choice (A), *menu*, can only be a noun, so the stem word *order* must also be a noun. But even just as a noun, *order* has many meanings. If you think of it as the command, as in "The general gave an order to the troops," you won't find an opposite. So what is another definition for *order*, besides command, that's also a noun?

You might come up with *pattern, organization*, or even *calm*. Now look through the choices. Choice (C), *chaos*, is the opposite of *pattern, organization*, and *calm*. It's the correct choice.

So another important strategy is to remember that many words have multiple meanings, and to consider other meanings if your first definition doesn't work.

Instant Replay: Sentence Completions and Antonyms

Sentence Completions

1. Use your own word.

2. Look for flag words.

3. Try the second blank first.

4. Try all the choices.

5. Read in your answer choice.

Antonyms

1. Define the word.

2. Come up with your own opposite word.

3. Put the word in context.

4. Identify the word's emotional charge.

5. Look for clues in word parts.

6. Look for clues in parts of speech.

7. Consider alternate meanings.

Day 5

Math Strategies: Problem Solving

Assignment for Today:

Learn problem-solving strategies for multiple-choice math problems.

MATH STRATEGY 1.

Scan the Choices

The answer choices on the GRE tell us a lot about how to solve the problem. Many people are surprised when they find out that the answer choices give away a lot of information. Here's an example.

What is the sum of the lowest factors of 8 and 6?

(A) −48

(B) −14

(C)   2

(D) 10

(E) 24

Can you think of the answer? Before you find out whether you got the right answer, think about this important rule: Always scan the answers before you work on a problem.

Did you think about your answers again? You have probably guessed by now that the correct answer is not choice (C), 2. If you scanned the answers before you solved this question, you may have seen that two of the answer choices were negative numbers. This should give you an important clue.

Yes, −6 is also a factor of 6 because −6 × −1 = 6 and −8 is a factor of 8 because −8 × −1 = 8. And so the correct answer is choice (B), −14.

Quite often, when you're asked to find the area or the circumference of a circle, you'll notice that the answer choices all have a π in them. This immediately tells you that you don't need to convert π to 3.14. You can leave π as π and work the problem.

So, remember this important strategy. Always scan the answers before you start a problem.

MATH STRATEGY 2.

See How It Ends

Here's a dandy shortcut to use when you multiply numbers. Suppose you were asked to multiply 356 and 39 and were given the following choices:

(A) 13,781

(B) 13,723

(C) 13,884

(D) 14,875

(E) 15,233

You should be able to tell that the right answer is choice (C). How? It's easy if you just "see how it

---

25

ends." To see how this works, let's take a problem that's more like the ones you'll find on the GRE:

Tickets to a concert cost $36 each. What is the total cost of each ticket if there is a 6% sales tax?

(A) $ 2.16

(B) $36.00

(C) $36.22

(D) $38.16

(E) $39.24

The first thing you should realize is that because of the sales tax, the total cost will be more than $36. At this point, you can knock out choices (A) and (B) because they are not more than $36.

One way to solve this problem is to find 6% of $36 and add that amount to $36. Another way is to find 106% of $36, and you would do that by multiplying 1.06 by 36.

$$\begin{array}{r} 1.06 \\ \times\, 36 \\ \hline \end{array}$$

What happens when you multiply the two 6's together? Your answer will end in a 6 because $6 \times 6 = 36$. In other words, the correct answer should be greater than $36 and it should end in a 6. Now look at your answer choices. Which answer choice is greater than $36 and ends in a 6? Answer choice (D), $38.16, has to be the correct answer. Notice that you could solve this problem without having to calculate the final answer!

Now back to the problem you saw at the beginning of this section:

$356 \times 39 =$

(A) 13,781

(B) 13,723

(C) 13,884

(D) 14,875

(E) 15,233

We know that 6 (from 356) $\times$ 9 (from 39) is 54, which means that the correct answer has to end in a 4. Only choice (C) 13,884, ends in a 4, so it must be the right answer.

Don't forget. Scan the choices, and always check how they end.

MATH STRATEGY 3.
Approximate

Sometimes you don't have to find the exact answer. You can approximate and get away with it. What's even better, if you approximate, you save time. And you can use that extra time on the more difficult problems. Here's an example.

If the weight of 33 boxes is 65 pounds, what is the weight of 49 boxes?

(A) 88

(B) 97

(C) 98

(D) 103

(E) 137

You can do this problem by approximating. Notice that the weight of 33 boxes is just a little less than twice 33, which is 66. This tells you that the weight of one box is a little less than 2 pounds. So 49 boxes must weigh just a little less than $49 \times 2 = 98$ pounds. So choice (C), 98, is too high (because we want our answer to be less than 98), which means that only choice (B), 97, is close enough to be the answer.

So remember, you can save a lot of time if you get in the habit of approximating. Before you work a problem, see if you can approximate your answer. This is a good strategy to use if the five answer choices are not close in value. If the answer choices are spread apart, that tells you that the right answer can be approximated.

MATH STRATEGY 4.
Work from the Choices

In high school, you learned to set up equations whenever you saw a word problem. This may be a good strategy some of the time. But most of the time, there's another strategy that is much faster. Suppose a problem goes like this:

Bill's wallet has $1, $5, and $10 bills. If he has a total of 12 bills, including 6 singles, that add up to $56, how many $10 bills does he have?

(A) 1

(B) 2

(C) 3

(D) 4

(E) 5

One way to do this problem is to set up one equation for the total amount of money that Bill has:

$S + 5F + 10T = 56$

where S is the number of singles, F is the number of $5 bills, and T is the number of $10 bills.

Then you'd need another equation for the total number of bills that Bill has:

$S + F + T = 12$

And then you have to solve the two equations.

This method works, but it's awfully slow. Here's a better way to do it. The secret is to work from the choices. To work from the choices, always start from choice (C) and then plug the answer back into the problem. So, let's plug in 3 as a possible answer.

Remember, we're looking for the number of $10 bills. Let's suppose Bill has three $10 bills. They total $30. He also has six singles, and so with three more bills he has nine bills. That means he has to have three $5 bills to get a total of 12 bills. But how do these numbers add up?

6 singles = $ 6

3 $10 bills = $30

3 $5 bills = $15

Total = $51

But this total is not enough, because we need $56. Let's look at the choices again. We know that choice (C) is too low. Zap it. If (C) is too low, we know that choices (B) and (A) are also too low. At this point, you should cross off choices (A), (B), and (C). Notice that if you wanted to guess, you now have a 50-50 shot. But let's keep going.

We'll plug in (D). If it works, great. If it doesn't work, we know (E) has to be the answer. So, let's try (D) and plug in 4 as the number of $10 bills that Bill has. If Bill has four $10 bills, then he has ten bills—

six singles and four $10 bills. Since he has a total of 12 bills, he must have two $5 bills.

6 singles = $ 6

4 $10 bills = $40

2 $5 bills = $10

Total = $56

This works, and so we know that the right answer is choice (D), 4.

So remember: Whenever you see word problems, consider starting from the answers and working your way back to the problem instead of taking the time to set up and solve equations. When you plug in values, start from choice (C). However, you should be aware of a couple of exceptions to the "start with (C)" rule.

Exceptions

If the problem says, "Find the *least* value, or the *smallest* angle, or the *lowest* integer," start from the lowest choice, usually choice (A). If the problem says, "Find the *most*, *largest*, or *greatest* value," start from the highest choice, usually choice (E). Here's an example:

What is the lowest positive factor of 24?

(A) 0

(B) 1

(C) 2

(D) 12

(E) 24

Since we're looking for the *lowest* positive factor, we start from choice (A). Is 0 a factor of 24? No. Zap (A). Let's look at choice (B), 1. Is 1 a factor of 24? Yes, it is. Is 1 positive? Yes, it is. And so this is the winner. Notice, you don't need to go further. So, remember: Whenever you can, plug in values and work from choices.

MATH STRATEGY 5.

Use Numbers for Unknowns

The people who write tests love things like P's and Q's and R's and X's. They talk about companies that manufacture T garments, about people who are X years older than their brothers, and about Q factors.

The best way to make sense out of this weird test language is to say it in English.

To do that, whenever you see P's, or Q's or X's, change them to numbers. Let's look at an example.

If a company produces q items in d days, how many items can it produce in m days?

(A) $\dfrac{qd}{m}$

(B) $\dfrac{dm}{q}$

(C) $\dfrac{qm}{d}$

(D) $\dfrac{d}{qm}$

(E) $\dfrac{m}{qd}$

The easiest way to solve this problem is to change q to an easy number, say 10. Then you can change d days to another easy number, like 1 day, and m to 2 days. Then, the question reads:

If a company produces 10 items in 1 day, how many items can it produce in 2 days?

Now if 10 items are produced in 1 day, it's easy to see that in 2 days, 20 items can be produced. With the values of $q = 10$, $d = 1$, and $m = 2$, see which choice gives you 20.

Choice (A): $\dfrac{10 \times 1}{2} = 5$

Choice (B): $\dfrac{1 \times 2}{10} = \dfrac{1}{5}$

Choice (C): $\dfrac{10 \times 2}{1} = 20$

Choice (C) works. But let's see what happens to the other choices.

Choice (D): $\dfrac{1}{10 \times 2} = \dfrac{1}{20}$

Choice (E): $\dfrac{2}{10 \times 1} = \dfrac{1}{5}$

As you can see, only choice (C) gives 20, and so it is the right answer. So remember, if you find yourself staring at a, b, c, q, r, and so on, just plug in your own numbers for these variables.

Instant Replay: Problem-Solving Strategies

1. Scan the choices.

2. See how it ends.

3. Approximate.

4. Work from the choices.

5. Use numbers for unknowns.

Math Strategies:
Quantitative Comparison and Diagrams

Assignment for Today:

Learn strategies for quantitative comparison and diagram questions.

QUANTITATIVE COMPARISON QUESTIONS

The quantitative comparison (QC) section of your math test looks something like this:

Common Quantity

Quantity in Column A	Quantity in Column B

Your task is to evaluate the quantity in each column to determine which column is greater. Compare the quantities and answer

(A) If Column A is greater than Column B

(B) If Column B is greater than Column A

(C) If Column A is equal to Column B

(D) If you cannot determine a definite relationship from the information given

Never answer (E)

Here's an easy example.

Column A	Column B

$$x = 2$$
$$y = 3$$

$x - y$	$y - x$

Notice that Column A is $2 - 3 = -1$, and Column B is $3 - 2 = 1$. This means that Column B is greater than Column A. So on your answer sheet you should mark B as your answer.

Here are some useful strategies for the QC section.

QC STRATEGY 1.

Substitute Values for Variables

Whenever you see variables like x, y, z, a, b, c, and so on in the QC section of your test, you should immediately start plugging in values for the variables to find out which column is greater.

Make sure that you plug in a wide range of values. First plug in 0 as a value of the variable, and see which column is greater. After that, plug in a positive number (1 is a good one) and then a negative number (–1, for example). If these three different values always give you the same answer, you've probably found the correct answer. However, as soon as you get two different results, you can stop because the right answer is Choice (D)—the greater column cannot be determined. Here's an example.

Column A	Column B

$$-3 < t < 3$$

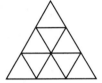

Start by plugging in values for t. We know that t can be 0 because we're told that t lies between –3 and 3. So plug in 0 for t. Then we get:

Column A = 0 and Column B = 0.

This tells us that the right answer might be Choice (C). But don't stop here. Plug in other values for t. For example, what happens if t is 3?

Column A = 3^2 = 9 and Column B = 3^3 = 27.

Here Column B is greater than Column A. Bingo! We got two different results—first C and now A. This immediately tells us that the correct answer is choice (D), it cannot be determined.

Notice that if you had stopped after plugging in 0 for t, your answer would have been incorrect. It's very important to plug in a wide range of values, including negative numbers.

QC STRATEGY 2.
Cancel If You Can

The QC questions on your test are designed for speed. The more shortcuts you know, the faster you can do the problems. One important shortcut is canceling. Whenever you can, you should cancel common terms before you do fancy computations. Let's take an example. Suppose you are asked to compare the perimeters of the two figures shown.

Column A	Column B

All small triangles are
equilateral with
sides of length 1.

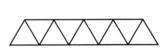

Perimeter of figure   Perimeter of figure

Perimeter simply means the distance around the outer edge of the figure. Before you actually calculate the distances, remember to cancel sides of triangles that are common to Column A and Column B. For every side that you consider in Column A, cancel a similar oÂde in Column B. You will see that nine sides are common to both columns. Just cross them out.

Column A	Column B

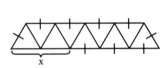

Now you're left with just two sides (marked "x") that remain in Column B. Column B has two extra sides, and so the right answer is B. Notice that it wasn't really necessary to calculate the perimeter of each triangle. Canceling out the common terms made this an easy problem.

QC STRATEGY 3.
Factor Out Common Terms

Before you do any calculation, you should first see if common terms can be factored out. You can then cancel the common terms and simplify your work. Let's compare these two quantities.

Column A	Column B

$$x \neq -7$$
$$x \neq -4$$

$$\boxed{\frac{x^2 - 49}{x+7}}$$ $$\boxed{\frac{x^2 - 16}{x+4}}$$

Did you notice what is common? Let's factor the quantities on the top of both fractions. The top of Column A, $x^2 - 49$, can be written as:

$$x^2 - 49 = (x+7)(x-7)$$

So, Column A can be written as:

$$\frac{x^2 - 49}{x+7} = \frac{(x+7)(x-7)}{(x+7)} = (x-7)$$

We can cancel the $(x+7)$ terms from the top and bottom to get $(x-7)$ for Column A.

Similarly, in Column B, $(x^2 - 16)$ can be written as:

$$x^2 - 16 = (x+4)(x-4)$$

So, Column B can be written as:

$$\frac{x^2 - 16}{x+4} = \frac{(x+4)(x-4)}{(x+4)} = (x-4)$$

We can cancel the $(x+4)$ terms from the top and bottom to get $(x-4)$ for Column B.

So we have $(x-7)$ in Column A and $(x-4)$ in Column B. No matter which value is taken by x, we can see that Column B will always be greater than Column A because Column B is only 4 less than x, whereas Column A is 7 less than x.

As you can see, factoring out the common terms will save you lots of time on the exam.

DIAGRAM QUESTIONS

As you well know, it is easy to make careless mistakes on the test. This is especially true if the problem is long and wordy. One good strategy to guard against careless mistakes is to make use of diagrams given in the problem. Feel free to mark on the diagram and write down the lengths of lines and values

of angles. If no diagram is given to you, see if you can draw one yourself.

Before you work on the following strategies, you should be aware of one special fact about your test: In the QC section of your test, *do not assume that diagrams are drawn to scale*. Angles that look perpendicular are not necessarily perpendicular; in fact, it's very likely that they're *not* perpendicular. Similarly, angles that look parallel may *not* be parallel.

Here are three very useful diagram strategies.

DIAGRAM STRATEGY 1.
Make a Sketch

It's very easy to drown in test language. To keep your head above water, you should get in the habit of drawing a diagram whenever you can. Use the margins of your test booklet for your sketches. Here's a good example of how a sketch can help:

> If the radius of a circle inscribed within a square is 5 feet, what is the perimeter of the square?

This question may look confusing, but it becomes simple if you draw a diagram. Let's see how we might do that.

We know that a circle of radius 5 is inscribed within a square. The diagram you draw may look something like this:

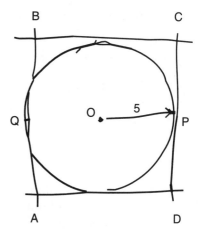

roblem asks you to find the perimeter of CD. Because *ABCD* is a square, we know that all four sides have the same length. *OP* is the radius of the circle, and its length is 5. This means that *OQ*, which is another radius, is also 5. So, *QP* = 5 + 5 = 10. If *QP* is 10, then *AD* is also 10. Now we know that one side of the square is 10, which means that all sides of the square are 10. So the perimeter of the square is

Perimeter = *AB* + *BC* + *CD* + *DA* = 10 + 10 + 10 + 10 = 40.

Notice that even though the problem didn't come with a figure, you were able to draw one and simplify your work considerably.

DIAGRAM STRATEGY 2.
Mark Up Given Diagrams

If a problem on your test comes with a diagram, you should get in the habit of marking on it. That way you minimize your chances of making careless mistakes. Marking on the given diagram also helps you keep focused and saves you time. Here's an example. Suppose a question on your test went something like this:

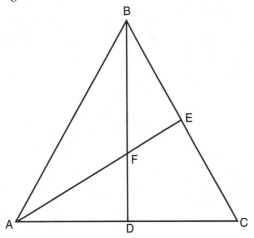

In the isosceles triangle *ABC* shown in the figure, ∠*BAC* = ∠*BCA* = 40°. *BD* bisects ∠*ABC* and *AE* is perpendicular to *BC*. What is ∠*BFE*?

We're told that ∠*BAC* is equal to ∠*BCA*, and each one is 40 degrees. We also know that *BD* bisects

∠*ABC*, which means that ∠*ABD* is equal to ∠*DBC*. Also, *AE* is perpendicular to side *BC*. Let's mark what we know.

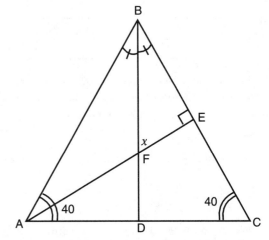

We want to find ∠*BFE*, marked *x* in the figure. First, let's look at triangle *ABC*. If the two bottom angles are each 40 degrees, they add up to 80 degrees, which means ∠*ABC* must be 100 degrees so that the three angles add up to 180 degrees. The two angles at the top are equal. So each angle must be 50 degrees.

Now look at triangle *BFE*. We know that ∠*B* = 50 and ∠*E* = 90. Together, they add up to 90 + 50 = 140 degrees. Because the three angles of any triangle must add up to 180 degrees, the measure of ∠*F* must be 180 − 140 = 40 degrees.

Notice how easy it becomes if you mark on the given diagram.

DIAGRAM STRATEGY 3.
Distort Given Diagrams

On the GRE, looks can be deceiving. Angles that look equal may not be equal and lines that look parallel may not be parallel. Every time you see two lines that look parallel, you should immediately assume that they're not parallel. In fact, you should distort those lines so that they look anything *but* parallel. In other words, don't hesitate to distort the given diagram. Here's an example.

Column A   **Column B**

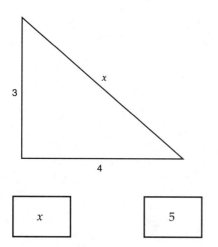

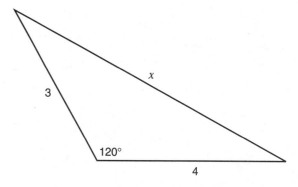

x		5

Suppose you're given a triangle as shown here. You're asked to compare the length of the side marked x with 5. So in Column A you have x, and in Column B you have 5.

When you see two sides marked 3 and 4, you might be tempted to think that the third side, x, is 5. Right? x would be 5 if the given triangle were a right triangle. But nothing in the problem says that it is a right triangle. In fact, you should assume that it is *not* a right triangle.

Let's see what happens if we distort the given diagram. Let's assume that the angle that looks like a 90-degree angle is, say, 30 degrees.

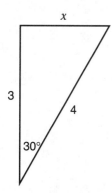

Notice that side x decreases from its original length if the bottom angle is 30 degrees. Similarly, watch what happens if the angle is, say, 120 degrees instead.

We can see that if the angle is 120 degrees, x becomes longer.

You've probably figured out by now that it's not possible to tell whether x is less than, equal to, or greater than 5, and so the right answer is choice (D), it cannot be determined. By distorting the given diagram, we were able to get the right answer.

Instant Replay: Quantitative Comparisons and Diagrams

Quantitative Comparisons

1. Substitute values for variables.

2. Cancel if you can.

3. Factor out common terms.

Diagrams

1. Make a sketch.

2. Mark up given diagrams.

3. Distort given diagrams.

Analytical Strategies: Analytical Reasoning

Assignment for Today:

Learn strategies for analytical reasoning questions.

ANALYTICAL REASONING QUESTIONS

Many GRE-takers find analytical reasoning questions to be especially complex and confusing. Questions of this type comprise 19 of the 25 questions in each GRE analytical section. They are divided among several sets of 3 to 7 questions each.

Every set begins by describing a certain situation. For example, you might be told that eight people will be speaking at a business meeting. You're then given a set of facts about the situation, such as the order in which certain people will speak. But you won't be told the exact order in which everyone will speak; you'll have to deduce at least part of that information from the given facts as you answer the various questions that follow.

Other typical situations in analytical reasoning questions concern the possible seating arrangements for people at a table, the choice of members to serve on different committees, the tenants who rent different apartments in a building, and the like. There are typically half a dozen questions about each situation.

ANALYTICAL REASONING STRATEGY 1.
Draw Pictures and Symbols

The best way to handle analytical reasoning questions is to draw pictures and symbols to help you visualize the situation and organize your thoughts. Here's an example of an analytical reasoning situation.

> Five automobiles sit from left to right in an auto dealership, each with a price tag on its window. The five cars are black, red, orange, green, and yellow. The prices are $1000, $2000, $3000, $4000, and $5000.

The key here is first to draw the five cars. "Draw" does not mean that you spend precious test time drawing V-8 engines and rack-and-pinion steering. Instead, make your cars the no-frills, stripped-down models. That is to say, draw five lines, as shown:

_____   _____   _____   _____   _____

Now let's list the five colors, each by their first letter: B (black), R (red), O (orange), G (green), and Y (yellow):

B

R

O

G

Y

and the five prices:

$1000

$2000

$3000

$4000

$5000

ANALYTICAL REASONING STRATEGY 2.

Watch Your Assumptions!

In this example as in all analytical reasoning problems, do not assume that the five colors or the five prices are in the order given. Nothing in the facts says that the colors or prices are in the order given. Unless something is stated or directly implied by the facts, never assume it to be so!

So what do you have? Doesn't seem like much, does it? It isn't, yet—but let's go on to the facts that are given about the situation. There are six of them, as follow:

(1) The last car on the right sells for $2000.

(2) The green car has at least one car on either side of it.

(3) The red car is in the middle.

(4) The black car costs $5000.

(5) The yellow car is to the right of the orange car.

(6) The $3000 car is to the immediate left of the red car.

OK, let's look at fact (1): The last car on the right sells for $2000. We can add this fact to our drawing:

_____ _____ _____ _____ _____
                                          $2000

ANALYTICAL REASONING STRATEGY 3.

Favor the "Definite" over the "Possible"

Now let's consider fact (2): The green car has at least one car on either side of it. What can you do with this fact? It's possible for the green car to be in places 2, 3, or 4. But there's an even better way to put this fact into your picture. Here's a hint: What do you know that's *definite* about the green car, not just what's possible?

You know that the green car cannot be at either end. "Not G" on the ends is *definite*, and that's better than putting in "possible-G," "possible-G," and "possible-G" in places 2, 3, and 4. And using only two "not-G's" shows the same information as using three "possible-Gs." Whenever you can, use fewer symbols. Avoid clutter. So let's add this information to our drawing:

G̶   G̶

_____ _____ _____ _____ _____
                                          $2000

Fact (3) says that the red car is in the middle. Let's add this information to our figure.

G̶   R   G̶

_____ _____ _____ _____ _____
                                          $2000

ANALYTICAL REASONING STRATEGY 4.

If Information Doesn't Fit in Your Chart, Put It Aside to Use Later

Fact (4) says that the black car costs $5000. You don't know exactly where the $5000 black car fits in the chart, so what do you do? Well, here's a question for you: What if you're doing a jigsaw puzzle and you find two pieces that fit, but you don't know *where* they fit in the puzzle? You'd probably put those two pieces off to one side to fit them in later. That's exactly what you do here, too. So put the B-$5000 to one side to use it later:

G̶   R   G̶
___   ___   ___   ___   ___
                           $2000

      B-$5000

ANALYTICAL REASONING STRATEGY 5.
Watch Out for General Phrases

Fact (5) says that the yellow car is to the right of the orange car. But "to the right" is a general phrase that means the yellow car could be *anywhere* to the right of the orange car, not necessarily exactly next to it. After all, on the map, New York City is to the *general* right of San Francisco. So what can you draw on your chart? For starters, you can be sure that the orange car is not at the right end, so you can mark that. And you also know that the yellow car cannot be on the left end. So mark that as well.

G̶Y̶   R   G̶O̶
___   ___   ___   ___   ___
                           $2000

      B-$5000

You might also draw an O to the left of Y somewhere in the diagram:

G̶Y̶   R   G̶O̶
___   ___   ___   ___   ___
                           $2000

      B-$5000 O . . . Y

Finally, fact (6) says that the $3000 car is to the immediate left of the red car. "To the immediate left" means that the $3000 car must be in spot number two, the space to the immediate left of the red car.

G̶Y̶ $3000   R   G̶O̶
___   ___   ___   ___   ___
                           $2000

B-$5000 O . . . Y

So we've used all the facts, but the chart isn't complete!

Not to worry: The test never gives you enough facts to complete a whole chart. That's because the questions will go something like this:

If the green car does not cost $3000, how much must the orange car cost?

(A) $1000
(B) $2000
(C) $3000
(D) $4000
(E) $5000

At this point, you don't know the price of the orange car, but you can begin to figure it out. The first step is lightly to mark where the green car goes. If the green car doesn't cost $3000, can you place it in the chart? Since the green car is not on either end, and in this question you're told it's not $3000, then the green car must be in place four. Write that in lightly:

G̶Y̶ $3000   R   G   G̶O̶
___   ___   ___   ___   ___
                           $2000

B-$5000 O . . . Y

Now where must the $5000 black car go? The $5000 black car can fit only in space one, since that's the only space that will accommodate both a color and a price.

B

G̶Y̶ $3000   R   G   G̶O̶
___   ___   ___   ___   ___
                           $2000

B-$5000 O . . . Y

So now, how must the orange and yellow cars be placed? Since the yellow car is to the right of the orange car, orange must be in space two, and the yellow car must be in space five:

B   O   Y

G̶Y̶ $3000   R   G   G̶O̶
___   ___   ___   ___   ___
                           $2000

B-$5000 O . . . Y

So the question asked, "How much must the orange car cost?" The answer is $3000.

ANALYTICAL REASONING STRATEGY 6.
Use Information Given in a Question
Only in That Question

Here's a critical point to remember: All information given in a question works *only* in that question, and not necessarily in other questions. Remember, this question went, "IF the green car does not cost $3000 . . . ." So for this question the green car does not cost $3000. But it might cost $3000 in another question. And all the other cars' prices and places you just determined are only for this question.

So, after you mark your answer for the question, what do you have to do? You've got to erase any information that was given in the question. But don't take out any of the *original* facts. So remember to bring a good eraser to the test. This is extremely important.

Let's look at one more question.

If the $1000 car is on one end, what color is the $3000 car?

(A) black

(B) red

(C) orange

(D) yellow

(E) green

First, let's bring back our drawing from the given facts:

~~G Y~~ $3000   R   ~~G O~~
_____   _____   _____   _____   _____
                                            $2000
        B-$5000 O . . . Y

And let's put $1000 at the left end.

$1000
~~G Y~~ $3000   R   ~~G O~~
_____   _____   _____   _____   _____
                                            $2000
        B-$5000 O . . . Y

So now you know that the $5000 black car has to go where? The $5000 black car must go in space four, since this is the only space open to both the color black and the price $5000.

$1000   B
~~G Y~~ $3000   R $5000   ~~G O~~
_____   _____   _____   _____   _____
                                            $2000
        B-$5000 O . . . Y

So now you know that the red car must cost $4000.

$1000 $4000   B
~~G Y~~ $3000   R $5000   ~~G O~~
_____   _____   _____   _____   _____
                                            $2000
        B-$5000 O . . . Y

And since the green car cannot be on an end, it must be in space two and cost $3000.

$1000   G $4000   B
~~G Y~~ $3000   R $5000   ~~G O~~
_____   _____   _____   _____   _____
                                            $2000
        B-$5000 O . . . Y

Which means orange and yellow must be in spaces 1 and 5, respectively.

O
$1000   G $4000   B   Y
~~G Y~~ $3000   R $5000   ~~G O~~
_____   _____   _____   _____   _____
                                            $2000
        B-$5000 O . . . Y

So now, what's the answer to the question, "What color is the $3000 car?" The answer is: green.

Now you've got to erase all the temporary information that you added for that question, but still keep the original facts. And in this way you go on to answer as many of the questions as possible about this set of facts.

ANALYTICAL REASONING STRATEGY 7.
Learn to Use Effective Symbols

When you're working on analytical reasoning questions, don't waste precious time inventing special symbol systems or trying to figure out ambiguous symbols. So it's a good idea to become familiar beforehand with the best, most effective symbols for facts commonly given on the test.

Suppose a fact on your test were as follows:

Mr. Adams and Ms. Bowers must work in the same office.

Think of what symbol you would use. Put the two letters representing their names next to each other:

AB

But if another fact were as follows:

Charles and Denise do not attend the same school.

Your symbol might look something like this:

~~CD~~

Or, for the statement "Harold and Iris live in an apartment building. Harold lives above Iris," your symbol might look something like this:

H
.
.
.
I

But what if the fact stated, "Harold and Iris live in an apartment building. Harold lives on the floor immediately above Iris"? Your symbol would look like this:

H
I

Notice the difference between "living above," which means anywhere above, and "living immediately above."

And the same holds true for "Pat sits to the right of Teri":

T . . . . P

and "Pat sits to the immediate right of Teri"

TP

Or: "Six houses are in a row. Vinny's house is between Linda's and Tom's":

____ ____ ____ ____ ____ ____

L . . . V . . . T

or

T . . . V . . . L

Or, an even simpler method:

____ ____ ____ ____ ____ ____

L/T . . . V . . . T/L

Notice that V is anywhere between T and L. They could be in places 1, 2, and 3 . . .

L/T   V   T/L   ____   ____   ____

. . . or in 2, 5, and 6:

____   L/T   ____   ____   V   T/L

And so forth.

How about, "If Bob goes to the party, then Fran will go, too"? Your symbol might look like this:

If B —> F

Notice that this is different from "Bob and Fran go to the party together," which is:

BF

How is the first situation different from the second? Because in the first situation, Fran *could* go to the party alone, without Bob.

Being able to use symbols quickly and effectively is an essential skill that you can learn and that will immensely improve your success on the GRE.

ANALYTICAL REASONING STRATEGY 8.

Know the Difference Among
Must Be, Could Be, and *Not*

Many GRE analytical reasoning questions fall into three basic categories:

- What *must* be true?

- What *could* be true?

- What's *not* true?

What does each of these mean? Here's an example:

Pat, Jean, and Mike are the only runners in a race. Pat finishes the race ahead of Mike. Which of the following must be true?

(A) Pat finishes in first place.

(B) Pat finishes in second place.

(C) Pat finishes in third place.

(D) Pat does not finish in second place.

(E) Pat does not finish in third place.

First, remember that the word *ahead* means anywhere ahead, not necessarily immediately ahead. So how did the three runners finish? Something like this:

$$P \ldots \ldots M$$

All you know is Pat finishes somewhere ahead of Mike. So the three could have finished:

Pat, then Mike, then Jean.

or . . .

Pat, then Jean, then Mike.

or . . .

Jean, then Pat, then Mike.

Or, more simply, we might write the following:

1st	2nd	3rd
P	M	J
P	J	M
J	P	M

So which answer has to be true? Pat could finish in first or second place. But *could be* true wasn't the question. The only answer that *must be* true is answer (E), Pat does not finish in third place.

In questions of this type, a good way to keep track of what's being asked is to circle the main word: *could, must,* or *not.*

Instant Replay: Analytical Reasoning

1. Draw pictures and symbols.

2. Watch your assumptions.

3. Favor the "definite" over the "possible."

4. If information doesn't fit in your chart, put it aside to use later.

5. Watch out for general phrases.

6. Use information given in a question only in that question.

7. Learn to use effective symbols.

8. Know the difference among *must be, could be,* and *not.*

Day 8

Analytical Strategies: Logical Reasoning

Assignment for Today:

Learn strategies for logical reasoning questions.

LOGICAL REASONING QUESTIONS

The second type of GRE analytical question is called logical reasoning. Each analytical section of the test will include six logical reasoning questions. The first three will follow the first analytical reasoning question set, and the last three will come at the end of the section.

Each logical reasoning question requires you to read a short passage and answer one question based on that passage. The passage will present a series of facts, and to select the right answer choice, you will need to draw the correct implications or conclusions regarding those facts.

A logical reasoning passage is usually structured like a syllogism, which is just a fancy word for a line of reasoning. Here's an example of a syllogism:

All dogs are brown.
Rover is a dog.
Therefore, Rover is brown.

Each of the first two lines is called a *premise*.

PREMISE —> All dogs are brown.
PREMISE —> Rover is a dog.

The last line is called a *conclusion*.

CONCLUSION —> Therefore, Rover is brown.

Given the two premises, the conclusion is valid. This is a logical line of reasoning.

For your test, it's not important whether the premises are true or false in real life. What's important is whether the reasoning is logical. For example, is the following reasoning logically valid?

All dogs are green.
Fred is a dog.
Therefore, Fred is green.

It doesn't matter that dogs aren't green in real life. What matters is that, given these premises, the conclusion is valid. How about this one?

All dogs are brown.
Bowser is a dog.
Therefore, Bowser barks.

Is this conclusion logically valid? Since most dogs bark, it's quite probable that Bowser barks. However, "probable" is not a logically valid conclusion. A logical conclusion is something that must be true, not just what could be true. So the given conclusion is not logically valid. Of course, the passages on your test aren't as straightforward as a syllogism. But within each passage will be the same elements: a premise or two and a conclusion.

41

LOGICAL REASONING STRATEGY 1.

Do These Questions Last

Since you have to read a passage for every logical reasoning question, these problems take time. So leave them until last, after you've answered the analytical reasoning questions that make up the rest of the test section.

LOGICAL REASONING STRATEGY 2.

First Read the Question

An effective strategy is always to read the question *first*. Since there's only one question for each passage, why not know what you're looking for *before* you read the passage? But don't also read the choices first, just the question.

LOGICAL REASONING STRATEGY 3.

Know Common Question Types

There are four basic types of GRE logical reasoning questions: conclusion, assumption, inference/implication, and strengthen or weaken.

Conclusion Questions

The first common logical reasoning question type asks you to draw a conclusion from the facts in the statement. In questions of this type, the conclusion is missing from the syllogism structure. Here is an example, using a simple line of reasoning:

> Pat and Miguel will go together to Fran's party only if food is served. Food will be served only if Fran does not have to spend her savings fixing her car. Fran's car is running well, and does not need to be fixed.
>
> Which of the following can be validly concluded from the passage above?
> (A) Pat will go alone to Fran's party.
> (B) Miguel will not go to Fran's party.
> (C) Food will not be served at Fran's party.

(D) Pat and Miguel will go together to Fran's party.

(E) Fran has to spend her savings to fix her car.

In this example, the passage gives you premises, and you must select the one answer choice that can be validly concluded. The premises tell you that Pat and Miguel will go together only if food is served. Food will be served only if Fran does not spend her savings fixing her car. Since Fran's car does not have to be fixed, food *will* be served, and so Pat and Miguel will go to the party together.

Questions that ask you to draw a conclusion can also be worded in other ways, as follow:

- What can be deduced?

- What necessarily follows?

- If the statements above are true, which of the following is also true?

- Which of the following must be true?

All of these are asking you the same question: Find the logically valid conclusion. And each of these requires you to choose the one answer that *must* necessarily follow from the passage—not what could or might follow.

Assumption Questions

In the second common logical reasoning question type, what's missing from the syllogism structure is one of the premises. A missing premise is called an *assumption*, and the question asks you to find the assumption in one of the answer choices. Here is an example, using just a simple syllogism structure:

> Bowser is a dog.
> Therefore, Bowser is brown.
>
> Which of the following is an assumption made by the author of the syllogism above?
> (A) Most dogs are brown.
> (B) Bowser is large.
> (C) Bowser is not a dog.
> (D) All dogs are brown.
> (E) All dogs bark.

What premise needs to be added to the syllogism above in order for it to be valid? Logically, to conclude that Bowser is brown, the premise "All dogs are brown" must be added to the argument.

Here's another assumption question:

We must pass an anti-pollution law for Dunn County. At present, no such legislation exists, nor has any ever existed in the county. The legislative process is in place, and the courts will uphold such legislation.

Which of the following is an assumption necessary for the passage above to be logically valid?

Before you look at any answers, can you think of a premise that's missing from this line of reasoning?

First, it helps to identify the conclusion. Can you find it? "We must pass an anti-pollution law . . . " is the conclusion. In order to conclude that "we must pass an anti-pollution law," what premise is needed? Is this the one you thought of?

Dunn County has, or anticipates having, a pollution problem.

Or, how about:

An anti-pollution law will be effective in dealing with Dunn County's pollution problem.

Notice that each of these is an unstated premise necessary to conclude that an anti-pollution law must be passed. If Dunn County had no pollution problem, there logically would be no need for a law. And the conclusion that we should pass an anti-pollution law also assumes that the law will work. After all, why propose a law if you don't believe it will be effective in solving the problem?

This is how the answer choices for this question might appear on the test:

(A) Anti-pollution laws are popular with a majority of concerned citizens.

(B) Anti-pollution laws have been used throughout the United States.

(C) An anti-pollution law may be effective in dealing with Dunn County's pollution problem.

(D) Dunn County is one of the more environmentally progressive counties.

(E) Dunn County is known for its enlightened citizenry.

Notice that some of the choices may help to support the passage. But only one choice is a premise that's *necessary* for the conclusion to be valid—choice (C).

Some other ways that the GRE may ask for an assumption—or unstated premise—are:

- Which of the following is assumed by the author of the passage?

- The passage presupposes which of the following statements?

- The passage relies upon which of the following assumptions?

Each of these is essentially the same question: "What is an unstated premise of the reasoning contained in the passage?"

Inference/Implication Questions

A third type of logical reasoning question asks you to draw an inference, or implication, from the facts in the passage. What exactly is an inference? An inference is merely the next step in a line of reasoning. Here is a very simple example of a question that asks you to draw an inference.

In the last election, 40 percent of the voting population was female. Which of the following can best be inferred from the passage above?

(A) Males have more political power in elections.

(B) Women are not as politically active as men.

(C) Men care more about election results than women.

(D) In the last election, a majority of voters were men.

(E) More men are registered voters than are women.

Several of these choices are possible, but they require large leaps in logic. However, one choice *directly* follows from the passage. Can you find the most direct inference?

Choice (D) is the answer. If 40 percent of the voters were female, then 60 percent of the voters must have been male, a majority of voters in the election.

Several of the incorrect choices sound possible, but the correct choice will not only be possible, it will *directly* follow from the statements in the passage.

Other ways in which logical reasoning questions ask you to draw an inference are as follow:

- Which of the following is the most reliable inference that can be drawn from the passage?

- Which of the following is implied by the passage above?

On the GRE, the words *inference, implication,* and *implied* all mean the same thing.

Strengthen-or-Weaken Questions

A fourth type of logical reasoning question is usually worded as follows:

Which of the following statements, if true, would strengthen the reasoning in the passage?

Note that the phrase "if true" means that you shouldn't argue with any of the answer choices. You should accept all the answer choices as if they were true in real life—even if they're not. Now, if all the choices are true, which one choice supports the reasoning in the passage? Here's an example:

In 1980 there were 35 condor sightings. In 1995, the number of condor sightings nearly doubled, to 60 sightings. Environmental laws were passed in 1980 to help protect the condor habitat. Therefore, environmental laws have increased the number of condors in the wild.

Which of the following statements, if true, would strengthen the reasoning in the passage?

(A) Environmental laws were also passed to protect the grizzly bear.

(B) Environmental laws were a fiercely debated issue in the United States Senate.

(C) Number of sightings do not accurately reflect a species' population.

(D) From 1980 to 1995, human destruction of natural habitats extinguished many animal species.

(E) The condor is still listed as a threatened species.

Let's look at each of the choices.

Choice (A): "Environmental laws were also passed to protect the grizzly bear." This has little bearing on the reasoning in the passage, which is about laws protecting condors, not laws protecting grizzlies. Eliminate it.

Choice (B): "Environmental laws were a fiercely debated issue in the United States Senate." This choice also is irrelevant to the reasoning in the passage. Eliminate it.

Choice (C): "Number of sightings do not accurately reflect a species' population." This choice casts doubt upon how accurately the numbers in the passage indicate the actual condor population. This choice *weakens* the reasoning in the passage, rather than strengthens it. Eliminate choice (C).

Choice (D): "From 1980 to 1995, human destruction of natural habitats extinguished many animal species." If that's true—and we are asked to assume that it is—then it helps support the argument that the laws protecting the condor were especially important in protecting it from the extinction that many other species suffered. This supports the reasoning in the passage. Circle it, but keep reading.

Choice (E): "The condor is still listed as a threatened species." That the condor is still listed as threatened certainly does not support the argument in the passage. Eliminate it.

Choice (D) is the correct answer.

This question asked, "What would *strengthen* the reasoning in the passage?" But you would use exactly the same strategy if the question had asked, "What would *weaken* the reasoning in the passage?" Here's how this works, using the same example:

In 1980 there were 35 condor sightings. In 1995, the number of condor sightings nearly doubled, to 60 sightings. Environmental laws were passed in 1980 to help protect the condor habitat. Therefore, environmental laws have helped to nearly double the number of condors in the wild.

Which of the following statements, if true, would weaken the reasoning in the passage above?

(A) Environmental laws were also passed to protect the grizzly bear.

(B) Environmental laws were a fiercely debated issue in the United States Senate.

(C) Number of sightings does not accurately reflect a species' population.

(D) From 1980 to 1995, human destruction of natural habitats extinguished many animal species.

(E) The condor is still listed as a threatened species.

If you remember, choices (A) and (B) were irrelevant to the logic of the argument, and choice (E) is only remotely relevant. Choice (D) strengthened the argument. Only choice (C) weakened the reasoning by calling into doubt the relationship between number of sightings and actual population. Choice (C) weakens the passage and is the correct answer.

Other ways that a logical reasoning question may ask you to find what would strengthen or weaken an argument are as follow:

• Which of the following statements, if true, would strengthen (or weaken) the reasoning in the passage above?

• Which of the following would support (or call into question) the validity of the author's conclusion?

• Which of the following would constitute evidence that the conclusion above is correct (or incorrect)?

• Which of the following, if true, would most effectively support (or challenge) the conclusion above?

• Which of the following additional information would support (or contradict) the argument in the above passage?

Instant Replay: Logical Reasoning

1. Do these questions last.
2. First read the question.
3. Know common question types.

    • Conclusion

    • Assumption

    • Inference/implication

    • Strengthen or weaken

Day 9 to Day 20

TEST 1

Questions and Answers

Explanations and Strategies

Test 1, Section 1: Math

Questions and Answers

Assignment for Today:

Take a sample GRE Math Test under actual test conditions. Allow yourself exactly 30 minutes to complete the 30 questions in this test.

Directions: *For questions 1–15, each question contains two quantities—one on the left (Column A) and one on the right (Column B). Compare the quantities and answer*

(A) if Column A is greater than Column B

(B) if Column B is greater than Column A

(C) if the two columns are equal

(D) if you cannot determine a definite relationship from the information given

Never answer E

In some questions, information appears centered between the two columns. Centered information concerns each of the columns for that question only. Any symbol in one column represents the same value if it appears in the other column.

	Column A	Column B
1.	$\left(\sqrt{20}\right)\left(\sqrt{5}\right)-\left(\sqrt{2}\right)\left(\sqrt{8}\right)$	$\left(\sqrt{50}\right)\left(\sqrt{2}\right)-\left(\sqrt{6}\right)\left(\sqrt{6}\right)$
2.	Interest owed on a loan of \$6000 at an annual rate of 10%.	Interest owed on a loan of \$12,000 at an annual rate of 5%.

Stefan misread a math problem and took the square root of x when he should have taken the square of x. He made no other mistake and his answer was a positive integer. Maria did the same problem correctly.

3.	(Maria's answer)$^{\frac{1}{2}}$	(Stefan's answer)^2

Column A	Column B

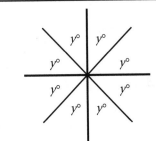

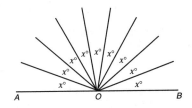

AOB is a line segment

4.
2x	y

Each boxer in the Lightweight category weighs 150 pounds or less. The average weight of 4 Lightweight boxers is 140 pounds and the combined weight of 2 of them is 290 pounds.

5.
Weight, in pounds, of the lightest of the 4 Lightweight boxers	120 pounds

Assume the tick marks are equally spaced.

6.
$\dfrac{A+C}{B+D}$	$\dfrac{2}{5}$

Column A	Column B

3 balanced coins are tossed at the same time.

7.
Probability of getting 2 heads and a tail	Probability of getting only 1 head

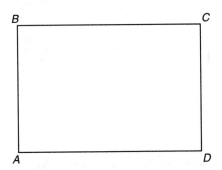

Perimeter of the rectangle *ABCD* is 24 and *AD* is twice *CD*.

8.
CD^2	AD

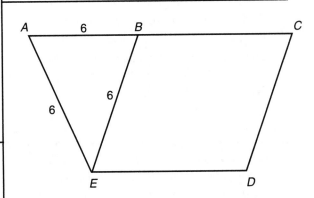

Perimeter of parallelogram *BCDE* = 30

9.
Area of *BCDE*	$27\sqrt{3}$

Column A	Column B

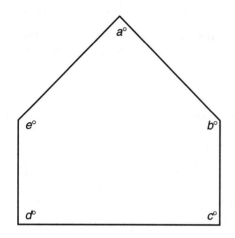

Note: Figure not drawn to scale

$$a° = b° = c°$$
$$d° = \frac{a° + b° + c°}{2}$$
$$e° = 2d°$$

	Column A	Column B
10.	$c°$	72

$$x < y \leq 1$$

	Column A	Column B
11.	$x^2 - y^3$	$x^3 - y^2$

Column A	Column B

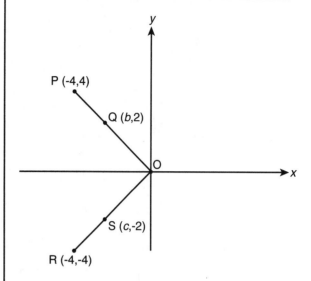

	Column A	Column B
12.	$b + c$	-4

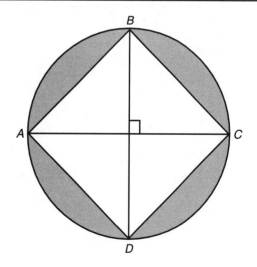

AC and BD are perpendicular bisectors

Radius of circle = 5

	Column A	Column B
13.	Area of shaded portion	25

Column A	Column B

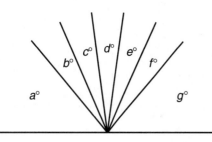

$a = g$

$b = c = d = e = f$

$a = 3d$

14. | $a + b$ | 65 |

A credit card PIN number consists of 4 digits from 0 through 9. The first digit cannot be 0.

15. | The total number of different possible PIN numbers. | 9^4 |

Directions: *Solve each problem and select the appropriate answer choice.*

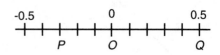

16. Tick marks in the figure above are equally spaced. If PQ is the diameter of a circle, what is the area of the circle?

(A) 0.01π

(B) 0.016π

(C) 0.04π

(D) 0.16π

(E) 0.64π

17. Three boxes—A, B, and C—together weigh 26 pounds. Box A weighs one-third as much as box B and box C weighs three times as much as box B. How many pounds does box B weigh?

(A) 2

(B) $3\frac{5}{7}$

(C) 6

(D) $8\frac{2}{3}$

(E) 13

18. If $\sqrt{y} = 9$, then $y^2 - \sqrt{y} =$

(A) $\sqrt{3} - 9$

(B) 0

(C) $9 - \sqrt{3}$

(D) 6552

(E) 6561

19. What is the value of $(p + p^2 + p^4 + q^3)$ when $p = -1$?

    (A) 0

    (B) q^3

    (C) $p + q^3$

    (D) $(1 + q)^3$

    (E) $1 + q^3$

20. If $\dfrac{x+3}{6} = \dfrac{12}{x+4}$, what is the positive value of x?

    (A) 2

    (B) 3

    (C) 5

    (D) $\sqrt{60}$

    (E) 12

Directions: Questions 21–25 are based on the given figure.

Distribution of Students at JFK School
and Lincoln School by Grade, 1984

JFK School	Grade	Lincoln School
(13%)	1	(11%)
(12%)	2	(13%)
(8%)	3	(15%)
(12%)	4	(10%)
(16%)	5	(9%)
(15%)	6	(14%)
(13%)	7	(15%)
(11%)	8	(13%)

Total enrollment = 1600   Total enrollment = 2400

21. How many students in JFK School are in 5th and 6th grades combined?

    (A) 240

    (B) 256

    (C) 310

    (D) 496

    (E) 552

22. How many grades in JFK School have more than or equal to the number of students in Lincoln School's 4th grade?

    (A) 1

    (B) 2

    (C) 4

    (D) 7

    (E) 8

23. How many students in Lincoln School are in 6th through 8th grades?

    (A) 42

    (B) 360

    (C) 624

    (D) 768

    (E) 1008

24. If 100 more students get enrolled in JFK School's 6th grade, and the number of students in other grades doesn't change, what percent of JFK's new total enrollment would be 6th graders?

    (A) 17.44

    (B) 18.17

    (C) 20.00

    (D) 21.25

    (E) 22.25

25. If JFK School's enrollment increases by 400 students, and Lincoln School's enrollment increases by 100 students, then JFK School's proportion of the two schools' total enrollment increases by approximately what percent?

    (A) 4

    (B) 7

    (C) 9

    (D) 20

    (E) 44

Directions: Solve each problem and select the appropriate answer choice, A–E. Circle the letter of your choice.

26. How many 4-digit numbers are there that consist of only *odd* digits?

    (A) 20
    (B) 625
    (C) 1024
    (D) 4500
    (E) 5000

27. For some integer m, let $\{m\}$ be defined by the equation $\{m\} = m (1 - m)$. If $n + 1 = \{n + 1\}$, then $n =$

    (A) –2
    (B) –1
    (C) 0
    (D) 1
    (E) 2

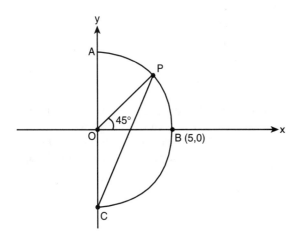

28. In the figure above, ABC is a semicircle with its center at the origin. What is the area of triangle OPC?

    (A) $\dfrac{25}{4}$

    (B) $\dfrac{25}{4}\left(\sqrt{2}+1\right)$

    (C) $\dfrac{25}{2\sqrt{2}}$

    (D) $\dfrac{25}{2}$

    (E) $\dfrac{25}{\sqrt{2}}$

29. Box A and box B have 6 cards each. Each card is marked with one integer, 1 through 6. Both boxes can have more than one card with the same integer, but the sum of all the integers in each box must be 18. Two of the cards in box A are 6's and two of the cards in box B are 5's. If one card is drawn from box A and one from box B, but neither a 6 nor a 5 is drawn, what is the *largest* possible sum of the integers on the cards drawn from the two boxes?

    (A) 3
    (B) 4
    (C) 7
    (D) 8
    (E) 12

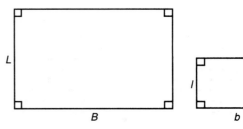

30. In the figure above, the ratio of the perimeter of the larger rectangle to the perimeter of the smaller rectangle is p. If $\dfrac{L-B}{l-b} = d$, what is $\dfrac{L^2-B^2}{l^2-b^2}$ in terms of p and d?

    (A) $p \times d$

    (B) $\dfrac{p}{d}$

    (C) $\dfrac{p^2 - d^2}{p^2 + d^2}$

    (D) $\dfrac{p+d}{p-d}$

    (E) $p - d^2$

Quick Answer Guide

Test 1, Section 1: Math

1. A	9. C	17. C	25. C
2. D	10. C	18. D	26. B
3. C	11. D	19. E	27. B
4. B	12. C	20. C	28. C
5. C	13. A	21. D	29. C
6. B	14. A	22. B	30. A
7. C	15. A	23. E	
8. A	16. D	24. C	

For explanations to these questions, see Day 10.

Day 10

Test 1, Section 1: Math
Explanations and Strategies

Assignment for Today:

Review the explanations for the Math Test you took on Day 9.

---

1. Correct choice (A)

As with most quantitative comparison problems, there are at least two ways to work to an answer: In this case, a fast way and a faster way! One fast way is to multiply the square roots in parentheses. So, in Column (A), you get $\sqrt{100} - \sqrt{16}$ which equals 10 – 4, or 6. In Column (B), you get $\sqrt{100} - \sqrt{36}$ which equals 10 – 6, or 4. So Column (A) is greater.

A faster way is to realize that the first set of parentheses is the same for each column (they both equal $\sqrt{100}$). So all you have to do is compare the second sets of parentheses: In Column (A), you have $-\sqrt{16}$ which equals –4. In Column (B), you have $-\sqrt{36}$ which equals –6. Since –4 is greater than –6, Column (A) is greater. (Don't forget about those minus signs!)

2. Correct choice (D)

The formula for finding interest is:

Interest = Loan amount × rate × time

Notice that we are given the loan amount ($6000 for Column A and $12,000 for Column B), and the annual rate (10% in Column A and 5% in Column B), but we don't know anything about the time period. For example, the loan in Column A may be for 5 years and the loan in Column B may be for just 1 month. We just don't know. So, the answer is choice (D).

3. Correct choice (C)

To solve this problem, let's plug in values for the unknowns. Let's assume that x is 25. Then, Stefan took the square root of 25, which means his answer was 5. Then Column B is:

(Stefan's answer)^2 = 5^2 = 25.

The correct answer required Maria to square x. So, with x as 25, Maria's answer was 25 × 25. Then, Column A is:

$$(25 \times 25)^{\frac{1}{2}} = \sqrt{25 \times 25} = 25$$

So, both columns are equal.

4. Correct choice (B)

Let's look at Column A first. We know that AOB is a straight line, which means that the total angle enclosed by AOB is 180 degrees. There are 9 angles, each x degrees. So each x is 180 ÷ 9 = 20 degrees.

So, if $x = 20, 2x = 40$.

Then, Column A $= 40$.

The 8 equal angles in Column B form a circle. We know that a circle has 360 degrees. So, if $8y = 360$, $y = 360 \div 8 = 45$.

Then, Column B $= 45$.

So, Column B is greater than Column A.

5. Correct choice (C)

We should work with total weights and not with average weights because averages have to be added with caution. We know that the average weight of the 4 boxers is 140 pounds. This means the total weight of the 4 boxers is $140 \times 4 = 560$. (Remember, total weight is the average times the number of boxers.)

We know that two of the boxers have a combined weight of 290 pounds. The heaviest possible weight that any boxer can have is 150 pounds. This means the lighter of the two can weigh a minimum of $290 - 150 = 140$ pounds. Now let's find the lighter of the *other* two boxers.

We know that four of them weigh 560 pounds and two of them weigh 290 pounds. Then, the other two must weigh $560 - 290 = 270$ pounds. Again, the lighter of these two boxers can weigh a minimum of $270 - 150 = 120$ pounds.

In both groups of two, to find the lighter boxer, we assume that the heavier boxer weighs the maximum possible amount, which is 150 pounds. This is the only way to make sure that the lighter boxer has the least possible weight.

So, Column A is 120 pounds, which is equal to Column B.

6. Correct choice (B)

We can determine the coordinates of the points we are interested in by just using the number line. Note that each tick mark is 2 units long.

$$\left. \begin{array}{l} A = -10 \\ B = -4 \\ C = 6 \\ D = 14 \end{array} \right\} \Rightarrow \frac{A + C}{B + D} = \frac{-10 + 6}{-4 + 14} = \frac{-4}{10} = -\frac{2}{5}$$

So, Column A is a negative value and Column B is a positive value, which means Column B is greater than Column A.

7. Correct choice (C)

If we toss 3 coins, these are the different outcomes:

Coin 1 Coin 2 Coin 3

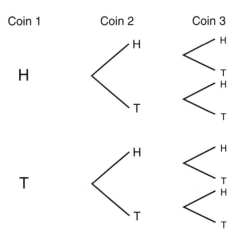

We notice that there are a total of eight possible outcomes: HHH, HHT, HTH, HTT, THH, THT, TTH, and TTT.

There are three outcomes with two heads and a tail (HHT, HTH, and THH), and so the probability is 3/8, which is Column A.

There are three outcomes with only one head (HTT, THT, and TTH) and so the probability is 3/8, which is Column B.

The two probabilities are equal and so the answer is choice (C).

8. Correct choice (A)

We are told that the perimeter is 24. Then, the sum of the length and width is 12 (because the perimeter is twice the sum of the length and width). That is,

$AD + CD = 12$

But, AD is twice CD. That is, $AD = 2(CD)$. So, let's plug in this value of AD in the equation. We get

$2(CD) + CD = 12$

Or $3\,CD = 12$

that is, $CD = 4$. If CD is 4, AD has to be 8. Then Column A $= 4^2 = 16$ and Column B $= 8$.

So, Column A is greater.

9. Correct choice (C)

To find the area of the parallelogram *BCDE*, we need its base, *ED*, and its height. Side *BE* is 6. Then, side *CD* is also 6 (in a parallelogram, opposite sides are equal). Together, these two sides sum to 12. We know the perimeter of *BCDE* is 30. If two of the sides add up to 12, the other two sides must add up to 30 – 12 = 18. So, side *BC* must be 9 and the base, *ED*, must also be 9. Got base, need height.

On to triangle *ABE*. It has the same height as the parallelogram. Each side of the triangle is equal in length, so it's an equilateral triangle.

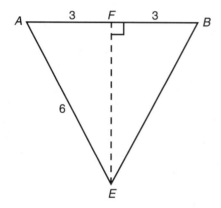

We can draw a perpendicular from *E* to *AB*. Then, *AF* = *BF* = 3. Then, from the right triangle *AFE*, we can find *FE* by using the Pythagorean theorem:

$$AE^2 = AF^2 + FE^2$$

Or, $$6^2 = 3^2 + FE^2$$

Or, $$27 = FE^2$$

So, $$FE = \sqrt{27} = \sqrt{9 \times 3} = 3\sqrt{3}$$

So, the height of the parallelogram is $3\sqrt{3}$. We know its base is 9. Then, its area = base × height.

$$= 9 \times 3\sqrt{3} = 27\sqrt{3}$$

So, Column A is equal to Column B.

10. Correct choice (C)

First, let's find the sum of all interior angles of the given figure. The sum of the interior angles of a polygon is $180 \times (n - 2)$, where *n* is the number of sides. For example, in a triangle (the number of sides is 3 and so *n* is 3), the sum of the angles is $180 \times (3 - 2) = 180 \times 1 = 180$.

So, the sum of the interior angles of the figure shown (with 5 sides) is: $180 \times (5 - 2) = 180 \times 3 = 540$.

We're asked to compare the value of angle *c* with 72 degrees. Let's suppose that *c is* 72 degrees. Let's see what happens if we plug this value back into the problem.

If *c* is 72, then *a* = 72 and *b* = 72 (because we're told: $a° = b° = c°$).

We also know that $d° = \dfrac{a°+b°+c°}{2}$. If *a*, *b*, and *c* are each 72, then, $d = \dfrac{72 + 72 + 72}{2} = \dfrac{216}{2} = 108$.

And, we know that *e* = 2*d*. So, if *d* = 108, then $e = 2 \times 108 = 216$.

Now, let's add up these values and see if they give us a total of 540 degrees.

$$a + b + c = 216$$
$$d = 108$$
$$e = 216$$

Then, total = 540

So, the value of *c is* 72 degrees, and the two columns are equal.

11. Correct choice (D)

The best way to solve this problem is to plug in values for *x* and *y*. Let's try the greatest possible value for *y*, which is 1, and 0 for *x* (which must be less than *y*).

Then, Column A = 0 – 1 = –1,

and Column B = 0 – 1 = –1.

This implies that the two columns are equal. Now, let's try *x* = –1 and *y* = 0.

Then, Column A = 1 – 0 = 1,

and Column B = –1 – 0 = –1.

Here, Column A is greater.

Because we get two different values, the correct choice is (D).

12. Correct choice (C)

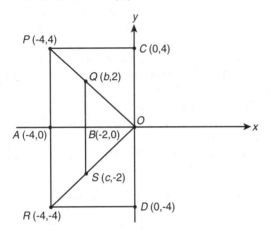

Let's first find the slopes of OP and OR. A slope is simply the ratio of the y-distance to the x-distance. From point O to point P, there is a y-distance of 4 (shown as OC), and there is an x-distance of -4 (shown as OA).

Then, slope of OP = $\dfrac{y\text{ - distance}}{x\text{ - distance}} = \dfrac{4}{-4} = -1$

This means, along the entire line OP, if we move 1 to the left, we have to move 1 upwards. Notice that to get to point Q, we need to move 2 upwards from the origin. This means we have to move $-1 \times 2 = -2$ on the x-axis. So, $b = -2$.

The slope of line OR is $\dfrac{y\text{ - distance}}{x\text{ - distance}} = \dfrac{-4}{-4} = 1$

This means, along line OR, if we move 1 to the left, we have to move 1 downwards. To get to point S, we move 2 downwards from the origin. So, we also need to move 2 to the left, which means the value of c is -2.

So, $b = -2$ and $c = -2$. Then, $b + c = -2 + -2$
$= -4$, and the two columns are equal.

13. Correct choice (A)

To find the area of the shaded portion, first let's find the area of the circle. Once we find the area of the circle, we can subtract from it the area of rectangle $ABCD$ (because everything is symmetrical, angle A = angle B = angle C = angle D, and so $ABCD$ is a rectangle), and we'll be left with the area of the shaded portion.

Area of circle = $\pi r^2 = \pi(5^2) = 25\pi$

Notice that rectangle $ABCD$ can be divided into four right triangles, each with height = base = radius = 5

Then,   area of each triangle = $\dfrac{1}{2}$ base × height

$= \dfrac{1}{2}$ radius × radius

$= \dfrac{1}{2}(5 \times 5) = \dfrac{25}{2}$

There are four such triangles in rectangle $ABCD$.

So,   area of rectangle $ABCD$ = 4 × area of each triangle

$= 4 \times \dfrac{25}{2} = 50$

So,   area of shaded portion = area of circle – area of $ABCD$

$= 25\pi - 50$

We have to compare this quantity in Column A with 25 in Column B. Notice that 25π is more than 75 because the value of π is a little more than 3 (it's roughly 3.14). We can approximate 25π to 78 or so. So, the area of the shaded portion is about $78 - 50$, which is about 28. No matter what its exact value, the area of the shaded portion is going to be more than 25, and so Column A is greater.

14. Correct choice (A)

To solve this problem, we need to find the value of a and b. We see that all angles add up to 180° because they form a straight line.

So, $a + b + c + d + e + f + g = 180$

Let's rewrite this equation using only a and b, because we need to compare $a + b$ in Column A with 65 in Column B.

Then, we can write $c = b$, $d = b$, $e = b$, $f = b$, and $g = a$.

So, $a + b + c + d + e + f + g = 180$ can be written as:

$a + b + b + b + b + b + a = 180$

Or, $2a + 5b = 180$

We also know that $a = 3d$ and $d = b$. So, $a = 3b$.

Then, $2(3b) + 5b$ $= 180$

Or, $6b + 5b$ $= 180$

Or, $11b$ $= 180$

Or, b $= \dfrac{180}{11}$

Because $a = 3b$, a $= \dfrac{180}{11} \times 3$

To get the value of $a + b$, we note that a is $3\left(\dfrac{180}{11}\right)$ and

b is $1\left(\dfrac{180}{11}\right)$. So, together, $a + b = 4\left(\dfrac{180}{11}\right) = \dfrac{720}{11}$.

If you divide this expression, you will find that it is 65 plus some (we don't need the exact amount, we only need to know that it's a bit more than 65). So Column A is 65 plus some and Column B is 65. The answer then is choice (A).

15. Correct choice (A)

Column A first. A PIN number has four positions and has a number in each position. In all positions except the first one, there are 10 possible numbers (0 through 9) that can fill that position. In the first position, since 0 is not allowed, there are nine possible choices. To get the total number of possible PIN numbers, we multiply these numbers together:

9 possibilities in the first position

$\times$ 10 possibilities in the 2nd position

$\times$ 10 possibilities in the 3rd position

$\underline{\times\ 10\ \text{possibilities in the 4th position}}$

= 9000 total possibilities.

There are a couple of ways that we can see that 9000 is greater than 9^4, the quantity in Column B. We could compute 9^4 directly (yuck) and see that it is less than 9000 ($9^4 = 6561$), or we could express Column A as 9×10^3 and Column B as 9×9^3, and choose Column A because $10^3 > 9^3$.

16. Correct choice (D) 0.16π

We're told that PQ is the diameter of the circle. We should first find the length of the diameter. From the figure we know that PQ is the sum of PO and OQ. PO is 0.3 (notice it's not -0.3 because distances cannot be negative) and OQ is 0.5. So, the diameter of the circle is $0.3 + 0.5 = 0.8$.

If the diameter is 0.8, the radius is half that, or 0.4.

If the radius is 0.4, the area $= \pi r^2 = \pi(0.4)^2 = 0.16\pi$.

17. Correct choice (C) 6

Word problems like these are best solved by plugging in the answer choices. As usual, we start from choice (C), 6. Because the question asked for the weight of box B, we plug in 6 pounds as its weight.

We're told that box C weighs 3 times as much as box B. So, if box B weighs 6 pounds, box C weighs 6 $\times$ 3 = 18 pounds. Now, box A weighs one-third as much as box B. So, if box B weighs 6 pounds, box A must weigh $\dfrac{1}{3} \times 6 = 2$ pounds.

Then,	weight of box A	=	2 pounds,
	weight of box B	=	6 pounds,
and	weight of box C	=	18 pounds.
Then,	the total weight = 26 pounds, which works, and so choice (C) is the right answer.		

18. Correct choice (D) 6552

Let's start with what we know. We know that $\sqrt{y} = 9$. Then, if we square both sides of this equation, $y = 81$.

Let's square this one more time to get $y^2 = 81^2$.

Before we find the value of 81^2, note that the question asks for the value of $y^2 - \sqrt{y}$, which means we'll have to square 81 and then subtract 9. If we square 81, the last digit will end in a "1" (because when you multiply 81 by 81, the last digit will be 1 $\times$ 1 = 1). Then, when we subtract 9, the last digit will have to be 11 − 9 = 2. There's only one answer that ends in a "2," choice (D). Here's a demonstration. We know that $y^2 = 81^2 = 81 \times 81 = 6561$ (ends in a "1"). Now, we need to subtract 9 because we want the value of $y^2 - \sqrt{y}$ and $\sqrt{y} = 9$. So, 6561 − 9 = 6552 (ends in a "2").

19. Correct choice (E) $1 + q^3$

This problem required us to see that one of the terms is a q, not a p like the others. Then, because we are not given the value of q, our answer choice must have a q-term in it. We can zap choice (A) right away. Then, let's plug in the value of (-1) for p. Then, we get:

$$p + p^2 + p^4 + q^3 = (-1) + (-1)^2 + (-1)^4 + q^3$$
$$= -1 + 1 + 1 + q^3$$
$$= 1 + q^3, \text{ which is choice (E).}$$

20. Correct choice (C) 5

We were told in high school to cross-multiply and solve for x. But here's a much faster method. Start from the choices and plug in values for x.

Remember, when plugging in values, we want to always start from choice (C). So, let's plug in values for $x = 5$.

Then, we get $\dfrac{5+3}{6} = \dfrac{12}{5+4}$

That is, $\dfrac{8}{6} = \dfrac{12}{9}$. Cross-multiplying, we get $72 = 72$

Hey, it works. So stop here. Of course, you can always cross-multiply and solve as presented. But we think plugging in values is faster.

21. Correct choice (D) 496

From the graph, we see that 16% of the students in JFK School are in 5th grade and 15% are in 6th grade. Thus, the total percent of students in JFK School who are in 5th and 6th grades is 15% + 16% = 31%.
We know that there are 1600 students in JFK School. SaÙ the total number of students in 5th and 6th grades is:
31% of 1600 = .31 × 1600 = 496.

22. Correct choice (B) 2

From the graph, we see that 10% of the students in Lincoln School are in 4th grade. There are a total of 2400 students in Lincoln School. This means that the number of students in 4th grade is 10% of 2400 = .10 × 2400 = 240.

Now we need to find out how many grades in JFK School have 240 or more students. The fastest way to find this is to look at the total enrollment in JFK School and see what percent constitutes 240 students. Because there are 1600 students in JFK School, we know that 10% of that would be 160. We need 80 more to get 240. If 10% is 160, then 5% must be 80. Now we see that 160 and 80 make 240, which means that we're looking for 15% or higher in JFK School. We see that grades 5 and 6 have 15% or more, which means that the number of grades with 240 or more students is 2.

23. Correct choice (E) 1008

We need to know the number of students in Lincoln School's 6th, 7th, and 8th grades. First, let's add up the percentages in these three grades: 14% + 15% + 13% = 42%. We know that there are 2400 students in that school. So now we need to find 42% of 2400.

We know that 10% of 2400 = 240. This means 40% is four times as much, or 240 × 4 = 960. We now need to find 2% more. But first, look at your answers. Only one answer, choice (E) 1008, is more than 960, which means that has to be the right answer. No need to go further.

24. Correct choice (C) 20.00

We know that 15% of all students in JFK are in 6th grade. This is .15 × 1600 = 240 students. If 100 more students get enrolled in 6th grade, the total number of students in 6th grade is 240 + 100 = 340.

But notice that when 100 more students get enrolled, the total enrollment of the school also goes up by 100. So the new enrollment is 1600 + 100 = 1700.

We now need to know what percent of 1700 is 340. We know that 10% of 1700 is 170, and so 20% is double that, which is 340. In other words 20% of all students are 6th graders.

25. Correct choice (C) 9

At present, JFK School's enrollment is 1600 out of 4000, or 40%. With the additions, JFK School's enrollment is 2000 out of a total of 4500, or 44.4%. So, the change is from 40 to 44, or 4 percent. To find percent increase, use the following formula:

$$\text{percent change} = \frac{\text{change}}{\text{starting point}} \times 100\%$$

$$= \frac{4}{44.4} \times 100\% = \frac{1}{11.1} \times 100 \approx 9\%$$

26. Correct choice (B) 625

We recall that an *odd* digit is one that is not a multiple of 2. So the question is asking how many four-digit numbers can we make using just the numbers 1, 3, 5, 7, and 9? To make a number, there are four digits that we have to fill, and there are five choices for what number to put in each position.

To calculate the total number of possible choices, we *multiply* the number of choices that we have for each position together—in this case $5 \times 5 \times 5 \times 5 = 5^4 = 625$ (if we could use *even* digits too, this number would be 10^4, or 10,000). Notice, you don't actually have to multiply this number. Once you figured out that it was $5 \times 5 \times 5 \times 5$, you could tell that the answer has to be choice (B). Why? Because that's the only answer that ends in a 5.

27. Correct choice (B) –1

To find an expression for $\{n + 1\}$, we apply the definition of the $\{\}$ operator:

$\{m\} = m (1 - m)$

To find $\{n + 1\}$, rewrite this equation and put "$n + 1$" everywhere that an "m" appears:

$\{n + 1\} = (n + 1) (1 - [n + 1])$

$= (n + 1) (1 - n - 1)$

$= (n + 1) (-n)$

$= -n^2 - n.$

So to solve the problem $n + 1 = \{n + 1\}$, we will want to solve the equation

$n + 1 = -n^2 - n.$

If we add $n^2 + n$ to both sides of this equation, we get

$n^2 + 2n + 1 = 0$

We recognize the left side of this expression as $(n + 1)^2$, and conclude that this equation is true only if $n = -1$, choice (B).

28. Correct choice (C) $\dfrac{25}{2\sqrt{2}}$

First, let's note that the radius of the semicircle is 5. We know this because the coordinates of B are (5,0), which means radius OB is 5. To find the area of the triangle, we need its base and its height. We can take OC as the base. We know that OC is also the radius of the semicircle, which is 5. So, the base of the triangle is 5. We now need its height.

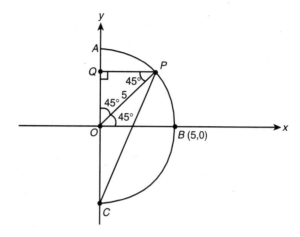

If we use OC as the base, we need a perpendicular from OC (or from an extension of OC) to the opposite corner. To find this perpendicular, let's draw PQ, 90 degrees on OA. Then, PQ is the height of the triangle. We need to find PQ.

Because $\angle POB$ is 45 degrees, $\angle POQ$ is also 45 degrees (because the two 45-degree angles form the 90-degree angle between the x- and y-axes). If $\angle POQ$ is 45 and $\angle PQO$ is 45, then $\angle OPQ$ must also be 45 degrees so that the three angles sum to 180 degrees. So, triangle PQO is a 45-45-90 triangle. Notice also that OP is another radius, which means OP is 5.

We know that in a 45-45-90 triangle, the hypotenuse is $\sqrt{2}$ times each perpendicular side. In other words, the hypotenuse, 5, is $\sqrt{2}$ times the height PQ. So, $5 = \sqrt{2} \, (PQ)$.

And, $\dfrac{5}{\sqrt{2}} = PQ.$

So, now we have base = 5 and height = $\dfrac{5}{\sqrt{2}}$

Then, area of triangle $OPC = \dfrac{1}{2} \times 5 \times \dfrac{5}{\sqrt{2}}$

$= \dfrac{25}{2\sqrt{2}}$

29. Correct choice (C) 8

We know that the total sum of all the cards in each box must be equal to 18. Box A has two cards that are already determined for us. Two of the cards are 6's. Therefore, the sum of the two cards in box A is 12. Thus the other four cards must sum to 6. Each card is numbered 1 through 6. We want three of the four cards to be as small as possible. Therefore, the three cards should be 1's. This leaves us with the fourth card as 3.

Sum of cards in box A: $6 + 6 + 1 + 1 + 1 + 3 = 18$.

For box B, two of the cards are 5's. This leaves us with four cards. Again, we want three of the four cards to be as small as possible. Let the three cards be 1's. This leaves the fourth card as 5. But recall that neither card was a 5 or a 6. Thus, the fourth card must be smaller than 5. We see that if the fourth card is 4 and one of the other cards is 2, we have:

Sum of cards in box B: $5 + 5 + 1 + 1 + 2 + 4 = 18$.

So, the largest possible sum of the two cards is $3 + 4 = 7$.

30. Correct choice (A) $p \times d$

There are a number of ways of working this problem. But first, let's make use of the given information to write an equation. We are told that the ratio of the perimeter of the larger to the smaller rectangle is p. That is,

$$\frac{\text{perimeter of larger rectangle}}{\text{perimeter of smaller rectangle}} = p$$

In terms of length and width, we know that the perimeter is $2(L + B)$ for the larger rectangle, and $2(l + b)$ for the smaller rectangle. Then the ratio of the two perimeters is

$$\frac{2(L + B)}{2(l + b)} = p, \text{ which can be reduced to}$$

$$\frac{(L + B)}{(l + b)} = p. \text{ Call this Equation (1).}$$

We are also told that $\frac{(L-B)}{(l-b)} = d$. Call this Equation (2). Now multiply Equation (1) and Equation (2) so that we get

$$\frac{(L+B)}{(l+b)} \times \frac{(L-B)}{(l-b)} = p \times d$$

Ah, both the numerator and the denominator are of the form $(a + b) \times (a - b)$ and are equal to $(a^2 - b^2)$.

Using the same formula, we multiply the numerators together and the denominators together to get

$$\frac{\left(L^2 - B^2\right)}{\left(l^2 - b^2\right)} = p \times d, \text{ which is choice (A).}$$

Don't be surprised that this was a difficult problem. It appears near the end of the exam; it is meant to be difficult.

But, let's see if there is an easier way to do the problem. If you don't like to deal with variables like p and d, give values to L, B, l, and b. To make calculations easy, let $L = 4$, $B = 2$, $l = 2$, and $b = 1$. Then, the ratio of the two perimeters is given by:

$$\frac{(L+L+B+B)}{(l+l+b+b)} = \frac{(4+4+2+2)}{(2+2+1+1)} = \frac{12}{6} = p = 2$$

Similarly, $\frac{(L-B)}{(l-b)} = \frac{(4-2)}{(2-1)} = \frac{2}{1} = d = 2$

We are asked to find $\left(\frac{L^2 - B^2}{l^2 - b^2}\right)$. Substituting our own values, we get

$$\frac{4^2 - 2^2}{2^2 - 1^2} = \frac{16 - 4}{3} = \frac{12}{3} = 4$$

Now look at the answer choices. Choice (A) is $p \times d$, which is equal to $2 \times 2 = 4$. As you can see, choice (A) gives us the required value, and so it is the right answer. At this point, we don't need to try the other choices.

Test 1, Section 2: Verbal

Questions and Answers

Assignment for Today:

Take a sample GRE verbal test under actual test conditions. Allow yourself exactly 30 minutes to complete the 38 questions in this test.

Directions: *For questions 1–7, one or more words have been left out of each sentence. Circle the answer, A–E, which contains the word or words that best fit the meaning of the entire sentence.*

---

1. The food server admitted that her work was just a job and that she was doing it for the sake of ____ and nothing else.

   (A) approbation

   (B) remuneration

   (C) emulation

   (D) exoneration

   (E) procrastination

2. According to the minority political party, the major problem with national health insurance reform, as a ____ alternative to more government spending, is that it's a tax ____.

   (A) purported..increase

   (B) cheery..standard

   (C) feasible..revolt

   (D) sarcastic..statement

   (E) toxic..shelter

3. Because the bulk of tax revenue comes from various sales taxes, the burden of payment falls ____ on the shoulders of poor and middle-income Americans who spend roughly 16 percent of their incomes on taxable goods, while the richest Americans spend only about 3.1 percent.

   (A) disproportionately

   (B) diminutively

   (C) lightly

   (D) inadequately

   (E) equitably

4. After the wind blew away the musician's music, she ____ so cleverly that the people watching were not ____ of the mishap.

   (A) extemporized..cognizant

   (B) digressed..unappreciative

   (C) improvised..warned

   (D) wafted..aware

   (E) denigrated..mindful

65

5. The dermatologist was ____ that the new surgical procedure he worked ten years to invent would be able to ____ all signs of having a tattoo.

(A) unwavering..expunge

(B) incredulous..erase

(C) sentient..obliterate

(D) timorous..eradicate

(E) euphoric..exacerbate

6. When the mayor announced her candidacy for the next term, she ____ the virtues of her past term while the reporters took copious notes and wished she weren't so ____.

(A) explained..taciturn

(B) expatiated on..garrulous

(C) expounded on..insidious

(D) gibbered about..erudite

(E) noted..talkative

7. After work, Miriam would go home and enjoy ____ with her husband and children, but at work she talked in lofty tones that were reminiscent of a ____.

(A) bantering..colloquy

(B) housework..discourse

(C) discussion..eulogy

(D) hoopla..secretary

(E) quibbling..scholar

Directions: For questions 8–16, determine the relationship between the two words given in capital letters. Then, from the choices listed A–E, select the one pair that has a relationship most similar to that of the capitalized pair. Circle the letter of that pair.

---

8. STATESMAN:GOVERNMENT::

(A) teacher:faculty

(B) potter:art

(C) raconteur:anecdote

(D) dowager:marriage

(E) shepherd:farm

9. COBBLER:OXFORDS::

(A) mason:mortar

(B) lapidary:stones

(C) haberdasher:linen

(D) chandler:candles

(E) agronomist:fertilizer

10. RIB:THORAX::

(A) tibia:fibula

(B) tendon:muscle

(C) pennant:flagpole

(D) odometer:dashboard

(E) grass:sidewalk

11. SURREPTITIOUS:CANDOR::

(A) stealthy:mystery

(B) confident:honesty

(C) fearless:pride

(D) fatuous:sense

(E) subtle:cunning

12. PAGE:TOME::

(A) ink:paper

(B) tree:forest

(C) rose:petal

(D) sky:sun

(E) thespian:stage

13. RAINBOW:EPHEMERAL::

(A) dolt:sagacious

(B) fanatic:zealous

(C) dinosaur:complacent

(D) connoisseur:stoic

(E) ocean:static

14. FORUM:DISCUSSION::

(A) papacy:absolution

(B) space:exploration

(C) parliament:legislation

(D) rostrum:peroration

(E) speakeasy:gossip

15. EXCORIATE:ABRADE::

(A) consent:decree

(B) demur:agree

(C) mar:burnish

(D) eschew:avoid

(E) proscribe:support

16. MNEMONIC:REMEMBER::

(A) amnesiac:forget

(B) euphoria:relax

(C) nostril:smell

(D) audio:hear

(E) glasses:see

Directions: Read each passage and answer the questions that follow. Base your answers only on what is stated or implied in the passage. Circle the letter of your answer choice.

Questions 17–24 are based on the following passage.

Before I became law editor for a farm paper, I used to doubt the genuineness of some of the absurd queries one occasionally sees propounded in the "Answers to Correspondents"
(5) columns of newspapers. Now I am almost prepared to believe that a Utah man actually wrote Bill Nye for information concerning the nature and habits of Limburg cheese, as a basis for experiments in the use of that substance as motive
(10) power.

Of the hundreds of queries that come to my office in the course of a year, most of them are commonplace enough, including such questions as what constitutes a lawful fence in Connecti-
(15) cut. But one correspondent in 50 unconsciously sends in a gem that gives the editor a smile with which to rest his tired countenance, albeit there is often concomitant pathos in the letters.

Many a pathetic domestic snarl is disclosed in
(20) amusing language. For instance, one woman wrote, "My husband's health is very poor and he is stubborn about making a will." She sought advice concerning her property rights, contingent

upon her spouse's "stubbornness" remaining
(25) with him to the end.

Sometimes the wife holds the upper hand, as illustrated by a Wisconsin farmer who complained: "Came to Wis., bought 160 A, put it in my Wife's name, and as soon as she found out
(30) that the law of Wis. gave the husband absolutely nothing, she will not give me *one cent*, or go a single place, or will not buy me any clothe, only working clothe. Now, can I compell her to pay me a salary, without leaving her. And I shopped
(35) three horses, one cow, one calf, one brood sow, wagon and harness, buggy and harness, and can *I* dispose of them?" This Mr. Bumble was told that he was at liberty to "go places" as he saw fit, could control the stock enumerated, and dic-
(40) tate the terms on which he would work in his wife's vineyard, but that the Wisconsin law makes her secure in the sole ownership of the farm which he unadvisedly caused to be conveyed to her.

(45) Another rebellious husband writes that he conveyed his property to his wife to defeat his judgment creditors. "Now I want my wife to Deed some of it back to me but she refuses to do that on account the feeling is not at best between
(50) us." He wanted to know if it wouldn't be a good plan to confess to the creditors, and get the property deeded "back to me as it was before as the hole Deal was a Fraud." The main objection to this plan being that it would enable the creditors
(55) to get the property, it was suggested that Friend Wife be permitted to retain control, especially since he could not compel her to revest title in him.

Another case is stated as follows: "The con-
(60) tents of case are—A newly married couple, the young lady having come to the decision that life is unbearable to live with her husband because she hates him and cannot bear his ways of manners. She wishes them to part, and he will not
(65) agree to it. And she thinks of going to her parents to live, and take her belongings that she had before being married with him, and the husband says no—what has she a right to do? Or does the belongings belong to him also?" Without

(70) encouragement to a domestic rupture, the correspondent was told that a woman's ownership of
personal property is not affected by her marriage.

A jilted girl sought advice about how to "fix"
her unfaithful sweetheart. He promised marriage
(75) three times, but as the wedding day approached
he "always had some excuse. If it weren't the
crops, it was the widow-women. If it weren't the
widow-women, it was something else. He never
had written his love for me in a letter. But when
(80) I was with him he was all love and kisses and
so on. He said in one of his letters, 'Make all you
can this fall in no matter what kind of work as it
may not last forever.' But he has backed out now
for good."

(85)   But problems of the heart are by no means the
only cause for correspondence. Rights between
employer and employee are frequently called
into question. One indignant woman employed
on a farm objected that the "landlord brought out
(90) a large worthless dog and we have been feeding
him, have been paying thirty dollars a sack for
flour and twenty-two dollars per week for corn
meal to feed him. We have asked several times
to take him away as we cannot afford to feed
(100) him. This mutt is no earthly account for any
thing and he seldom gets up. He just lies there,
wagging his tail, eager for his meals. We don't
need or want him here and have told him so."

I disclaim any intention to unduly discredit
(105) the intelligence or high-mindedness of any of my
correspondents for, as already intimated, the
freak letters are few as compared with the general run of submissions. My observations in reading thousands confirm my belief that most
(110) people, regardless of their wealth or walk in life,
stand upon an equal plane intellectually and
morally, when fair allowance is made of individual opportunities and environment. I may
smile for a moment or two over the occasional
(115) rude spelling or unschooled language of one
writer out of 50, but I sober up when I reflect that
he or she may have earned a larger percentage
of dividend on the opportunities presented than
I have on mine.

17. The main purpose of this passage most likely is to
   (A) examine the different types of commonly occurring domestic disputes
   (B) describe the failed schemes of people who try to outwit the law
   (C) analyze the legal recourse available to people in oppressive situations
   (D) determine the role of a newspaper in helping its readers through advice columns
   (E) validate the authenticity of strange but heartfelt submissions that newspapers publish

18. The word "conveyed" in line 44 most likely means
   (A) trusted
   (B) transported
   (C) transferred
   (D) bequeathed
   (E) bypassed

19. The author probably wades through submissions to the paper with
   (A) incessant laughter
   (B) weary disillusionment
   (C) restrained contempt
   (D) profound disbelief
   (E) infrequent smiles

20. The author relates the story of Mr. Bumble the farmer in order to
   (A) warn farmers that Wisconsin law can be dangerous
   (B) emphasize that some wives are suffering in silence while waiting for a chance to gain the upper hand
   (C) highlight a turning point in the forces that brought about the liberation of women
   (D) illustrate the pitfalls of not taking legal advice before trusting someone even as close as a wife
   (E) to entertain the reader with a pathetic but amusingly worded domestic dispute

21. The essential difference between the Limburg cheese letter and the letter in paragraph three is that the Limburg cheese letter was

    (A) a freak letter whereas the other letter was commonplace

    (B) merely absurd whereas the other letter was amusing

    (C) written by a Utah man and the other letter by a Connecticut woman

    (D) an information query while the other letter was for legal advocacy

    (E) concerned with powerful odors and the other letter with stubbornness

22. In this passage, the author probably uses excerpts from submissions

    (A) so readers may judge for themselves the extent to which farming communities are petty and illiterate

    (B) because they possess an amusing flavor that is lost if converted to polished prose

    (C) to lend authenticity to what might otherwise be unconvincing narrative

    (D) to show that pathetic snarls can have an amusing facet if only linguistically

    (E) so the reader may not misinterpret the information or suspect the author of fabrication

23. From the various examples used in the passage, the reader can conclude that

    (A) the farm paper is based in Utah or Wisconsin

    (B) Wisconsin law stipulates that in a farm the wife secures sole ownership

    (C) hating your husband's unbearable manners is sufficient grounds for divorce

    (D) large dogs are capable of consuming 62 dollars' worth of meal in a week

    (E) some farm people were not hesitant to solicit advice from newspapers

24. Which of the following can be inferred from the advocacy given in one or more of the cases mentioned?

    (A) The farm and livestock do belong to his wife, but Mr. Bumble may decide how he wants to work on it.

    (B) If a Deal was based on Fraud it can be rendered null and void.

    (C) A wife retains control over her personal property even if her husband raises a dispute.

    (D) A general statement in a letter is not legally considered as a sign of intent to marry.

    (E) A landlord has the right to add livestock or animals to a farm without the tenant's consent.

Questions 25–27 are based on the following passage.

One of the strangest facts in literary criticism is that, after more than 40 years of intense and occasionally even feverish activity on the part of scholars of Beckman, the question of what is
(5) Beckman's "Song to Me" is still a legitimate one. If the poem were a brief and much-mutilated fragment containing part of a single episode, the present state of criticism would be understandable and excusable. But of this poem we have
(10) nearly all that was written or planned by the author. Though incomplete, the extant copy contains 21,258 lines, and it obviously can never have been intended to contain much more. We have, therefore, in the present version, nearly all
(15) that he intended to write.

Moreover, we have, as an indication of the meaning of the poem, the title given by the author himself. And we have a positive and definite statement not only of the main features of
(20) the narrative as far as it is preserved to us but also of the principal incident of the unwritten portion.

Why, then, are not the purpose and meaning of the poem clear and well recognized? Several
(25) reasons may be suggested.

In the first place, much of the study devoted to this poem has been concerned not with the interpretation of the author's meaning but with the discovery of the sources of his materials. What

(30) suggested the temple? And the figures on the walls? And the treeless desert? Did the eagle come from Ovid, or from Dante, or from folklore? Whence came the ice-capped mountain and the revolving house? Correct answers to these ques-

(35) tions would be interesting. If rightly used, they might be important. But they could hardly, in any event, contribute largely to the interpretation of the poem, for an author's meaning depends not upon where he got his material, but upon what

(40) use he makes of it.

That students of Beckman should persist in interpreting him allegorically is strange. As a matter of fact, his work is singularly free from allegory in the strict sense of the term. The mere

(45) presence of nonhuman actors, whether animal or mythological or even personified abstractions, does not create allegory. For this, there must be symbolism of action or of character. But a debate between two girls concerning their lover is not

(50) allegory, even if birds take sides and debate and fight, and the decision is left to the god of love or his representative.

25. According to the passage, Beckman scholars benefit from all of the following EXCEPT

   (A) the extant copy of the poem has 21,258 lines

   (B) "Song of Me" has always been published as the author intended

   (C) Beckman himself gave the work a title

   (D) the principal incident surrounding the poem is clear

   (E) the present version of the poem is faithful to Beckman's intention

26. The author of the passage implies that an allegorical reading of Beckman's work is "strange" because

   (A) allegories are common in the Bible and Beckman was not religious when he wrote this poem

   (B) the poem lacks personified abstractions

   (C) "Song to Me" does not suggest that the plot or the characters are symbolic of anything

   (D) Beckman used other works to explore allegory

   (E) birds and other animals are the actors instead of people

27. According to the passage, in order to understand "Song to Me" more fully, scholars should

   (A) examine the competing editions of the text to see what Beckman's intended meaning was

   (B) discover the sources for the elements of Beckman's work

   (C) view the poem as an extended allegory of opposing forces

   (D) abandon current lines of scholarship and further explore basic questions about meaning and purpose

   (E) balance their research between criticism and interpretation

---

Directions: *For questions 28–38, select the lettered choice most nearly opposite in meaning to the word given in CAPITAL letters. Circle the letter of your choice.*

---

28. UNANIMOUS:

   (A) luminous

   (B) agreeable

   (C) discordant

   (D) united

   (E) uniform

29. DELINQUENT:
   (A) juvenile
   (B) mischievous
   (C) delayed
   (D) early
   (E) delicate

30. ROTUND:
   (A) angular
   (B) tall
   (C) stout
   (D) straight
   (E) dietetic

31. FORTHRIGHT:
   (A) furthermost
   (B) fatuous
   (C) fatalistic
   (D) furtive
   (E) fortuitous

32. LATENT:
   (A) dormant
   (B) rubber
   (C) patent
   (D) plastic
   (E) paternal

33. GALE:
   (A) storm
   (B) breeze
   (C) monsoon
   (D) anemometer
   (E) blizzard

34. MELLIFLUOUS:
   (A) melodious
   (B) superfluous
   (C) grating
   (D) superficial
   (E) melancholy

35. WAX:
   (A) melt
   (B) wave
   (C) dull
   (D) shine
   (E) wane

36. FALLACIOUS:
   (A) irrational
   (B) valid
   (C) indifferent
   (D) faulty
   (E) logical

37. PERVIOUS:
   (A) permeable
   (B) previous
   (C) pernicious
   (D) prescient
   (E) impenetrable

38. ORBICULAR:
   (A) round
   (B) convoluted
   (C) planetary
   (D) straight
   (E) visionary

Quick Answer Guide

Test 1, Section 2: Verbal

1. B	11. D	21. D	31. D
2. A	12. B	22. C	32. C
3. A	13. B	23. E	33. B
4. A	14. C	24. C	34. C
5. A	15. D	25. B	35. E
6. B	16. E	26. C	36. B
7. A	17. E	27. D	37. E
8. C	18. C	28. C	38. D
9. D	19. E	29. D	
10. D	20. E	30. A	

For explanations to these questions, see Day 12.

Test 1, Section 2: Verbal
Explanations and Strategies

Assignment for Today:

Review the explanations for the Verbal Test you took on Day 11.

---

1. Correct choice (B) remuneration

The sentence makes it pretty clear that the server is working just for the money. So to find the right answer, select the word that has something to do with earning money. Choice (B) fits just right. *Remuneration* means compensation or money.

The food server said her work was just a job and that she was doing it for the *remuneration* and nothing else.

2. Correct choice (A) purported..increase

You can find the right answer to this question by using a different strategy for each blank. First, think of what word you might use for the second blank. The sentence should tell you that having national health care is going to raise taxes. Choice (A) fits beautifully here. Now try the elimination strategy for the first blank. Again, nothing works very well here except *purported* in choice (A).

According to the minority political party, the major problem with national health insurance reform, as a *purported* alternative to more government spending, is that it's a tax *increase*.

3. Correct choice (A) disproportionately

Note the flag word, "because," at the beginning of the sentence. This tells you that the last part of the sentence is caused by the first part.

The sentence tells us that the tax burden is nearly five times greater for poor and middle-income Americans than for rich Americans. In other words, the tax load is lopsided. An adverb that means uneven or inequitable would fit the context nicely. So choice (A), *disproportionately*—which means unevenly distributed—is the correct answer.

Because the bulk of tax revenue comes from various sales taxes, the burden of payment falls *disproportionately* on the shoulders of poor and middle-income Americans who spend roughly 16 percent of their incomes on taxable goods, while the richest Americans spend only about 3.1 percent.

4. Correct choice (A) extemporized..cognizant

The sentence itself gives you some major clues even before you see the possible choices. First off, if a musician loses her music, she will either have to stop playing or make stuff up as she goes along. The sentence indicates that the musician is clever, so you can be fairly sure she made stuff up. The people watching did not notice what she did. So look for words that fit these ideas. Choice (A) works best.

After the wind blew away the musician's music, she *extemporized* so cleverly that the people watching were not *cognizant* of the mishap.

5. Correct choice (A) unwavering..expunge

The easy part about this question is deciding what kinds of words will adequately fill the blanks—something like "hopeful" and "erase." The hard part is knowing which words have these meanings. Choice (A) offers *unwavering*, which means solidly confident, and *expunge*, which means to remove all evidence of existence. This is the best choice.

The dermatologist was *unwavering* that the new surgical procedure he worked ten years to invent would be able to *expunge* all signs of having a tattoo.

6. Correct choice (B) expatiated on..garrulous

The best bet for finding the correct choice is to simply read in the choices, eliminating those that don't work well. Then you will have to make some fine distinctions about which choice best fits the context of the sentence. All in all, (B) works best. To *expatiate* is to elaborate. This works well for a politician. *Garrulous* means talkative—another good word for a politician.

When the mayor announced her candidacy for the next term, she *expatiated on* the virtues of her past term while the reporters took copious notes and wished she weren't so *garrulous*.

7. Correct choice (A) bantering..colloquy

The sentence clues and the flag word "but" indicate that the first blank is best filled by a word that means "light talk," while the second word should mean "serious talk." (A) is the best choice here. *Bantering* means playful kidding. A *colloquy*, in contrast, is a serious conference.

After work, Miriam would go home and enjoy *bantering* with her husband and children, but at work she talked in lofty tones that were reminiscent of a *colloquy*.

8. Correct choice (C) raconteur:anecdote

statesman—a person skilled in the art of government.
government—the control of the actions of a community or nation.

A *statesman* is a person skilled in the art of *government*.

Is a *raconteur* skilled in the art of *anecdote*? Yes. A *raconteur* is a person skilled in relating *anecdotes* interestingly (an expert teller).

9. Correct choice (D) chandler:candles

cobbler—a person who makes shoes.
oxfords—shoes, something worn on the foot.

A cobbler makes oxfords.

Does a *chandler* make *candles*? Yes! A *chandler* is a candle maker. Therefore, *cobbler* is to oxfords as *chandler* is to *candles*.

10. Correct choice (D) odometer:dashboard

rib—one of the 24 bones that cover the thorax.
thorax—the front part of the body, between the neck and the belly; the chest.

A *rib* is part of the *thorax*.

Is an *odometer* part of the *dashboard*? Yes. An *odometer* is an instrument that shows the number of miles traveled, and is part of the dashboard in an automobile.

11. Correct choice (D) fatuous:sense

surreptitious—to be secretive.
candor—honesty and sincerity.

To be *surreptitious* means to lack *candor*.

Does being *fatuous* mean to lack *sense*? Yes. To be *fatuous* is to be silly and inane.

12. Correct choice (B) tree:forest

page—a single sheet of paper in a book.
tome—a large or scholarly book.

A *tome* consists of many *pages*.

Does a *forest* consist of many *trees*? Yes. Therefore, a *tome* consists of many *pages* in the same way that a *forest* consists of many *trees*.

13. Correct choice (B) fanatic:zealous

ephemeral—lasting a very short time.
rainbow—a short-lived phenomenon in the sky

A characteristic of a rainbow is that it is ephemeral.

Is a *fanatic zealous?* Yes! A *fanatic* is one who exhibits intense devotion or *zeal.* Therefore, *rainbow* is to *ephemeral* as *fanatic* is to *zealous.*

14. Correct choice (C) parliament:legislation

forum—an assembly for the discussion of public affairs.

discussion—debate, exchange of views, examination by argument.

A *forum* is a body of people assembled for *discussion.*

Is a *parliament* a body assembled for *legislation?* Yes. *Parliament* is the legislative body of representatives that makes or enacts laws.

15. Correct choice (D) eschew:avoid

excoriate—to wear off the skin.
abrade—to rub away by friction.

To *excoriate* is the same as to *abrade.*

Is to *eschew* the same as to *avoid?* Yes.

16. Correct choice (E) glasses:see

mnemonic—a device used to aid memory.
remember—to recall.

A *mnemonic* is a device used to help one *remember.*

Are *glasses* a device used to help one *see? Glasses* are a device used to correct poor vision, thus enabling a person to *see* more clearly.

17. Correct choice (E)

This passage seems to contain a series of anecdotes or different incidents. In this case, the first paragraph contains clues that tie them together.

In the first sentence, the author admits he used to question the validity or genuineness of submissions in newspaper columns. The author then lists a number of strange cases he received, news of which convinced him that unusual submissions were authentic.

18. Correct choice (C)

"Convey" can mean "transport, transmit, communicate" or, in a legal context, "transfer" (titles, deeds, property, etc.). The context here is legal. Besides, none of the other choices make sense when you talk about property, such as a farm.

19. Correct choice (E)

Lines 15-17 tell us that "one correspondent in 50 unconsciously sends in a gem that gives the editor a smile with which to rest his tired countenance." This implies that 49 out of 50 submissions don't make the editor smile. "Infrequent (or occasional) smiles" describes this nicely. The other choices don't come close.

20. Correct choice (E)

The author is trying to tell the reader that advice columns describe real problems or situations, even if they seem funny or strange. Given this purpose, only choice (E) makes sense. The other choices assume that the author is trying to give advice.

21. Correct choice (D)

This choice sounds too superficial or easy. But all the other choices have something wrong with them. We know the former was written for "information concerning the nature and habits of Limburg cheese" (lines 7-8). We know the latter was for "advice concerning her property rights" (line 23). That's enough evidence to support this choice.

22. Correct choice (C)

What sounds like a personal judgment really has to do with the author's main purpose in the passage. The author is out to entertain readers and convince them that advice columns are not made up. Keeping this in mind, it becomes obvious that choice (C) is the best answer. One good way of supporting the authenticity of a column and making it more believable is to have different submissions, each with its own characteristics.

23. Correct choice (E)

This looks like a simple choice. It doesn't say much. But the other choices can be ruled out because of obvious inaccuracies. The passage speaks of farm people who asked for advice. Logical inference: Some farm people were not hesitant to solicit advice from newspapers.

24. Correct choice (C)

The question is very specific. Which of the following can be inferred from the *advocacy* given, *not* from the descriptions or disputes. Examine each choice carefully against the passage. In lines 70-72, " . . . the correspondent was told that a woman's ownership of personal property is not affected by her marriage." So a wife's dispute with her husband cannot affect personal property.

25. Correct choice (B)

According to the passage, all the statements given are helpful to Beckman scholars except (B). The passage says nothing about the publication history of the poem. Furthermore, the publication history would be less beneficial to these specific scholars than the other facts, which deal with Beckman's idea about what the poem should be and mean.

26. Correct choice (C)

In order to have allegory, the author states, "there must be symbolism of action or of character." Because the author argues against reading "Song of Me" as an allegory, we can safely conclude that the poem does not suggest this kind of symbolism.

27. Correct choice (D)

It should be clear that the author wants scholars to get away from two current lines of research: sources of materials and allegorical criticism. In many ways, the author is asking his colleagues to get back to the basic questions of purpose and meaning without wandering off into more alluring (and, to him, less productive) scholarship. The author here is still eager to see great scholarship done on meaning and purpose.

28. Correct choice (C) discordant

Unanimous means in complete agreement.

   Discordant means in disagreement, clashing, conflicting. It's the opposite of *unanimous.*

29. Correct choice (D) early

Delinquent means late, failing in duty, or unpaid.

   Early means premature or before its time. Is early the opposite of *delinquent*? As *delinquent* can mean late (such as "your payment is delinquent"), this is a good choice.

30. Correct choice (A) angular

Rotund means rounded or chubby.

   Angular means lean or sharp-edged. Is *angular* the opposite of *rotund*? Yes.

31. Correct choice (D) furtive

Forthright means straight to the point.

   Furtive means sneaky, surreptitious. Is *furtive* the opposite of *forthright*? Yes, to be indirect (*furtive*) is the opposite of straight to the point (*forthright*).

32. Correct choice (C) patent

Latent means potential, concealed or hidden.

   Patent means obvious or exposed (among other meanings). It's nearly opposite of *latent.*

33. Correct choice (B) breeze

Gale means a very strong wind.

   Breeze means a light wind. Is a breeze the opposite of a gale? Yes—a breeze is a light wind whereas a gale is a strong wind.

34. Correct choice (C) grating

Mellifluous means smooth or pleasant sounding.

   Grating means hard, unpleasant. Is *grating* the opposite of *mellifluous*? Yes—sweet musical sounds would be *mellifluous*, not *grating.*

35. Correct choice (E) wane

Wax means grow larger.

   Wane means grow smaller in size. Is *wane* the opposite of *wax*? Yes, *wax* means grow larger in size.

36. Correct choice (B) valid

Fallacious means faulty, false, or negative.

   Valid means sound, true, or reasonable. Is *valid* the opposite of *fallacious*? Yes, the two words provide you with several excellent opposite meanings.

37. Correct choice (E) impenetrable

Pervious means penetrable.

   Impenetrable means impervious. Is *impenetrable* the opposite of *pervious*? Yes.

38. Correct choice (D) straight

Orbicular means round, bulb-shaped.

    Straight means shallow. Is *straight* the opposite of *orbicular*? Yes, planets move in round—not *straight*—orbits.

Test 1, Section 3: Analytical

Questions and Answers

Assignment for Today:

Take a sample GRE analytical test under actual test conditions. Allow yourself exactly 30 minutes to complete the 25 questions in this test.

Directions: The following questions are based either on a brief passage or a number of conditions. For each question, circle the best answer among the choices given. You may wish to draw diagrams to help you answer some of the questions.

Questions 1–4 are based on the following.

The Western Derby is a race held annually at Bayshore Racetrack. There are eight gates at the racetrack, but only seven horses are entered in this race—Julius Caesar, King's Bounty, Longshot, Man Among Boys, Nocturnal, Odyssey, and Phantom. One of the gates is left empty. The horses are at the gate, waiting for the race to begin.

Gate 1, on the inside of the racetrack, is occupied.

Phantom is at a gate inside of Nocturnal.

The number of gates separating Julius Caesar and King's Bounty equals the number of gates separating Longshot and Man Among Boys.

Nocturnal and Odyssey are next to each other.

1. If Odyssey is at Gate 2, which of the following must be true?

   (A) Nocturnal is at the innermost gate.

   (B) King's Bounty is at the outermost gate.

   (C) A horse occupies the outermost gate.

   (D) Phantom is at the innermost gate.

   (E) The outermost gate is not empty.

2. Which of the following is a possible assignment for the horses, from the inside to the outside?

   (A) Phantom, King's Bounty, Julius Caesar, Odyssey, Nocturnal, Man Among Boys, Longshot, vacant

   (B) vacant, Phantom, Julius Caesar, Longshot, King's Bounty, Man Among Boys, Nocturnal, Odyssey

   (C) Longshot, Man Among Boys, Nocturnal, vacant, Phantom, Odyssey, King's Bounty, Julius Caesar

   (D) Julius Caesar, King's Bounty, Longshot, Phantom, vacant, Man Among Boys, Nocturnal, Odyssey

   (E) Phantom, Julius Caesar, Nocturnal, vacant, Odyssey, King's Bounty, Longshot, Man Among Boys

3. If Julius Caesar is at Gate 6, King's Bounty is at Gate 7, and Odyssey is at Gate 4, which of the following must be true?

   I. Longshot is at Gate 1.

   II. Nocturnal is at Gate 5.

   III. Man Among Boys is at Gate 2.

   IV. Gate 8 is vacant.

   (A) I and II only

   (B) II and III only

   (C) II and IV only

   (D) I, II, and III only

   (E) I, II, III, and IV

4. If Julius Caesar and King's Bounty are at the second and fourth gates, respectively, all of the following can be true EXCEPT

   (A) Phantom is at Gate 1

   (B) Man Among Boys is at Gate 3

   (C) Longshot is at Gate 6

   (D) Odyssey is at Gate 7

   (E) Nocturnal is at Gate 7

5. Studies have shown that families who install smoke detectors and own fire extinguishers have a reduced risk of losing a child in a house fire. Therefore, no family who installs smoke detectors and owns a fire extinguisher will lose a child in a house fire.

Of the following, the best criticism of the argument above is that the argument does not

   (A) take into account the possibility of losing a child in a house fire despite all precautionary measures

   (B) indicate that fire extinguishers are effective during early stages of a fire

   (C) cite the fact that smoke detectors have proven to be effective in waking sleeping children during a house fire

   (D) differentiate between the two major causes of house fires: cooking and heating

   (E) take into account that families who buy smoke detectors are also more likely to purchase fire insurance

6. LSD is a drug known to cause synesthesia, a phenomenon in which sensory input somehow becomes interchanged in the brain: a person with synesthesia might smell a symphony, hear sunlight, or taste a pinprick. While most cases are drug induced, some people suffer from synesthesia in various forms since birth.

Which of the following can be most safely inferred from the information above?

   (A) Synesthesia is not always a drug-induced phenomenon.

   (B) Some great artists of this century have been known for their synesthetic proclivities.

   (C) LSD is an addictive drug.

   (D) Synesthesia is rarely bothersome to those who experience it.

   (E) Synesthesia at birth is a result of mothers who have tried LSD.

7. Palindromes are easier to solve than acrostics, but acrostics are more difficult to create than palindromes. Rebuses are more difficult to solve than acrostics, yet rebuses are easier to create than palindromes.

If the above information is true, then it must also be true that

   (A) acrostics are more difficult to create than rebuses

   (B) palindromes are more difficult to solve than rebuses

   (C) rebuses are easier to solve than acrostics

   (D) acrostics are easier to create than rebuses

   (E) rebuses are easier to solve than palindromes

Questions 8–13 are based on the following.

In a baseball field, one team can practice at a time. There are seven teams—the Aces, the Bears, the Cubs, the Ducks, the Eagles, the Falcons, and the Giants. The baseball field is open seven evenings a week from Monday to Sunday (Sunday being considered the last day of the week), and the allocation of practice times is governed by the following rules:

On any evening, only one team can play.

The Aces must practice on Monday.

The Ducks practice exactly one day before the Falcons practice.

The Falcons practice exactly one day before the Giants practice.

The Cubs and the Bears must practice earlier in the week than the Eagles.

8. The latest day in the week that the Bears can practice is
   (A) Tuesday
   (B) Wednesday
   (C) Thursday
   (D) Friday
   (E) Saturday

9. If a person went to the baseball field on three consecutive evenings, he or she could see which of the following teams in the order listed?
   (A) the Falcons, the Giants, the Cubs
   (B) the Falcons, the Giants, the Ducks
   (C) the Aces, the Ducks, the Cubs
   (D) the Bears, the Cubs, the Falcons
   (E) the Ducks, the Eagles, the Falcons

10. One week, the Cubs practiced on Wednesday and the Ducks practiced the next day. That week, the Bears must have practiced on
   (A) Monday
   (B) Tuesday
   (C) Friday
   (D) Saturday
   (E) Sunday

11. If the Giants practice on Thursday, the Eagles and the Ducks must practice on which days, respectively?
   (A) Sunday and Tuesday
   (B) Saturday and Tuesday
   (C) Friday and Wednesday
   (D) Wednesday and Thursday
   (E) Tuesday and Monday

12. If the Falcons practice on Saturday, the Eagles must practice on what day?
   (A) Tuesday
   (B) Wednesday
   (C) Thursday
   (D) Friday
   (E) Sunday

13. The practice schedule has to adhere to which of the following?
   (A) The Ducks practice earlier in the week than the Eagles.
   (B) The Falcons practice on a later day than the Eagles.
   (C) The Falcons practice earlier in the week than the Giants.
   (D) The Cubs practice earlier in the week than the Ducks.
   (E) The Bears practice earlier in the week than the Cubs.

Questions 14–19 are based on the following.

Nine athletes attend a sports banquet. Three of the athletes—J, K, and L—are varsity football players; two of the athletes—M and N—are varsity basketball players. The other four athletes—O, P, Q, and R—belong to the hockey club. All nine athletes will be seated at three small tables, each seating three athletes. The athletes must be seated according to the following rules:

O and J do not sit at the same table.

P sits together with at least one of K or M.

There can be at most only one football player at a table.

There can be at most only one basketball player at a table.

14. Suppose just one varsity athlete sits at a certain table, and that athlete happens to be J. If so, who else sits with J?

    (A) P, Q

    (B) P, R

    (C) Q, R

    (D) O, Q

    (E) O, P

15. If a table consists of L, Q, and R, which of the following trios sits at one of the other tables?

    (A) K with M and O

    (B) K with N and O

    (C) J with M and O

    (D) J with K and N

    (E) M with N and P

16. Which trio could sit together?

    (A) P, R and O

    (B) M, N and O

    (C) K, N and O

    (D) K, M and O

    (E) J, Q and O

17. J and M are seated at one table. Which of the following are possible seating arrangements for the remaining two tables?

    (A) K with O and R, L with N and P

    (B) K with P and Q, L with O and R

    (C) K with L and W, N with Q and R

    (D) L with N and O, K with Q and R

    (E) O with P and Q, K with N and R

18. Which of the following must be true?

    (A) J is sitting with a basketball player.

    (B) Exactly one hockey player is sitting at L's table.

    (C) No hockey players sit at one table.

    (D) A basketball player is sitting with O.

    (E) A football player sits with two hockey players.

19. Which of the following pairs will not sit with P?

    (A) J, M

    (B) K, L

    (C) K, M

    (D) K, O

    (E) L, M

Questions 20–22 are based on the following.

A university has a procedure for registering and recording complaints. Due to strict bureaucractic regulations, the following system of passing complaints must be observed:

A is the first registrar to receive all incoming complaints.

F is the recorder and final adminstrator to handle a complaint.

Personnel B, C, D, and E may pass complaints only as follows:

A to B

B to either C or D

C to either B or E

D to C

E to either D or F

20. Which is an acceptable path for a complaint to follow, passing from A?

    (A) B to C to D to F

    (B) B to D to C to F

    (C) B to C to E to F

    (D) B to E to F

    (E) D to C to F

21. If a complaint is received and is handled by each personnel member only one time, which of the following could be one of the passes?

    (A) A to C

    (B) C to B

    (C) C to F

    (D) D to C

    (E) E to D

22. Between which two personnel may a complaint pass by means of two different paths without any duplication of passes?

    (A) B to E

    (B) C to D

    (C) C to E

    (D) D to B

    (E) E to B

23. Wine, cheese, butter, and raisins are all examples of early techniques to preserve food. In modern times, food scientists have developed other techniques such as dehydration, hermetic sealing, and radiation. Of these, radiation is the most controversial because preliminary studies have shown that radiation alters the natural chemical bonds in fruits and vegetables. Instead of providing salutary effects, eating radiated produce may well introduce irritating chemicals into the body, creating a possible health hazard.

    Which of the following, if true, supports the conclusion that eating radiated produce poses a possible health hazard?

    (A) Radiation affects only those chemical bonds associated with water, that is, hydrogen and oxygen.

    (B) Radiation kills microorganisms that hasten food decay.

    (C) The radiation-induced bonds are unlike any of those found in non-radiated produce.

    (D) Certain microorganisms, namely those found in yogurt cultures, are essential for proper digestion.

    (E) Radiation has no effect on foods preserved by drying.

24. Blue Blood, Inc., is a private blood products company that buys blood only from qualified donors. To qualify, a person must weigh at least 105 pounds, must not have taken malaria medication in the last three years, must never have had hepatitis, and must never have used intravenous drugs.

    Blue Blood nurses know that traveling has an effect on the possibilities for blood donation: Everyone who travels to Malaysia is required to take malaria medication; no one who enters Singapore can have ever used intravenous drugs; everyone traveling to Gorisimi gets hepatitis.

    Which of the following situations would not automatically disqualify a person from selling blood to Blue Blood?

    (A) traveling to Malaysia two years ago

    (B) having once weighed 110 pounds and now weighing 95 pounds

    (C) being denied admission to Singapore

    (D) traveling to Gorisimi five years ago

    (E) using intravenous drugs that were legal at the time

25. Before marriage, couples should be tested for AIDS and any other sexually communicable diseases. Negative results will guarantee the health and safeness of their marriage.

    Which of the following is an assumption of the argument in the passage above?

    (A) Current state laws require couples who are planning to get married to be tested for infectious disease in order to prevent possible health problems in the future.

    (B) There are many infectious diseases that can be sexually transmitted from one individual to another.

    (C) Fortunately even if a test proves positive for a communicable disease, couples can still lead healthy marriages by taking the proper precautions.

    (D) Due to advances in medical research over the years, infectious diseases that used to be fatal can now be effectively treated.

    (E) All the diseases detectable through testing have no incubation period and the results of these tests can immediately indicate whether or not the individual has the disease.

Quick Answer Guide

Test 1, Section 3: Analytical

1. D	8. E	15. B	22. B
2. A	9. A	16. C	23. C
3. C	10. B	17. D	24. C
4. C	11. A	18. E	25. E
5. A	12. C	19. B	
6. A	13. C	20. C	
7. A	14. C	21. D	

For explanations to these questions, see Day 14.

Test 1, Section 3: Analytical
Explanations and Strategies

Assignment for Today:

Review the explanations for the Analytical Test you took on Day 13.

Questions 1–4:

From the facts, the following chart and symbols can be drawn:

```
—   —   —   —   —   —   —   —
1   2   3   4   5   6   7   8
^
H
P . . . . . . . N
ON or NO
```

And circle the entire third statement, which is difficult to chart, to help you keep it in mind.

1. Correct choice (D)

From the question, Odyssey is in gate 2:

```
        O
—   —   —   —   —   —   —   —
1   2   3   4   5   6   7   8
```

Since Nocturnal is next to Odyssey, it has to be at either gate 1 or 3.

If Nocturnal is at gate 1, then:

```
N   O
—   —   —   —   —   —   —   —
1   2   3   4   5   6   7   8
```

But this does not allow Phantom to be on the inside of Nocturnal. So Nocturnal must be at gate 3. Then the only gate free on the inside of it is gate 1, which is where Phantom must be:

```
P   O   N
—   —   —   —   —   —   —   —
1   2   3   4   5   6   7   8
```

2. Correct choice (A)

This is the only answer where the sequence fits all the facts.

```
P   K   J   O   N   M   L   x
—   —   —   —   —   —   —   —
1   2   3   4   5   6   7   8
```

Phantom is on the inside of Nocturnal; Nocturnal is adjacent to Odyssey; gate 1 is occupied by Phantom; King's Bounty and Julius Caesar are adjacent, as are Man Among Boys and Longshot. Viola! We've found our assignment!

3. Correct choice (C)

If Julius Caesar is at gate 6, King's Bounty is at gate 7, and Odyssey is at gate 4, a diagram can be drawn as:

			O		J	K	
—	—	—	—	—	—	—	—
1	2	3	4	5	6	7	8

Since Julius Caesar is adjacent to King's Bounty, Longshot must be adjacent to Man Among Boys. Thus, Longshot and Man Among Boys must occupy two of the three gates from 1 to 3.

L/M	L/M						
M/L	M/L		O	J	K		
—	—	—	—	—	—	—	—
1	2	3	4	5	6	7	8

Since Nocturnal must be adjacent to Odyssey, it must occupy either gate 3 or gate 5. However, Nocturnal must be at a gate such that there is a gate inside of it available for Phantom. So Nocturnal must be at gate 5, and Phantom can be either at gate 1 or gate 3:

P							
L/M	L/M						
M/L	M/L	P	O	N	J	K	x
—	—	—	—	—	—	—	—
1	2	3	4	5	6	7	8

Therefore, the only conditions that we are certain of are conditions II and IV, which specify that Nocturnal is at gate 5 and the vacant gate is gate 8, the outermost gate.

4. Correct choice (C)

If Longshot is to be at gate 6, then Man Among Boys must be at gate 8 so that the number of gates between them is the same as the number of gates between Julius Caesar and King's Bounty.

	J		K		L		M
—	—	—	—	—	—	—	—
1	2	3	4	5	6	7	8

If this is the case, then there are no longer two consecutive gates for Nocturnal and Odyssey.

5. Correct choice (A)

This question asks you to select the choice that would weaken the claim that no family that takes certain precautions against house fires will lose a child in a fire. The best strategy is to read the choices and eliminate those that are irrelevant or that strengthen (rather than weaken) the argument. If you do this, you are left with choice (A). Indeed, precautions such as smoke detectors and fire extinguishers are no guarantee that children will not die in house fires. Note that the passage says "reduced risk," not "no risk."

6. Correct choice (A)

Your job is to find a statement that is a safe inference based on the information in the passage. The best way to find the right answer is to read each choice and eliminate those that cannot be safely inferred. Be careful not to be distracted by answer choices that are merely "true"; instead, you must find one that the passage implies.

The best choice here is (A): that synesthesia is not always a drug-induced phenomenon. The last sentence makes this inference quite clear: "Some people suffer from synesthesia in various forms since birth." This implies that LSD has nothing to do with some cases of synesthesia.

7. Correct choice (A)

This question is like a mini-logic game. To solve this quickly you must write out two categories and fill in the information from the passage. The categories are "solve" and "create."

According to the passage, the solving levels, from easy to hard, go like this:

SOLVING: palindrome, acrostic, rebus

(rebus is at the hard end).

The creating levels, listed easy to hard, are

CREATING: rebus, palindrome, acrostic

(acrostic is at the hard end).

Once you have this information down, just check the choices against it. The only one that works is (A): Acrostics are more difficult to create than rebuses. This is true because "rebuses are easier to create than palindromes" and "acrostics are more difficult to create than palindromes." This makes acrostics more difficult to create than rebuses.

Questions 8–13:

From the facts, we have:

$$\frac{A}{M}$$

DFG

C – –

      E

B – –

8. Correct choice (E)

From the facts, we can see that the Bears cannot practice on Sunday because the Eagles must practice at a later day than the Bears. However, the Bears can practice on Saturday. For example, the following is an acceptable schedule with the Bears on Saturday:

A	D	Tu	G	C	B	E
—	—	—	—	—	—	—
M	Tu	W	Th	F	Sa	Su

9. Correct choice (A)

We get this answer by eliminating all the other choices. All the other choices are flawed. The Falcons and the Giants have to practice consecutively in that order, and it is possible for the Cubs to practice right after the Giants. For example,

A	D	F	G	C	B	E
—	—	—	—	—	—	—
M	Tu	W	Th	F	Sa	Su

10. Correct choice (B)

For this question, we have:

A		C	D			
—	—	—	—	—	—	—
M	Tu	W	Th	F	Sa	Su

Because the Ducks, Falcons, and Giants must practice in that order on consecutive days, and because the Eagles must practice after the Bears and the Cubs, we have the following order:

A	B	C	D	F	G	E
—	—	—	—	—	—	—
M	Tu	W	Th	F	Sa	Su

So the Bears must practice on Tuesday.

11. Correct choice (A)

For this question, we have:

A					G	
—	—	—	—	—	—	—
M	Tu	W	Th	F	Sa	Su

Because the Ducks, Falcons, and Giants must practice in that order on consecutive days, the Ducks must play on Tuesday:

A	D	F	G			
—	—	—	—	—	—	—
M	Tu	W	Th	F	Sa	Su

Since the Eagles must practice after both the Cubs and the Bears, the Eagles must practice on Sunday.

12. Correct choice (C)

For this question, we have:

A					F	
—	—	—	—	—	—	—
M	Tu	W	Th	F	Sa	Su

Because the Ducks, Falcons, and Giants must practice in that order on consecutive days, we have:

A			D	F	G	
—	—	—	—	—	—	—
M	Tu	W	Th	F	Sa	Su

If the Eagles are to practice after both the Bears and the Cubs as the rules state, then they must practice on Thursday.

13. Correct choice (C)

We can see from the last rule that the Giants must practice the next day after the Falcons.

Questions 14 –19:

From the facts, we have
    VARS Foot = J, K, and L
    VARS Bask = M, N
        Hock = O, P, Q, R

   Q̸J̸

PK or PM or PKM

  — — —   — — —   — — —

14. Correct choice (C)

For this question, we have J at a table with no other varsity athlete.

J

___ ___   ___ ___   ___ ___

This means the other two seats must be taken up by two of O, P, Q, and R. However, one of the facts states that O and J cannot be at the same table. P also cannot sit at this table because he sits with either K or M, who are both varsity athletes, and there are no varsity athletes other than J at this table. Thus, the two other athletes must be Q and R.

15. Correct choice (B)

If L, Q, and R are at one table, then the two other tables must have J, K, M, N, O, and P.

L Q R

___ ___   ___ ___   ___ ___

J and K must sit at different tables and M and N must sit at different tables because no two varsity athletes from the same sport sit at the same table. Also, since O and J do not sit at the same table, O must sit with K. So for the other two tables we have

J M P   K N O   J N P   K M O

___ ___   ___ ___ or ___ ___   ___ ___

The second possibility listed above is not valid because it violates the fact that if P is at a table, either K or M must be there too. Thus, the correct seating arrangement is the one on the left, above.

16. Correct choice (C)

O, K, and N can sit at a table if J, M, and P sit at one table and L, Q, and R sit at the other:

O K N   J M P   L Q R

___ ___   ___ ___   ___ ___

17. Correct choice (D)

We arrive at this choice by eliminating the choices that have flaws. For this seating arrangement, we have

J M P   L N O   K Q R

___ ___   ___ ___   ___ ___

This choice satisfies all the facts above.

18. Correct choice (E)

Since no table has two varsity athletes from the same sport, and there are three football players, each table must have one football player. Since there are four hockey players and only three tables, at least one table will have two hockey players.

19. Correct choice (B)

Since K and L are both football players, they do not sit at the same table together. Thus, P does not sit at the same table as these two athletes.

Questions 20–22:

From the facts, we have

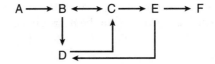

20. Correct choice (C)

From the diagram, we know that a complaint can travel from A to B to C to E to F.

21. Correct choice (D)

We arrive at this answer by eliminating all the other choices. The complaint could travel from A to B to D to C to E and then out to F.

22. Correct choice (B)

A complaint may go from C to D either via E or via B.

23. Correct choice (C)

Your task here is to find a statement that strengthens the conclusion about the possible danger of radiating produce. The best strategy is to read through the answer choices and eliminate those that weaken the conclusion and those that are not relevant.

Choice (C) is the best choice. Although this statement doesn't provide solid evidence for the dangers of radiation, it does raise concern about the effects of radiation because the new bonds are unlike anything else normally found in produce. This rests on an assumption that natural is good and unnatural is bad, a line of thinking that is widely accepted. In any event, this is the only statement that strengthens the claim.

24. Correct choice (C)

Your challenge in this question is to find the choice that would *not* automatically disqualify someone from selling blood to Blue Blood. The best way to do this is to go through the choices like a true/false test, eliminating those choices that make a person ineligible. By doing this, you will find that (C) is the only possibility. Being denied admission to Singapore does not necessarily mean that the person has used intravenous drugs. There may be other reasons, such as political unrest, that could get in the way of traveling to Singapore. Therefore, a person who has been denied admission to Singapore may still be eligible to sell blood.

25. Correct choice (E)

Usually when people get infected with a communicable disease, their immune system begins to develop antibodies to the viruses causing the disease. The tests used for detection specifically look for these antibodies. The activation of these antibodies is not immediate. Therefore, an individual may be infected but still test negative. The passage assumes that none of the diseases go into this "sleep period." Antibodies are immediately activated upon initial infection and no "sleep period" occurs.

Test 1, Section 4: Math

Questions and Answers

Assignment for Today:

Take a sample GRE math test under actual test conditions. Allow yourself exactly 30 minutes to complete the 30 questions in this test.

Directions: For questions 1–15, each question contains two quantities—one on the left (Column A) and one on the right (Column B). Compare the quantities and answer

A   if Column A is greater than Column B

B   if Column B is greater than Column A

C   if the two columns are equal

D   if you cannot determine a definite relationship from the information given

Never answer E

In some questions, information appears centered between the two columns. Centered information concerns each of the columns for that question only. Any symbol in one column represents the same value if it appears in the other column.

	Column A	Column B
1.	$\dfrac{3}{4} - \dfrac{2}{3}$	$\dfrac{3}{4} - \dfrac{2}{5}$
2.	$0.7p + 0.006q$	$0.7p + 0.06q$
3.	Area of a circle with radius π	Circumference of a circle with radius π

Column A	Column B		Column A	Column B

The number of cells in an
organism doubles every hour.

The organism has 1 cell at noon.

4. | Number of cells in the organism at 3:00 p.m. of the same day | 6 |

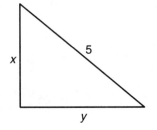

The ratio $x{:}y$ is 3:5

5. | $15x$ | $9y$ |

8. | $\sqrt{x^2+y^2}$ | $\sqrt{5^2}$ |

m is a positive integer

$n = m\,(m + 1)\,(m + 2)$

m, n, and p are factors of 60

$m \neq n \neq p$

9. | 1 | The remainder when n is divided by 6 |

6. | Highest possible value of the average (arithmetic mean) of m, n, and p | 20 |

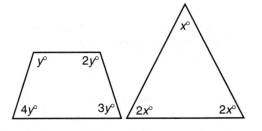

Note: Figure not drawn to scale

7. | $2ab - 1$ | $4ab - 1$ |

10. | y | x |

Column A	Column B

11.

The number of integers between 8 and 8^4	The number of integers between −8 and $(-8)^4$

$n > 0$

12.

$\dfrac{n}{0.44}$	$\dfrac{0.56}{n}$

$x = -1$

13.

$\dfrac{5x + \dfrac{4}{3}}{3}$	$\dfrac{4x + \dfrac{5}{3}}{3}$

Let #x# denote the sum of the tens digit of x and the units digit of x. For example, #14# = 1 + 4 = 5.

Let {y} denote #y + 5#. For example, {19} = #24# = 2 + 4 = 6.

14.

{53} − #44#	53 − 44

Column A	Column B

The six sides of a cube are each assigned a different number between 1 and 6 and the cube is tossed without any systematic pattern.

15.

The probability that the cube will land on the same side twice in a row.	The probability that the cube will land on the number 3 twice in a row.

Directions: *For questions 16–30, solve each problem, and select the appropriate answer choice, A–E. Circle the letter of your choice.*

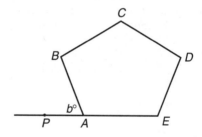

16. *ABCDE* is a regular pentagon. What is angle *PAB*, denoted by *b*, in the figure above?

(A) 36

(B) 72

(C) 100

(D) 108

(E) Cannot be determined

17. A square with a diagonal of length $5\sqrt{2}$ has the same area as circle O. What is the radius of circle O?

(A) $\dfrac{5}{\sqrt{\pi}}$

(B) $\dfrac{5}{2\sqrt{\pi}}$

(C) $\dfrac{25}{2\pi}$

(D) $\dfrac{25}{\pi}$

(E) 5

18. Five lamps, each with a different colored light bulb, are used to light up a room. If each lamp can be either on or off, and any combination of the lamps may be on at one time, in how many ways can the room be lit (including having all lamps off)?

(A) 5

(B) 7

(C) 10

(D) 25

(E) 32

19. Jerry, Kerry, and Larry divide 60 jelly beans among themselves in the ratio 3:4:5, respectively. The number of jelly beans Larry got was how many more than the average number (arithmetic mean) of jelly beans that each person got?

(A) 1

(B) 5

(C) 7

(D) 13

(E) 25

20. If x and y are factors of 24, what is the least possible value of their sum?

(A) –25

(B) –24

(C) 10

(D) 11

(E) 24

Questions 21–26 are based on the following figure.

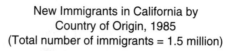

New Immigrants in California by
Country of Origin, 1985
(Total number of immigrants = 1.5 million)

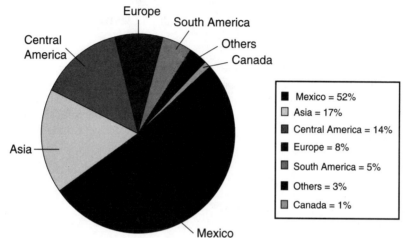

Legend:
■ Mexico = 52%
□ Asia = 17%
■ Central America = 14%
■ Europe = 8%
■ South America = 5%
■ Others = 3%
□ Canada = 1%

Central America	
El Salvador	97,000
Nicaragua	83,000
Honduras	18,000
Guatemala	8,000
Others	4,000

South America	
Colombia	34,000
Ecuador	24,000
Peru	10,000
Others	7,000

Asia	
Philippines	109,000
India	42,000
Israel	38,000
Iran	33,000
China	21,000
Others	12,000

Europe	
Italy	42,000
France	33,000
Portugal	19,000
Ireland	14,000
Others	12,000

21. According to the chart, approximately how many new immigrants were from Mexico in 1985?

(A) 52,000

(B) 78,000

(C) 520,000

(D) 720,000

(E) 780,000

22. New immigrants from the Philippines represent approximately what percent of new Asian immigrants?

(A) 7

(B) 17

(C) 43

(D) 87

(E) 109

23. Approximately how many more new immigrants are from Europe than from South America?

    (A) 45,000
    (B) 75,000
    (C) 195,000
    (D) 300,000
    (E) 450,000

24. Approximately what percent of total new immigrants were from El Salvador and Colombia?

    (A) 9
    (B) 13
    (C) 19
    (D) 28
    (E) 46

25. If there were 480,000 new immigrants from Mexico in 1984, what is the approximate percent increase in the number of new immigrants from Mexico from 1984 to 1985?

    (A) 38
    (B) 62
    (C) 109
    (D) 162
    (E) 217

26. If $a(8 - 5) = 8 - \dfrac{5}{a}$, then what is a possible value for a?

    (A) $-\dfrac{5}{3}$
    (B) 1
    (C) $\dfrac{5}{3}$
    (D) 5
    (E) 8

27. If $5050 \times 0.5y = 126{,}250$, then $5050 \div y^2 =$

    (A) 2.02
    (B) 2.2
    (C) 101
    (D) 202
    (E) 12,625,000

$$P = 4900 \times 10^n$$

$$-3 < n < 3$$

28. According to the rules above, how many different integer values of n will make P a perfect square?

    (A) 1
    (B) 2
    (C) 3
    (D) 4
    (E) 5

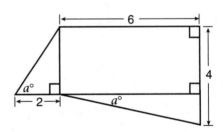

29. The figure above consists of two right triangles and one rectangle. What is the area of the figure?

    (A) 12
    (B) 16
    (C) 20
    (D) 24
    (E) cannot be determined

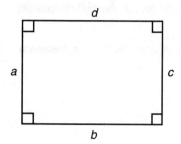

Note: Figure not drawn to scale.

30. What is one half the perimeter of the rectangle $abcd$ if its area is 50 and $a^2 + b^2 = 125$?

(A) 15

(B) $15\sqrt{2}$

(C) 25

(D) 30

(E) 225

Quick Answer Guide

Test 1, Section 4: Math

1. B	9. A	17. A	25. B
2. D	10. C	18. E	26. C
3. A	11. B	19. B	27. A
4. A	12. D	20. A	28. C
5. C	13. B	21. E	29. B
6. A	14. B	22. C	30. A
7. D	15. A	23. A	
8. D	16. B	24. A	

For explanations to these questions, see Day 16.

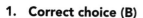

Day 16

Test 1, Section 4: Math
Explanations and Strategies

Assignment for Today:

Review the explanations for the Math Test you took on Day 15.

---

1. Correct choice (B)

Notice that "$\frac{3}{4}$" is in both columns. So we can cancel this term and not even consider it. So, we're really comparing $-\frac{2}{3}$ in Column A and $-\frac{2}{5}$ in Column B.

We know that $\frac{2}{3}$ is approximately .667. So $-\frac{2}{3}$ is about -0.667. And, $\frac{2}{5}$ is 0.4. So $-\frac{2}{5}$ is -0.4.

So, Column A = -0.667. Column B = -0.4.

Then, Column B is greater because it's a smaller negative number.

2. Correct choice (D)

Both columns have the quantity $0.7p$, and so we can get rid of it from both sides. Then we are really comparing $0.006q$ in Column A and $0.06q$ in Column B.

Let's plug in values for q and compare the columns.

If $q = 0$, in Column A, $0.006q = 0$ and in Column B, $0.06q = 0$.

This says that both columns are equal.

But, if $q = 1$, then $0.006q = 0.006$ (Column A) and $0.06q = 0.06$ (Column B), and so Column B is greater. Because we get two different results, we can conclude that the correct answer is (D).

3. Correct choice (A)

For Column A, we need to find the area of a circle with radius π. We know that the area of a circle is πr^2, where r is the radius. If we take the radius of the circle to be π,

Column A = Area of circle = $\pi r^2 = \pi(\pi)^2 = \pi^3$.

Circumference of a circle is given by the formula: $2\pi r$. If π is the radius, then,

Column B = Circumference of circle = $2\pi r = 2\pi(\pi) = 2\pi^2$.

So, we're comparing π^3 in Column A with $2\pi^2$ in Column B. Notice that we can cancel π^2 from both sides, so that we compare π in Column A with 2 in Column B.

Then Column A = π = 3.14 and Column B = 2.

So, Column A is greater.

4. Correct choice (A)

If the organism has 1 cell at noon, then, at 1:00 p.m., it will have 2 cells (double of 1). At 2:00 p.m., it will have 4 cells (double of 2), and at 3:00 p.m. it will have 8 cells (double of 4). So, Column A is greater than Column B.

5. Correct choice (C)

To solve this problem, we can first find an equation that relates x and y. Because $x{:}y$ is 3:5, we can say

$$\frac{x}{y} = \frac{3}{5}$$

$$5x = 3y$$

Solving for x, we get

$$x = \frac{3}{5}y$$

To determine the value of $15x$ in terms of y, we can multiply both sides of this equation by 15, giving us:

$$15x = \frac{15 \times 3}{5}y$$

$$= 9y$$

Here we see that $15x$ equals $9y$, so the values in both columns are equal.

6. Correct choice (A)

Let's first find the factors of 60. The easiest way is to start from 1 and list all numbers that divide evenly into 60. They are 1, 2, 3, 4, 5, 6, 10, 12, 15, 20, 30, and 60.

(On the test, to see if you have all the factors or not, take the first number (1) and multiply it by the last (60), take the second number (2) and multiply it by the second from the last (30), and work your way inward. All the products should be 60. For example, 1×60, 2×30, 3×20, 4×15, 5×12, and 6×10 all give you 60.)

Anyway, to find the largest possible value of the average, take the three largest factors—20, 30, and 60. Their sum is $20 + 30 + 60 = 110$. Their average is $110 \div 3 = 36$ and change.

So, Column A is slightly more than 36 and Column B is 20. So, Column A is greater than Column B.

7. Correct choice (D)

Let's first eliminate the "–1" from each side. (You can always eliminate equal numbers, but not necessarily equal letters, from each side.) So we're really comparing $2ab$ in Column A with $4ab$ in Column B.

Now let's plug in our special value of zero for either a or b. If $a = 0$, Column A = 0 and Column B = 0. So the columns could be equal. Now let's plug in 1 for a and b. Then, Column A = $2(1)(1) = 2$, and column B = $4(1)(1) = 4$. Now B is greater than A.

As soon as we get two different results, the answer has to be choice (D), cannot be determined.

8. Correct choice (D)

This triangle looks like it's a right triangle. BUT, there's nothing that says it is. So watch it!

IF the triangle were a right triangle, AND if 5 were the hypotenuse, then Columns A and B would be equal. But, in the given triangle, we have no way of knowing.

For example, if $x = 2$ and $y = 4$, then Column A would be equal to $\sqrt{20}$ and Column B would be equal to $\sqrt{25}$, which means Column B would be greater. But what would happen if $x = 3$ and $y = 5$? Then, Column A would be greater. This tells us that the correct answer is (D).

9. Correct choice (A)

The best way to do this problem is to plug in values for m. Let's say that m is 1. Then, $n = 1 \times 2 \times 3 = 6$. The remainder when 6 is divided by 6 is 0, and so Column B is 0. Then, Column A is greater than Column B.

If m is 2, then $n = 2 \times 3 \times 4 = 24$. Again, the remainder (when 24 is divided by 6) is zero, and so Column A is greater than Column B.

If m is 3, then $n = 3 \times 4 \times 5 = 60$. The remainder is again 0 and Column A is greater than Column B.

We could try this a couple of more times, but, we'll find that n will always be a multiple of 6. In other words, n divided by 6 will always have a remainder of 0. So, Column A will always be greater than Column B.

10. Correct choice (C)

To solve this problem, we must know that the sum of all the interior angles of any figure is $180(n - 2)$, where n is the number of sides. In a triangle, $n = 3$, and so the sum of all angles is $180(3 - 2)$, which is $180(1)$, or $180°$.

Let's apply this to Column B. We know that all three angles have to add up to 180°. That is, $x + 2x + 2x = 180$

Or, $5x = 180$

Then, $x = 36°$.

So,   Column B is 36°

Let's use our formula to find the sum of all interior angles in Column A. The figure has four sides, and so $n = 4$. Then, the sum of all interior angles is $180(4 - 2) = 180(2) = 360°$.

There are four different angles. Let's add them up and make the sum equal to 360°.

Then $y + 2y + 3y + 4y = 360$

That is, $10y = 360$

Or, $y = 36°$

So,   Column A = Column B = 36°

The correct answer is choice (C).

11. Correct choice (B)

Let's work this problem in terms of a number line. Then, the integers described in Column A go from positive 8 to 8^4. All of them lie on the positive side of the number line.

To work Column B, we need to remember that a negative number taken to an *even* power is *positive*. For example, $(-3)^2$ is positive 9. So, $(-8)^4$ is a positive number, and in fact $(-8)^4 = 8^4$. So, in terms of our number line, the integers described in Column B go from -8 to 8^4. Clearly, there are more integers in Column B because Column B includes the negative integers from -8 to 0, whereas Column A doesn't.

12. Correct choice (D)

We know that n is a positive number. So, let's plug in different positive values for n and see what answers we get.

To make things easy, let's first plug $n = 0.44$. That way, we can cancel the numerator and denominator in Column A.

If $n = 0.44$, Column A $= \dfrac{0.44}{0.44} = 1$.

Column B $= \dfrac{0.56}{0.44}$, which is greater than 1 (because it's a top-heavy fraction).

So, when $n = 0.44$, Column B is greater than Column A.

Now let's try $n = 0.56$ (so that we can cancel the top and the bottom in Column B).

If $n = 0.56$, Column A $= \dfrac{0.56}{0.44} > 1$ (top-heavy fraction).

Column B $= \dfrac{0.56}{0.56} = 1$.

Now Column A is greater than Column B. Because we get two different results, the right answer is choice (D).

13. Correct choice (B)

Before we plug in values for x, we can cancel the 3s in the denominator from both sides. So, we are really comparing:

$5x + \dfrac{4}{3}$ in Column A and $4x + \dfrac{5}{3}$ in Column B.

Now, let's plug in the value of $x = -1$.

Column A $= -5 + \dfrac{4}{3} = -5 + 1.33 = -3.67$

Column B $= -4 + \dfrac{5}{3} = -4 + 1.67 = -2.33$

Because Column B has a smaller negative number, Column B is greater.

14. Correct choice (B)

Column B is easy. It's $53 - 44 = 9$.

Now, let's work Column A.

{53} = #53 + 5# = #58# = 5 + 8 = 13. And #44# = 4 + 4 = 8. So,

{53} − #44# = 13 − 8 = 5. Therefore, Column A is 5 and Column B is 9, and Column B is greater than Column A.

15. Correct choice (A)

An easy way to solve probability problems is to use the formula:

$$\text{probability} = \frac{\text{favored outcome}}{\text{total outcomes}}$$

The trick here is to find what the total number of outcomes is. If we toss a cube once, there are six possible ways the cube could land: 1–2–3–4–5–6. For every number that comes up on the first toss, there are six possibilities for the second toss. That is, if 1 comes up the first time, there are six possibilities for the second: 1–2–3–4–5–6. This is true for every side of the cube, as shown in the diagram below:

Toss #1	Possibilities for Toss #2
1	1 2 3 4 5 6
2	1 2 3 4 5 6
3	1 2 3 4 5 6
4	1 2 3 4 5 6
5	1 2 3 4 5 6
6	1 2 3 4 5 6

There are a total of 36 ways the cube can land.

In Column A, there are six favored outcomes (1-1, 2-2, 3-3, etc.) and so the probability is: $\frac{6}{36}$, or $\frac{1}{6}$. In Column B, there is only one favored outcome (3-3) and so the probability is $\frac{1}{36}$. So, Column A is greater.

16. Correct choice (B) 72

We're told this is a *regular* pentagon, which means all sides are equal and so all interior angles are equal. To find the total interior angle of a figure, we can use the formula:

Interior angle = $180(n - 2)$, where n is the number of sides in the figure.

(If you forget the formula, think about a triangle, for which $n = 3$ because it has 3 sides. Then the formula gives you $180(3 - 2)$, which is $180(1)$, or 180.)

In a pentagon, $n = 5$ because it has five sides. Then,

Interior angle = $180(5 - 2) = 180(3) = 540$

This is the sum of all interior angles. Because there are five such angles, each interior angle is $540 \div 5$, which is $108°$.

But $108°$ is not the right answer, mind you. We're asked for angle b. Notice that PAE forms a straight line. If angle EAB is $108°$ (1 interior angle), then angle b must be $180 - 108 = 72°$, which is choice (B).

17. Correct choice (A) $\frac{5}{\sqrt{\pi}}$

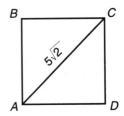

For problems like this, it's helpful to draw a diagram, such as the one shown above. We're told that diagonal AC of square $ABCD$ is $5\sqrt{2}$. Notice that side AD is equal to side CD (both are sides of a square) and, in the triangle ADC, AC is the hypotenuse. Let's say side $CD = x =$ side AD.

Then, $(5\sqrt{2})^2 = x^2 + x^2 = 2x^2$

Taking the square root, we get $5\sqrt{2} = \sqrt{2}\,x$

We can cancel the $\sqrt{2}$ from both sides of the equation so that

$5 = x$

(Actually, we could have found the length of CD by noting that ADC is a 45-45-90 triangle whose hypotenuse is $\sqrt{2}$ times the length of one of the sides.)

So, the length of each side of the square is 5. Then, its area is 25. We're told that the circle has the same area as the square. So, if the area of the square is 25, the area of the circle is also 25. Now, let's plug 25 into the formula for the area of a circle, πr^2, so that:

$25 = \pi r^2$

Dividing by π, we get $\frac{25}{\pi} = r^2$

Taking the square root, $\frac{5}{\sqrt{\pi}} = r$, which is the answer.

18. Correct choice (E) 32

We see that any lamp may be either on or off, so in deciding how to light the room, for each lamp we must choose one of two possible choices. To count the number of ways that more than one lamp can light the room, we *multiply* the number of choices together.

For example, with two lamps, there are *four* possibilities: both lamps off, both lamps on, the first lamp on and the second lamp off, and the first lamp off with the second lamp on. With three lamps, there are eight combinations. With four lamps, there are 16 combinations. And with five lamps, there are 32 possible ways of having the lamps on and off.

As each lamp has two possible modes (on or off), the math is:

$2 \times 2 \times 2 \times 2 \times 2 = 2^5 = 32$

19. Correct choice (B) 5

Let's first figure out the sum of the three individual ratio numbers, which is 3 + 4 + 5 = 12. Then,

Jerry got $\dfrac{3}{12} \times 60 = 15$ jelly beans,

Kerry got $\dfrac{4}{12} \times 60 = 20$ jelly beans,

and Larry got $\dfrac{5}{12} \times 60 = 25$ jelly beans.

Check to see that these three numbers add up to 60 (15 + 20 + 25 = 60).

We know that there was a total of 60 jelly beans shared by three people. Then, the average number of jelly beans each person got has to be 60 ÷ 3 = 20. So, Larry got 25 – 20 = 5 more than the average, which is choice (B).

20. Correct choice (A) –25

Let's look at the choices: two negative numbers. This should give us a clue. Remember, –24 × –1 gives us 24. So, both –24 and –1 are factors of 24. Now the problem is easy. The lowest value of the sum of two factors of 24 is (–24 + –1), which is equal to –25, choice (A).

21. Correct choice (E) 780,000

The title of the chart says that the total number of new immigrants was 1.5 million. We know from the chart that 52% of new immigrants were from Mexico. So, the number of new immigrants from Mexico = 52% of 1.5 million = 52% of 1,500,000.

Notice that 52% means slightly greater than half of 1.5 million. We know that half of 1.5 million is 750,000. Now we should look for an answer that is slightly greater than 750,000. So, the closest answer would be choice (E) 780,000.

22. Correct choice (C) 43

Let's first find the total number of immigrants from Asia.

Total Asian immigrants = 109,000 + 42,000 + 38,000 + 33,000 + 21,000 + 12,000

= 255,000

We know that the total number of immigrants from the Philippines is 109,000. So now we need to answer the question: 109,000 is what percent of 255,000?

Notice that half (or 50%) of 255,000 would have been about 125,000. So we can approximate 109,000 as a little below 50%. Now look for an answer that is slightly below 50%. Choice (C), 43, is the best answer.

23. Correct choice (A) 45,000

Of all new immigrants, 8% were from Europe and 5% were from South America. So, there were 8% – 5% = 3% more immigrants from Europe than South America. We know that the total number of new immigrants is 1.5 million. So now we should find 3% of 1.5 million.

Then, 3% of 1.5 million = .03 × 1,500,000

= 45,000.

24. Correct choice (A) 9

From the figure, we see that 97,000 new immigrants came from El Salvador and 34,000 new immigrants came from Colombia. Thus, a total of 131,000 new immigrants came from El Salvador and Colombia combined. We know that there were a total of 1.5 million new immigrants. So now the question is:

131,000 is what percent of 1.5 million? To find the required percent, we can use the formula:

$$\text{Required percent} = \frac{131,000}{1,500,000} \times 100\%$$

$$= \frac{131}{1,500} \times 100\% = \frac{131}{15} \approx 9$$

So the correct answer is choice (A), 9.

25. Correct choice (B) 62

In 1985, from the figure, 52% of all new immigrants were from Mexico. We know that the total number of new immigrants was 1.5 million. So, the total number of new immigrants from Mexico in 1985 = 52% of 1.5 million = .52 × 1.5 million = .78 million = 780,000.

In 1984, the number of new immigrants from Mexico was 480,000. Then, the increase in the number of new immigrants from Mexico = 780,000 − 480,000 = 300,000. To find the percent increase, we can use the formula:

$$\text{percent increase} = \frac{\text{increase}}{\text{number in 1984}} \times 100\%$$

$$= \frac{300,000}{480,000} \times 100\% = \frac{300}{480} \times 100\% = \frac{30}{48} \times 100\%$$

$$= \frac{5}{8} \times 100\%$$

$$= 62.5\%$$

So, the closest answer is choice (B), 62.

26. Correct choice (C) $\frac{5}{3}$

The easiest way to work this problem is to plug the value for a back into the problem and see if it works. Before we do that, let's simplify the given equation. So that

$$a(8-5) = 8 - \frac{5}{a} \text{ becomes}$$

$$3a = 8 - \frac{5}{a}$$

As usual, we start from choice (C). So, let's plug

in $a = \frac{5}{3}$. Then, $3 \times \frac{5}{3} = 8 - \dfrac{\frac{5}{5}}{3}$

Or, $5 = 8 - 5 \times \frac{3}{5}$

Or, $5 = 8 - 3 = 5$

So, this value of a works and choice (C) is the right answer.

27. Correct choice (A) 2.02

We are given:
$5050 \times 0.5y = 126,250$
Dividing both sides by 5050, we get:
   $0.5y = 25$
Dividing both sides by 0.5, we get:
   $y = 50$

Now that we know the value of y, we can solve the problem:
   $5050 \div y^2 = 5050 \div (50)^2 = 5050 \div 2500$

$$= \frac{5050}{2500}$$

$$= 2.02$$

28. Correct choice (C) 3

Not an easy problem, that's for sure. The key is to realize that 49 will be a perfect square if it has 0, 2, 4, 6, 8, . . . zeros after it. In other words, 49 (no zeros) is a perfect square (7 × 7), 4,900 (two zeros) is a perfect square (70 × 70), 490,000 (four zeros) is a perfect square (700 × 700), and so on.

So, let's plug in values for n, remembering that n can be equal to −2, −1, 0, 1, or 2. Don't forget: n cannot equal −3 or 3.

If $n = -2$, $P = 4,900 \times 10^n = 4,900 \times 10^{-2} = 49$. (A perfect square).

(When you multiply by 10^{-2}, it's like dividing by 100).

If $n = -1$, $P = 4,900 \times 10^{-1} = 490$. (Not a perfect square).

If $n = 0$, $P = 4,900 \times 10^0 = 4,900$. (A perfect square).

(Multiplying by 10^0 is the same as multiplying by 1 because anything raised to the power of 0 is equal to 1.)

If $n = 1$, $P = 4{,}900 \times 10^1 = 49{,}000$. (Not a perfect square).

If $n = 2$, $P = 4{,}900 \times 10^2 = 490{,}000$. (A perfect square).

There are three perfect squares (when $n = -2, 0,$ or 2), which means n can have three different values.

29. Correct choice (B) 16

The trick to this problem is to rearrange the two triangles and one rectangle to form one large right triangle. Two possible results are:

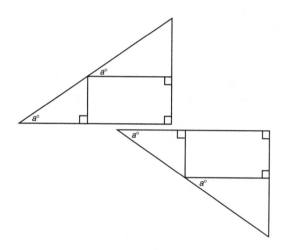

We know this is a right triangle because the two angles labeled a are equal and both start from parallel lines (the rectangle's sides).

With the newly drawn figure, we use $A = \dfrac{1}{2}bh$ to calculate the area of the large right triangle:

$$A = \frac{1}{2}bh$$
$$= \frac{1}{2} \times (6+2) \times 4$$
$$= 16$$

30. Correct choice (A) 15

The perimeter of the rectangle is $a + b + c + d$, which is the same as $2(a + b)$. In other words, $(a + b)$ is half the perimeter.

Note also that $(a + b)^2 = a^2 + b^2 + 2ab$. But $(a + b)$ is half the perimeter. So, we can write the above equation as:

(half the perimeter)$^2 = a^2 + b^2 + 2ab$. Call this equation #1.

But we are told that $a^2 + b^2 = 125$. Also, the area of the rectangle is ab, which we are told is 50. Then $2ab = 100$.

Let's substitute these two values in equation #1. We get:

(half the perimeter)$^2 = 125 + 100 = 225$. That is,

(half the perimeter) $= \sqrt{225}$, which is 15, choice (A).

Test 1, Section 5: Verbal

Questions and Answers

Assignment for Today:

Take a sample GRE Verbal Test under actual test conditions. Allow yourself exactly 30 minutes to complete the 38 questions in the test.

Directions: For questions 1–7, one or more words have been left out of each sentence. Circle the answer, A–E, that contains the word or words which best fit the meaning of the entire sentence.

---

1. The president's speech contained common words and simple examples mainly because her advisors counseled her to be more _____ instead of being so erudite.

   (A) accessible
   (B) gregarious
   (C) mercenary
   (D) sanctimonious
   (E) saturnine

2. Soon after Mary ascended the English throne in 1553, Parliament voted to reinstate the medieval law that _____ heresy by burning the perpetrator at the stake.

   (A) rewarded
   (B) mollified

   (C) usurped
   (D) punished
   (E) welcomed

3. During the final meeting of the convention, the chairperson _____ that nominations to _____ a party candidate would begin.

   (A) observed..hire
   (B) lamented..constrain
   (C) indicated..impoverish
   (D) clarified..congratulate
   (E) announced..elect

4. The Olympic gold medalist found that her fame was _____ because by the time she arrived home, no one even remembered what she had achieved.

   (A) resilient
   (B) salient
   (C) ephemeral
   (D) lascivious
   (E) lucrative

5. The Sophists taught that influencing forces can be ____ systematically and can be understood through the use of a ____ mind.

(A) mitigated..banal

(B) analyzed..disciplined

(C) conjectured..controlled

(D) dispelled..decrepit

(E) categorized..charlatan

6. The owner of the small-town movie theater was a(n) ____ man who regularly ____ films he thought would be objectionable to his conservative clientele.

(A) pious..expurgated

(B) avaricious..promoted

(C) fastidious..emasculated

(D) disputatious..censored

(E) churlish..attenuated

7. The clearest symbol of the village architect is not a ____ for a simple facade, but the automatic allocation of space for an outhouse that stems from a long and deeply ____ way of life.

(A) penchant..ingrained

(B) prescription..unsanitary

(C) decree..treasured

(D) propensity..urban

(E) yearning..nascent

Directions: For questions 8–16, determine the relationship between the two words given in capital letters. Then, from the choices listed A–E, select the one pair that has a relationship most similar to that of the capitalized pair. Circle the letter of that pair.

---

8. TRUCK:HAUL::

(A) bicycle:race

(B) towel:clean

(C) mentor:guide

(D) road:detour

(E) synapse:feel

9. FAMINE:FOOD::

(A) feast:fowl

(B) market:stall

(C) drought:rain

(D) shoe:foot

(E) cough:wheeze

10. VINTNER:WINE::

(A) professor:students

(B) poet:anthologies

(C) historian:artifacts

(D) physicist:trees

(E) baker:bread

11. SPACE:COSMONAUT::

(A) kitchen:utensil

(B) hangar:pilot

(C) building:architect

(D) frontier:pioneer

(E) market:grocer

12. OFFICE:METIER::

(A) sauna:sweat

(B) leisure:home

(C) engine:power

(D) atelier:artistry

(E) moat:water

13. TOURNIQUET:BLOOD::

(A) thermometer:fever

(B) computer:information

(C) ligature:stitch

(D) moratorium:repayment

(E) check:money

14. PROMISCUOUS:HARLOT::

(A) puissant:stallion

(B) materialistic:bourgeois

(C) pernicious:detective

(D) incorrigible:thief

(E) sleazy:hotel

15. PLENARY:ASSEMBLY::

(A) bountiful:harvest

(B) saturated:solution

(C) legislative:council

(D) terrestrial:earth

(E) constitutional:monarchy

16. CIRCUMSPECT:INDECOROUS::

(A) circumambient:surrounded

(B) circumstantial:incidental

(C) circumnavigable:global

(D) circumlocutory:terse

(E) circumvolutory:coiled

Directions: Read each passage and answer the questions that follow. Base your answers only on what is stated or implied in the passage.

Questions 17–20 are based on the following passage.

If we only had a Walt Whitman for London! Whitman is one of the voices of the earth, and it is only in Whitman that the paving stones really speak, with a voice as authentic as the voice of
(5) the hills. He knew no distinction between what is called the work of nature and what is the work of man. He left out nothing; what still puzzles us is the blind, loving, embracing way in which he brings crude names and things into his vision—
(10) the name of a trade, a street, a territory—no matter what syllables it might carry along with it. He created a vital poetry of cities. It was only a part of what he did; but since Whitman there is no gainsaying it any more.
(15) It has been said of Whitman that he is mere bathybius, that he is in literature in the condition of protoplasm, that he is a maker of poems in solution, and that he remains an expanse of crystallizable substances, waiting for the structural
(20) change that never came. I think that Stendhal invented the latter phrase in his cold and penetrating study of the physiology of love, *De l' Amour*. He discovered for himself a method of unemotional, minute, slightly ironical analysis,
(25) which has fascinated modern minds.

In the case of Whitman, what is evident in his pages is that men played a greater part in his life's drama than women. As his life is a mixture of lawful and lawless propensities and rebellious
(30) instincts, there is no coordination in his vagabond existence between such clashing qualities in so strange a temperament. He gives one an extraordinary sense of bodily sensations. He sees nothing really spiritual in flesh—he is too much
(35) of a materialist. Certain of his vices are indecent; yet how often one sees in nature indecency! To be immodest or prurient is an inherent vice: Whitman is neither.

17. The author apparently believes that Walt Whitman's writing is

(A) cold and penetrating

(B) immodest and prurient

(C) quixotic and whimsical

(D) earthy and authentic

(E) obscure and forgotten

18. Which of the following best describes the author's tone in the discussion of Whitman's writing?

(A) sarcastic

(B) laudatory

(C) disparaging

(D) droll

(E) dispassionate

19. Which of the following statements about Whitman can be inferred from the passage?

(A) He lived a life of hermetic solitude.

(B) He spent much of his time in cafés.

(C) He wrote honestly, if indecently.

(D) He wrote extensively about his romances with women.

(E) He saw the world chiefly in spiritual terms.

20. The phrase "mere bathybius" in lines 15-16 is used in the passage to indicate the

    (A) clarity of Whitman's prose and poetry

    (B) unsurpassed literary genius of Whitman

    (C) uncategorizable nature of Whitman's talent

    (D) prototypicality of Whitman's genius

    (E) fascinating nonsentimentality of Whitman's mind

Questions 21–27 are based on the following passage.

The undergraduate college, during the last two decades, has been the target of a great deal of miscellaneous criticism, and no one knows as well as those on the inside how much it is de-
(5) served. The college has been accused, in some cases with reason, of crimes against almost all nature of educational misdemeanors and felonies: of laxness in teaching, of flabbiness in discipline, of prehistoric business methods; of
(10) overemphasis on athletics; of providing opportunities for falsified and dubious research; and, in general, of a failure to comprehend and to meet its responsibilities. That many of the attacks upon it have been unintelligent there can be no
(15) doubt, but the discussion aroused, even by such biased caviling, has been helpful and stimulating.

It is a curious but undoubted fact that the stimulus leading to the reformation of institutions very seldom comes from within. Whether
(20) it be the church, the business corporation, the governmental office, or the school, some outside irritation seems to be necessary before the inertia of custom can be shaken off. So, too, it is with the university; only recently have the criticisms
(25) and barbs of non-academicians moved the academy to reconsider its goals and operations.

The progress made during the last several decades has certainly been enormous, and it is still going on. In the better institutions, there has been
(30) little less than a revolution. As to the others, the process of improvement is very rapid.

Mr. Keppel's review of the results achieved—and of the present state of undergraduate instruction throughout the country—is very timely as
(35) well as exceedingly interesting. His experience as

secretary of Columbia University and dean of Columbia College has given him contact with all phases of educational administration. He approaches his subject with a clear mind, with free-
(40) dom from insularity and complete acquaintance with educational progress, so that his book is an authoritative statement of the present stage of the evolution of our undergraduate institutions. He has, withal, an understanding of the psychology
(45) of college students, a thorough and sympathetic appreciation of their virtues, their foibles, and their needs, and he never fails to keep in mind the fact that the college must be adapted to the student, rather than the student to the college.

(50) The book opens with an analysis of the various types of institutions offering the bachelor's degree, and of the strengths and weaknesses of each of these types. This is followed by a discussion of the raw material with which the college
(55) works: the equipment—moral, intellectual and physical—which students bring with them, the social organization of student life, their athletics, and their religious, moral, and intellectual development. Mr. Keppel then passes to a
(60) consideration of the administrative and educational machinery of the college and to its finished product, the alumni.

There can be no doubt that the tone of student life has greatly improved during the last 20 years.
(65) There is much less alcohol abuse than there once was, less boisterousness and less lawlessness. If morality has declined, there is a larger emphasis on the social obligation of the individual. Although some of us, but not Mr. Keppel, believe
(70) that intercollegiate athletics, as presently conducted, cost more than they are worth, we are very ready to admit that even here there has been improvement.

21. The primary purpose of this passage is to
 (A) delineate the virtues of the best colleges
 (B) critique undergraduate education
 (C) review a recently published book
 (D) show how education has changed in the past two decades
 (E) demonstrate the eroding social fabric of the U.S.

22. According to the passage, undergraduate education has recently been accused of all of the following EXCEPT
 (A) lazy teaching
 (B) fabricated research
 (C) outdated business methods
 (D) disregard for student needs
 (E) neglected responsibilities

23. The word "dubious" in line 11 is used to mean
 (A) dishonest
 (B) ambiguous
 (C) doubtful
 (D) vague
 (E) questionable

24. The author implies that a university is similar to a church in that both
 (A) require outside impetus to bring about internal change
 (B) are leaders in advocating social causes
 (C) discipline their members to achieve a higher aim
 (D) must be adapted to fit the needs of their members
 (E) put top priority on teaching social responsibility

25. In comparing the progress made in universities during the last several decades, the passage implies that
 (A) better institutions have a long way to go before they can lay claim to a revolution
 (B) better institutions have changed more

 (C) private colleges have resisted the trend to change
 (D) Mr. Keppel has outlined ten key steps to success
 (E) non-academicians have overstepped their boundaries

26. In describing the qualifications of Mr. Keppel, the passage mentions all of the following EXCEPT that he
 (A) was dean of Columbia College
 (B) understands how students think
 (C) has studied evolution in present stages
 (D) is sympathetic to college students
 (E) is a good thinker

27. According to the passage, Mr. Keppel believes that intercollegiate athletic programs
 (A) cost more than they are worth
 (B) are overemphasized
 (C) need to be reformed
 (D) are worthwhile endeavors
 (E) create a sense of camaraderie among students

Directions: *For questions 28–38, select the lettered choice most nearly opposite in meaning to the word given in CAPITAL letters. Circle the letter of your choice.*

---

28. HYPERBOLE:
 (A) overstatement
 (B) hypnotism
 (C) deemphasis
 (D) rhythm
 (E) stanza

29. EXTEMPORANEOUS:
    (A) fastidious
    (B) prepared
    (C) contemporaneous
    (D) informal
    (E) informed

30. FACETIOUS:
    (A) flippant
    (B) facile
    (C) gratuitous
    (D) grave
    (E) fractious

31. POLEMIC:
    (A) kudos
    (B) persiflage
    (C) anathema
    (D) rubric
    (E) platitude

32. UNDAUNTED:
    (A) dauntless
    (B) remiss
    (C) amiss
    (D) intimated
    (E) dispirited

33. ALACRITY:
    (A) elasticity
    (B) finality
    (C) intervention
    (D) procrastination
    (E) hypocrisy

34. TRADUCE:
    (A) defend
    (B) defray
    (C) betray
    (D) bewilder
    (E) detract

35. GRANDILOQUENT:
    (A) euphuistic
    (B) aphonic
    (C) cryptic
    (D) euphonic
    (E) reticent

36. ACCRETION:
    (A) secretion
    (B) reparation
    (C) agglomeration
    (D) dearth
    (E) contrition

37. VISCERAL:
    (A) vertiginous
    (B) impalpable
    (C) virulent
    (D) impeccable
    (E) incorporeal

38. PROPINQUITY:
    (A) confluence
    (B) resonance
    (C) perspicacity
    (D) iniquity
    (E) distance

Quick Answer Guide

Test 1, Section 5: Verbal

1. A	11. D	21. C	31. A
2. D	12. D	22. D	32. E
3. E	13. D	23. E	33. D
4. C	14. B	24. A	34. A
5. B	15. B	25. B	35. E
6. A	16. D	26. C	36. D
7. A	17. D	27. D	37. E
8. C	18. B	28. C	38. E
9. C	19. C	29. B	
10. E	20. C	30. D	

For explanations to these questions, see Day 18.

Test 1, Section 5: Verbal

Explanations and Strategies

Assignment for Today:

Review the explanations for the Verbal Test you took on Day 17.

1. Correct choice (A) accessible

Flag words: "instead of." The correct choice will mean the opposite of *erudite*, which means scholarly, educated. *Accessible* means simple or understandable. This would describe what the president is trying to do with her simple examples and common words.

The president's speech contained common words and simple examples because her advisors counseled her to be more *accessible* instead of being so erudite.

2. Correct choice (D) punished

Reading through the sentence should give you some idea of which word will fill in the blank. The sentence describes a medieval attitude toward heresy. Heresy is religious dissent or disobedience. You can probably guess that the attitude is not positive. Choice (D) fits well. Heretics were *punished*.

Soon after Mary ascended the English throne in 1553, Parliament voted to reinstate the medieval law that *punished* heresy by burning at the stake.

3. Correct choice (E) announced..elect

The best way to find the missing words is to read the sentence and anticipate the choices. Because the

sentence describes actions taking place during a political convention, you can expect to find words that relate to politics. The first blank should have a word like "said"; both *indicated* and *announced* work well. The word "select" would fit well in the second blank; of the choices given, *elect* works best.

During the final meeting of the convention, the chairperson *announced* that nominations to *elect* a party candidate would begin.

4. Correct choice (C) ephemeral

Ephemeral, or short-lived, is the best answer here. If the medalist's fame has died before she even gets home, that's pretty short.

The Olympic gold medalist found that her fame was *ephemeral* because by the time she arrived home, no one even remembered what she had achieved.

5. Correct choice (B) analyzed..disciplined

Your best approach here is to read the choices and eliminate the ones that don't make sense. In doing this, you'll find that choice (B) works well, much better than the other choices.

The Sophists taught that influencing forces can be *analyzed* systematically and can be understood through the use of a *disciplined* mind.

6. Correct choice (A) pious..expurgated

Reading through the choices is the best way to find the right words. The important thing is to find a word pair that fits the overall meaning of the sentence. Choice (A) turns out to be the best answer. *Pious* means earnestly religious. To *expurgate* is to cut out material. These two words make sense together and with the rest of the sentence.

The owner of the small-town movie theater was a *pious* man who regularly *expurgated* films he thought would be objectionable to his conservative clientele.

7. Correct choice (A) penchant..ingrained

There's a flag: "but." However, it's still a complicated sentence requiring context clues. So, start with the second blank first. Try to understand the sentence's meaning: What is characteristic of the village architect? It's the *automatic habit* of setting aside space for an outhouse. (An outhouse is an outside restroom or lavatory.) Something automatic must be deeply fixed. That's *ingrained*, which means "firmly fixed or deeply rooted."

Penchant means "strong inclination or liking." Plug in both. Makes sense, doesn't it?

The clearest symbol of the village architect is not a *penchant* for a simple facade but the automatic allocation of space for an outhouse that stems from a long and deeply *ingrained* way of life.

8. Correct choice (C) mentor:guide

truck—a motor vehicle used for hauling things
haul—to transport
   A *truck* is used in order to *haul*.

   To find the right answer, you need to see that hauling is the defining characteristic of a truck. Here's a sentence that can help you determine the right answer: If it can't haul, it can't be defined as a truck.

   Is a *mentor* used in order to *guide*? Yes. In fact, the defining characteristic of *mentor* is that he or she is a *guide*, just as the defining characteristic of a *truck* is that it can *haul*.

9. Correct choice (C) drought:rain

famine—lack of food
food—something you eat
   A *famine* is a lack of *food*.

   Is a *drought* the lack of *rain*? Yes, so *drought* has the same relationship to *rain* as *famine* does to *food*.

10. Correct choice (E) baker:bread

vintner—someone who makes wine
wine—alcoholic beverage made from grapes
   A *vintner* is someone who makes *wine*.

   Does a *baker* make *bread*? Yes! Therefore, *vintner* is to *wine* as *baker* is to *bread*.

11. Correct choice (D) frontier:pioneer

space—the expanse where the solar system and beyond exist.
cosmonaut—a Russian astronaut, someone who travels through space.
   A *cosmonaut* is someone who travels through *space*.

   Is a *pioneer* someone who travels through a *frontier*? A *frontier* is an unexplored territory. A pioneer might travel through a frontier, exploring it just as a cosmonaut explores space. So this is the right answer: *space* is to *cosmonaut* as *frontier* is to *pioneer*.

12. Correct choice (D) atelier:artistry

office—a room or set of rooms in which business is transacted.
metier—a skilled trade; a craft or expertise.
   An *office* is one place where a person can conduct his or her *metier*.

   Is an *atelier* a place where a person can conduct his or her *artistry*? Yes. An *atelier* is a workshop or artist's studio.

13. Correct choice (D) moratorium:repayment

tourniquet—a device that halts the flow of blood.
blood—fluid circulating in the vertebrate vascular system.
   A *tourniquet* halts the flow of *blood*.

   Does a *moratorium* halt or arrest *repayment*? Yes. A *moratorium* is a legally authorized delay in an action or the payment of a debt.

14. Correct choice (B)
materialistic:bourgeois

promiscuous—indiscriminate in choice of sexual partners.
harlot—a lewd woman, a prostitute.

A *harlot* is *promiscuous*.

Is the *bourgeois* materialistic? The *bourgeois* is middle-class: wrapped up in *materialistic* concerns, ruled by property values, or lacking in artistic taste. Is it characteristic for the *bourgeois* to be *materialistic*? Typically, yes. A tough one.

15. Correct choice (B) saturated:solution

plenary—full, complete.
assembly—a formal gathering or meeting.

A *plenary assembly* is an *assembly* attended by all members. It is a full or complete *assembly*.

Is a *saturated solution* full or complete? A *saturated solution* contains the greatest amount of material that can be dissolved in it.

16. Correct choice (D) circumlocutory:terse

circumspect—careful or proper.
indecorous—not careful or improper.

Circumspect means nearly the opposite of *indecorous*.

Does *circumlocutory* mean nearly the opposite of *terse*? Yes. *Circumlocutory* means using lots of words. *Terse* means using few words. Therefore, *circumspect* is to *indecorous* as *circumlocutory* is to *terse*. Yes, this was a tough one.

17. Correct choice (D)

Throughout the passage, the author extols the virtues of Whitman's writing. In the first paragraph, the author tells us that Whitman was one of the "voices of the earth," who spoke with a voice "as authentic as the hills."

18. Correct choice (B)

The passage, largely a celebration of Whitman's writing, could thus be called "laudatory," which means relating to or expressing praise.

19. Correct choice (C)

In the first paragraph, the author tells us that Whitman "left nothing out" of his writing, and in the last paragraph we are told that his life was "a mixture of lawful and lawless propensities" and that "certain of his vices are indecent." The implication is that Whitman wrote about life as he saw it, and that what he saw might make more than a few readers blush.

20. Correct choice (C)

What in the world is "bathybius"? Look at what follows this word. The protoplasm-like virtues of Whitman: "poems in solution," "crystallizable," and "waiting for structural change." Protoplasm is not settled. It's always moving, taking on a different shape. So a choice that reflects such a changeable and unsettled quality would be a possible meaning.

Something constantly changing would likely be uncategorizable.

21. Correct choice (C)

This passage is a book review, plain and simple. Even though the first three paragraphs make no mention of a book, the fourth paragraph makes it clear that the author is responding to a book recently written by Mr. Keppel. The fifth paragraph continues the review by outlining the book, topic by topic. Of course, along the way the author of the passage also gets a few words in about education.

22. Correct choice (D)

Paragraph one contains a list of accusations about undergraduate colleges. All of the responses listed are in paragraph one except choice (D), disregard for student needs. Therefore, this is the right answer.

23. Correct choice (E)

In the context of the sentence, the best meaning for "dubious" is "questionable." The author is saying that colleges have been accused of providing opportunities for falsified and questionable research—questionable meaning both in truthfulness and in value.

24. Correct choice (A)

Paragraph two compares a university to a number of other institutions, including a church. The point is that all these institutions require "outside irritation" before they change. The university, the author says, is no different. Therefore, outside criticism often leads to change.

25. Correct choice (B)

In paragraph three, the author is saying that all the colleges are changing rapidly, but that the better institutions have changed more. The author describes the change as a "little less than a revolution," which is quite drastic.

26. Correct choice (C)

Paragraph four lists Keppel's qualification to write a book on undergraduate institutions. Check which choice is *not* mentioned in the passage. If you are careful, you'll find that the words in choice (C) are mentioned ("evolution" and "present stages"), but they are not used in the same sense as in (C). Therefore, (C) is the choice that is not mentioned.

27. Correct choice (D)

The correct answer to this question is not immediately clear; you have to find the answer by finding its opposite. In the last paragraph, the author states that some people are against intercollegiate athletics, but *not* Mr. Keppel. From this, we can safely infer that Mr. Keppel feels athletic programs are worthwhile.

28. Correct choice (C) deemphasis

Hyperbole means overstatement.

Deemphasis means understatement. Is *deemphasis* the opposite of *hyperbole*? Yes—one means understatement, the other overstatement.

29. Correct choice (B) prepared

Extemporaneous means impromptu, at the spur of the moment, not planned.

Prepared means planned in advance. Is *prepared* the opposite of *extemporaneous*? An impromptu speech would not be planned in advance.

30. Correct choice (D) grave

Facetious means not serious.

Grave means somber, serious. Is *grave* the opposite of *facetious*? Yes, *grave* means somber or very serious, the opposite of *facetious*, which means not serious.

31. Correct choice (A) kudos

Polemic means an attack on the principles of another.

Kudos means praise. Is *kudos* the opposite of *polemic*? Yes, at least given the other choices.

32. Correct choice (E) dispirited

Undaunted means not discouraged.

Dispirited means deprived of enthusiasm. Is *dispirited* the opposite of *undaunted*? Yes, whereas a *dispirited* person would be discouraged, or deprived of enthusiasm, an *undaunted* person would be enthusiastic despite possible obstacles.

33. Correct choice (D) procrastination

Alacrity means prompt response.

Procrastination means to put off (delay) intentionally and habitually. Is *procrastination* the opposite of *alacrity*? Yes, to put off intentionally and habitually is not a prompt response.

34. Correct choice (A) defend

Traduce means malign, to make malicious statements.

Defend means to ward off attack. Is *defend* the opposite of *traduce*? Yes, one word is defensive, the other offensive.

35. Correct choice (E) reticent

Grandiloquent means a lofty or pompous speaking style.

Reticent means restrained in expression. Is *reticent* the opposite of *grandiloquent*? Yes, a grandiloquent speaking style is the opposite of a restrained style of expression.

36. Correct choice (D) dearth

Accretion means accumulation, adding up.

Dearth means an inadequate supply. Is *dearth* the opposite of *accretion*? Yes, if you accumulate something, you probably have a lot of it, which is the opposite of *dearth*, not having enough of something.

37. Correct choice (E) incorporeal

Visceral means bodily or corporeal.

Incorporeal means having no material body or form. Is *incorporeal* the opposite of *visceral?* Yes, *incorporeal* and corporeal *(visceral)* are opposites.

38. Correct choice (E) distance

Propinquity means nearness.

Distance means degree or amount of separation. Is *distance* the opposite of *propinquity?* Yes, the two words have opposite meanings.

Test 1, Section 6: Analytical

Questions and Answers

Assignment for Today:

Take a sample GRE Analytical Test under actual test conditions. Allow yourself exactly 30 minutes to complete the 25 questions in this test.

Directions: *The following questions are based either on a brief passage or a number of conditions. For each question, circle the best answer among the choices given. You may wish to draw diagrams to help you answer some of the questions.*

Questions 1–7 are based on the following.

A Buick, a Chevy, a Dodge, a Ford, a Honda, a Nissan, a Porsche, and a Toyota are all candidates for a race. The five spots for the race are assigned as follows:

> The inside position is position 1; the outside position is position 5.
>
> Should the Buick be selected, it will occupy the inside position.
>
> The middle position will be assigned to either the Honda or the Nissan.
>
> If the Porsche is selected, then the Dodge will be next to it.
>
> At least one of the Buick and the Toyota is selected.

1. If the Toyota is next to the outside, then which car cannot be in the outside position?
   - (A) Dodge
   - (B) Honda
   - (C) Ford
   - (D) Chevy
   - (E) Porsche

2. Suppose that position 2 is assigned to the Porsche. What other car is also assigned to the race?
   - (A) Chevy
   - (B) Nissan
   - (C) Toyota
   - (D) Honda
   - (E) Buick

3. If the Nissan is on the inside, then which of the following assignments is made?
   - (A) The Toyota to position 5
   - (B) The Porsche to position 2
   - (C) The Dodge to position 4
   - (D) The Honda to position 3
   - (E) The Porsche to position 4

4. Suppose the outside position is assigned to the Porsche. None of the following arrangements is possible EXCEPT

(A) The Ford is next to the Chevy

(B) The Dodge occupies the inside

(C) The Buick is next to the Dodge

(D) The Toyota is next to the Honda

(E) The Honda occupies position 4

5. Which of the following is a possible race lineup, from inside to outside?

(A) Chevy, Porsche, Nissan, Toyota, Ford

(B) Toyota, Chevy, Ford, Dodge, Porsche

(C) Buick, Honda, Porsche, Dodge, Ford

(D) Porsche, Dodge, Honda, Nissan, Buick

(E) Dodge, Porsche, Nissan, Honda, Toyota

6. Suppose the Ford is immediately between the Honda and the Nissan. Which assignment necessarily follows?

(A) The Toyota is assigned a position.

(B) The Honda is assigned an even-numbered position.

(C) The Ford is assigned an even-numbered position.

(D) The Nissan is not assigned an odd-numbered position.

(E) The Chevy is assigned the outside position.

7. Suppose the Honda is assigned the inside position. If the Dodge is not among the remaining cars assigned, which of the following lists the other cars that are not assigned?

(A) Buick and Ford

(B) Buick and Chevy

(C) Buick and Porsche

(D) Buick and Toyota

(E) Chevy and Nissan

8. A survey performed by the county health department found that people who belong to private health clubs were closer to their ideal bodies than people who were not members of health clubs. The department director then concluded that health club membership better enables people to achieve their ideal body weight.

Which of the following statements, if true, would most seriously weaken the director's conclusion?

(A) People who don't belong to health clubs exercise more often than people who do belong to health clubs.

(B) Most county inhabitants can't afford to join a private health club.

(C) Private health clubs give their members personalized health advice.

(D) Children under 16 years of age were not part of the survey.

(E) Most people who join health clubs were already at or near ideal body weight prior to joining.

9. The number of students in a freshman course at MIT ranges from 20 to 100. Each course has one professor. If a freshman course has more than 50 students, it must have at least one Graduate Teaching Assistant (GTA) helping the professor.

Assuming the above rules are followed, which of the statements below can be inferred about courses at MIT?

(A) Some freshman courses with 60 students do not have a GTA.

(B) None of the freshman courses with 50 students have a GTA.

(C) Courses with more than 50 students that are not freshman level have a GTA.

(D) Some freshman courses with more than 80 students have a GTA.

(E) Freshman courses with more than 200 students usually have more than one GTA.

10. Jake proclaimed, "The banning of smoking in public places has done absolutely no good in making people healthier. The number of new and different smoking-related diseases incurred by cigarette smokers has not decreased at all!"

All of the following statements, if true, are valid objections to the above argument EXCEPT

(A) Smoking-related diseases are caused by long-term, prolonged exposure to smoke.

(B) Secondary smoke has been proven to be as harmful as primary smoke and can be directly attributed to respiratory cancers.

(C) The effects of toxins contained in cigarette smoke are cumulative and thus continual exposure will eventually lead to an increased frequency of smoking-related diseases.

(D) The smoking of cigarettes has been clinically proven to relax one's body and increase the defensive capacity of one's immune system.

(E) Cigarette smoke contains charcoal and tar, which have been proven to be carcinogenic, accounting for most cancer deaths.

Questions 11–14 are based on the following.

A city has seven subway stations—Arlington, Boylston, Cambridge, Dedham, Elliot, Fenway, and Gingham. The city's subway system has four lines, and passengers can transfer between the lines. The routes are as follows:

The blue line goes from Arlington to Boylston to Cambridge to Dedham to Elliot and back to Arlington.

The green line goes from Boylston to Fenway back to Boylston.

The red line goes from Cambridge to Elliot back to Cambridge.

The yellow line goes from Dedham to Gingham back to Dedham.

Each line makes stops at each of its stations.

Each station is one mile from the next consecutive station.

11. Which of the following two stations are consecutive stops on any one line?
(A) Arlington and Fenway
(B) Boylston and Arlington
(C) Cambridge and Arlington
(D) Dedham and Cambridge
(E) Elliot and Cambridge

12. The least number of stations between Arlington and Elliot that a passenger could encounter is
(A) 1
(B) 2
(C) 3
(D) 4
(E) 5

13. Which lines, in order, form the most direct way to travel from Gingham to Cambridge?
(A) Blue to Green to Red
(B) Green to Blue to Yellow
(C) Yellow to Blue to Red
(D) Red to Blue
(E) Yellow to Blue

14. A train coming from Fenway has to stop where?
(A) Arlington
(B) Boylston
(C) Cambridge
(D) Dedham
(E) Elliot

Questions 15–18 are based on the following.

Abe, Bill, Chad, Don, Evan, Frank, and Greg want to return home after partying all night. They decide to take two cabs based on these guidelines:

Abe and Greg always ride in the same cab.

Frank must ride in the first cab if Chad rides in the first cab.

Bill won't ride in the second cab if Don is in the second cab.

Three or more passengers will ride in each cab.

15. Who of the following CANNOT be one of the three passengers in the second cab if Abe is already one of the three?
    (A) Bill
    (B) Chad
    (C) Don
    (D) Evan
    (E) Frank

16. Which of the following is a possible arrangement of the seven friends in the two cabs?
    (A) Cab #1: Abe, Chad, Don, Frank
        Cab #2: Bill, Evan, Greg
    (B) Cab #1: Abe, Chad, Frank, Greg
        Cab #2: Bill, Don, Evan
    (C) Cab #1: Bill, Chad, Evan, Frank
        Cab #2: Abe, Don, Greg
    (D) Cab #1: Bill, Evan, Frank, Greg
        Cab #2: Abe, Chad, Don
    (E) Cab #1: Chad, Evan, Frank
        Cab #2: Abe, Bill, Don, Greg

17. Which of the following must be false?
    (A) Bill and Don ride in the first cab.
    (B) Frank and Greg ride in the first cab.
    (C) Abe, Evan, and Frank ride in the first cab.
    (D) Abe and Chad ride in the second cab.
    (E) Don, Evan, and Chad ride in the second cab.

18. If the second cab takes Bill and Frank, what must be true?
    (A) Abe and Chad ride together.
    (B) Abe and Evan ride together.
    (C) Chad and Don ride together.
    (D) Chad and Evan ride together.
    (E) Don and Greg ride together.

Questions 19–22 are based on the following.

A gardener waters her six favorite plants, currently located on displays 1 through 6 at the local county fair. The gardener is superstitious and always follows these procedures when watering:

As long as there is no conflict with the following procedures, a blooming plant is always watered before a non-blooming plant. In every instance, the following procedures always take precedence:

She waters the plant in display 6 before watering the plants in displays 1 and 5.

She waters the plant in display 2 after watering the plants in displays 1 and 4.

She never waters the plant in display 4 immediately before or immediately after watering the plant in display 3.

19. If plant 4 is blooming, which of the following can be a valid sequence for watering?
    (A) 4 1 3 2 6 5
    (B) 4 3 2 6 1 5
    (C) 4 6 5 1 3 2
    (D) 6 1 5 4 3 2
    (E) 6 4 2 1 5 3

20. If plants 2 and 5 are blooming, which of the following must be true?

   (A) The fourth plant watered is the plant in display 1.
   (B) The sixth plant watered is the plant in display 3.
   (C) The third plant watered is the plant in display 4.
   (D) The first plant watered is the plant in display 5.
   (E) The second plant watered is the plant in display 6.

21. If plants 2 and 4 are blooming, and plants 1, 3, 5, and 6 are not blooming, which of the following is an acceptable order to water the plants?

   (A) 4 2 6 3 1 5
   (B) 4 6 1 5 2 3
   (C) 4 6 1 2 5 3
   (D) 6 4 1 2 3 5
   (E) 6 4 2 5 1 3

22. If only plants 1, 2, 4, and 6 are not blooming, which of the following is a valid order of watering?

   (A) 3 5 6 4 1 2
   (B) 3 6 5 4 1 2
   (C) 6 3 1 5 4 2
   (D) 6 5 1 3 2 4
   (E) 6 5 1 4 2 3

23. It wasn't until the last century that people became aware of mercury poisoning, which causes liver damage, among other things. At the turn of the century, one manufacturer of electrical switches denied that his workers were being exposed to dangerous levels of mercury because no worker had been diagnosed with liver disease. The labor board closed the factory, citing other factors; however, many workers contracted liver disease years later and were left without legal claim. A recent labor advocate now argues that mercury poisoning was directly responsible for the workers' cases of liver disease.

Which of the following statements, if true, supports the labor advocate's claim?

   (A) Workers who are at risk are responsible to advocate their own working conditions.
   (B) The factory workers' incidence of liver disease is no different from those of the general population.
   (C) The effects of mercury poisoning take years to be diagnosed.
   (D) Mercury, a cumulative poison, is not easily discharged from the body.
   (E) The factory workers tended to drink excessive amounts of alcohol, which causes liver disease.

24. To reduce traffic noise for residential property near highways, urban planners have begun building sound walls between highways and homes. These walls have proven effective. As a result, the property values of homes near highways have increased, because ambient noise—such as highway noise—reduces residential property value. However, the sound walls have had an unexpected consequence: Noise from the highway is reflected off the sound walls and is projected farther into the community, typically affecting areas about one-half mile away from the highway. This phenomenon has been labeled "sound skip" and is most noticeable at night and in cold weather.

Which of the following conclusions can most properly be drawn if the statements above are true?

(A) Urban planners who advocate sound walls are intentionally deceiving their communities.

(B) The cost of sound walls has been paid for by the increase in property taxes of those living near the highways.

(C) Sound walls will cause a reduction in property values for homes located about one-half mile away from the highway.

(D) Sound skip is more noticeable in cold weather because fewer activities are taking place in most neighborhoods.

(E) Sound walls usually eliminate ambient sound for homes near highways.

25. The average yearly income for college professors in Pedrasco County is $38,000. In the same county, the average yearly income for phlebotomists is $28,000. However, on average, phlebotomists have a higher net worth than college professors.

Which of the following, if true, would help to account for the phenomenon described above?

(A) Pedrasco County places lower taxes on income gained through professional education.

(B) College professors are paid on the academic year, while phlebotomists are paid on the calendar year.

(C) Phlebotomists work fewer hours and therefore have more time for pursuing hobbies.

(D) College professors acquired more debts during their education.

(E) Net worth calculations fail to account for inherited properties.

Quick Answer Guide

Test 1, Section 6: Analytical

1. E	8. E	15. E	22. B
2. C	9. D	16. C	23. C
3. D	10. D	17. C	24. C
4. D	11. E	18. E	25. D
5. E	12. B	19. C	
6. C	13. C	20. B	
7. C	14. B	21. C	

For explanations to these questions, see Day 20.

Test 1, Section 6: Analytical
Explanations and Strategies

Assignment for Today:

Review the explanations to the Analytical Test you took on Day 19.

Questions 1–7:

From the facts, we can set up the following chart:

$$
\begin{array}{ccccc}
 & & \text{H/N} & & \\
\rule{1cm}{0.4pt} & \rule{1cm}{0.4pt} & \rule{1cm}{0.4pt} & \rule{1cm}{0.4pt} & \rule{1cm}{0.4pt} \\
1 & 2 & 3 & 4 & 5 \\
\end{array}
$$

$$
\begin{array}{c}
\text{B} \\
\text{if P => PD or DP;} \qquad \rule{1cm}{0.4pt} \text{ and/or T} \\
1
\end{array}
$$

1. Correct choice (E)

If the Porsche was in position 5, as the choice suggests, then we can see from above that the Dodge must be in position 4 (since there is no position 6). However, the question states that the Toyota is in position 4. Thus, the Porsche cannot be in position 5.

2. Correct choice (C)

If, as the question states, the Porsche is in position 2, then we can determine from the chart above that the Dodge must also be selected, and it must be adjacent to the Porsche. Since the middle position must be occupied by either the Honda or the Nissan, the Dodge must be in position 1. Since the Buick can no longer be in position 1, the last condition in the chart dictates that the Toyota must also have been assigned to the race.

3. Correct choice (D)

Position 3 must be occupied by either the Honda or the Nissan. Thus, if the Nissan is assigned at position 1, as the question states, then the Honda must be in position 3.

4. Correct choice (D)

If the Porsche is assigned to position 5, then the Dodge must be assigned to position 4:

$$
\begin{array}{ccccc}
 & & \text{H/N} & \text{D} & \text{P} \\
\rule{1cm}{0.4pt} & \rule{1cm}{0.4pt} & \rule{1cm}{0.4pt} & \rule{1cm}{0.4pt} & \rule{1cm}{0.4pt} \\
1 & 2 & 3 & 4 & 5 \\
\end{array}
$$

If the Honda is assigned to the middle position and the Toyota is assigned to position 2, this creates an acceptable arrangement:

$$
\begin{array}{ccccc}
\text{M} & \text{T} & \text{H} & \text{D} & \text{P} \\
\rule{1cm}{0.4pt} & \rule{1cm}{0.4pt} & \rule{1cm}{0.4pt} & \rule{1cm}{0.4pt} & \rule{1cm}{0.4pt} \\
1 & 2 & 3 & 4 & 5 \\
\end{array}
$$

All the other choices cause conflicts.

5. Correct choice (E)

You arrive at this answer by elimination. All the other choices have flaws. In this choice, the Porsche is assigned to position 2, which specifies that the Dodge must be assigned to position 1. Because the

Buick was not assigned to the inside position, then the Toyota must be assigned. Finally, the Nissan occupies position 3, which satisfies the facts.

6. Correct choice (C)

If the Ford is immediately between the Nissan and the Honda, then it must be adjacent to position 3. Thus, the Ford is assigned to either position 2 or 4, both even-numbered positions.

7. Correct choice (C)

If the Dodge was not assigned, then the Porsche cannot be assigned either. If the Honda is assigned to the inside position, then the Buick cannot be assigned because it must be assigned to the inside position. Thus, we have three cars out of eight which are not assigned.

8. Correct choice (E)

Your task here is to find the statement that weakens the director's conclusions that health club membership better enables people to achieve their ideal body weights. The safest way to find the right answer is to read through the choices and eliminate the ones that are wrong. You should be able to eliminate all the choices fairly easily except (E). Choice (E) states that people who join health clubs are already close to their ideal body weight. This challenges the director's claim because people who join health clubs are already in good shape before they even walk in the door, so it likely isn't the health club membership itself that is enabling people to get to their desired body weight.

9. Correct choice (D)

"If a freshman course has more than 50 students, it *must* have . . . GTA." Since 80 is more than 50, *all* courses with 80 students must have GTAs.

Since *some* is part of *all*, it is true that "*Some* freshman courses with more than 80 students have a GTA."

10. Correct choice (D)

The correct answer objects to the argument by stating a fact that smoking is not harmful to one's body. This response actually states that the body's immune system will become stronger and that with smoking, one's overall health will improve. The other choices do not support the argument by pointing out the alternative reasons for the continued presence of diseases related to smoking.

Questions 11–14:
From the facts, we can draw the following diagram:

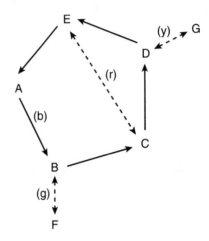

Blue Line: A —> B —> C —> D —> E
Green Line: B <—> F
Red Line: C <—> E
Yellow Line: D <—> G

11. Correct choice (E)

A passenger can travel from E to C directly on the Red Line.

12. Correct choice (B)

The most direct way for a passenger to go from A to E is A —> B —> C on the Blue Line and then go C —> E on the Red Line. There are two stations between A and E: B and C.

13. Correct choice (C)

First take the Yellow Line from G to D. From there, the most direct way to C is the Blue Line from D to E and the Red Line from E to C.

14. Correct choice (B)

The Green Line is the only line with a station at F, and its only other stop is B. Thus, any passenger who leaves F must stop at B.

Questions 15–18:
From the facts, we can make the following notes:

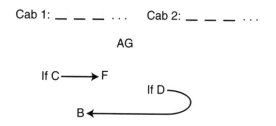

15. Correct choice (E)

For this question, if A is in cab 2, then G must also be in cab 2. F cannot be in cab 2 because there is only one spot left in cab 2. If F takes that spot, then C must be in cab 1, and the guidelines require that in that case F must also be in cab 1.

16. Correct choice (C)

In this choice, A and G are together in cab 2; C and F are both in cab 1; D is in cab 2, and B is in cab 1.

17. Correct choice (C)

If A, E, and F are all in cab 1 as this choice suggests, then G must also be in cab 1. This means that D, B, and C must be in cab 2. However, if D is in cab 2, the guidelines specify that B cannot also be in cab 2.

18. Correct choice (E)

If B and F are in cab 2, then C must also be in cab 2 because otherwise F must be in cab 1. In addition, D must be in cab 1 because he cannot be in cab 2 with B. Since A and G must also be in the same cab, and three spots in cab 2 have already been taken, A and G must both be in cab 1. Thus, D and G must be in the same cab.

Questions 19–22:
From the facts, we can draw the following:

$$<\!\!\text{———}4\text{———}\!>|$$
$$6 .. 1 .. 2 \quad \cancel{34} \text{ or } \cancel{43} \quad \text{Bloom} .. \text{Non-bloom}$$
$$|<\!\!\text{———}5\text{———}\!>$$

19. Correct choice (C)

For this question, we know that plant 4 is blooming, and since no plant has to be watered before 4, plant 4 will be watered first due to the bloom/non-bloom rule. In this choice, plant 6 is watered before plants 5 and 1; plant 2 is watered after plants 1 and 4; and plants 3 and 4 are not watered adjacently.

20. Correct choice (B)

For this question, we know that plants 2 and 5 must be watered as soon as possible. Thus, plant 6 is watered first, plant 5 is watered second, plants 1 and 4 are watered third and fourth (not necessarily in that order), and plant 2 is watered fifth. Thus, plant 3 must be watered sixth.

21. Correct choice (C)

We arrive at this answer by eliminating all the other choices. For this question, we know that plants 2 and 4 must be watered as soon as possible without violating the other facts. This means that plant 4 should be watered first, and plant 2 should be watered fourth. In this choice, both of these conditions are met, and plants 6 and 1 are watered before plant 2, and plants 5 and 1 are watered after plant 6.

22. Correct choice (B)

For this question, we know that plants 3 and 5, since they are blooming, must be watered as soon as possible without violating the other facts. This means that plant 3 should be watered first, plant 6 second, and plant 5 third. In addition to these conditions, this choice also satisfies the facts that plants 1 and 4 must be watered before plant 2.

23. Correct choice (C)

Your task here is to find the statement that supports the labor advocate's claim that mercury poisoning led to liver disease in the factory workers. Because the effects of mercury poisoning take years to show up, the factory workers wouldn't be diagnosed with liver disease until many years later. This is exactly what happened. Of course, this is not proof; it's just support for the advocate's claim.

24. Correct choice (C)

What you need to do here is to find a statement that is a logical conclusion to the facts in the passage. Choice (C) states that sound walls will reduce property values for those homes about one half mile away from the highway. This is true because sound walls reflect ambient noise one half mile and because ambient noise reduces property value. Therefore, sound walls reduce property values for places one half mile away from the highway.

25. Correct choice (D)

Your task in this question is to find a statement that explains why college professors have a lower net worth than phlebotomists, even though they earn more each year. If you eliminate the choices that are irrelevant (B and E) and those that are contradictory to the passage (A and C), you will end up with (D), which is the correct answer. Choice (D) suggests that college professors acquired more debt during their education, which would logically lead to less overall total net worth. In other words, the professors aren't worth as much because they are still paying off school loans from their many years of education.

Day 21 to Day 29

TEST 2

Questions and Answers

Explanations and Strategies

Day 21

Test 2, Section 1: Math

Questions and Answers

Assignment for Today:

Take a sample GRE Math Test under actual test conditions. Allow yourself exactly 30 minutes to complete all 30 questions in this test.

Directions: For questions 1–15, each question contains two quantities—one on the left (Column A), and one on the right (Column B). Compare the quantities and answer

- (A) if Column A is greater than Column B
- (B) if Column B is greater than Column A
- (C) if the two columns are equal
- (D) if you cannot determine a definite relationship from the information given

Never answer (E)

In some questions, information appears centered between the two columns. Centered information concerns each of the columns for that question only. Any symbol in one column represents the same value if it appears in the other column.

Column A	Column B

$$\frac{12x}{5} = \frac{3}{y}$$

| 1. | 5 | $4xy$ |

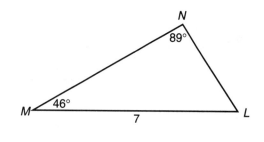

| 2. | MN | NL |

Column A	Column B

$$y^5 - y^5 = 0$$

$$xy \neq 0$$

3.

$\dfrac{x^2}{y^4}$	$\dfrac{1}{xy}$

Let $\langle u|v|w \rangle = \dfrac{u}{v} + \dfrac{v}{w}$, where u, v, and w are integers, and $v \neq 0$ and $w \neq 0$.

4.

$\langle 4|-2|-1 \rangle$	0

$$-7 \leq y < 4$$

5.

The greatest possible value of $-8y$	The greatest possible value of $14y$

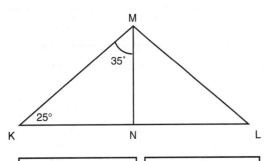

6.

KN	NL

Column A	Column B

Clyde's bicycle has wheels of radius 8 inches. Donna's bicycle has wheels of radius 16 inches. During a race, each wheel of Clyde's bicycle turns 60 times per minute, and each wheel of Donna's bicycle turns 30 times per minute.

7.

The distance traveled by Clyde's bicycle every minute	The distance traveled by Donna's bicycle every minute

In December, a $100 sweater was discounted 20%. In April, the sweater was placed on a clearance rack and the discounted price was cut in half.

8.

Total price of the sweater in April, including a 6% sales tax	$46

$$x > y > 0$$

9.

$\left(7\dfrac{x}{y}\right)^2 + \left(2\dfrac{x}{y}\right)^2$	$\left(9\dfrac{x}{y}\right)^2$

Column A	Column B

g is an even integer, and $16 \le g \le 20$.

h is an odd integer, and $5 \le h \le 15$.

$$g = 2h$$

10.

$g + h$	27

k is a negative integer

11.

$\dfrac{1}{k^5 + k^3}$	$\dfrac{1}{k^5}$

Let the operation # have the property that $x \# y = -(y \# x)$ for all real numbers x and y.

12.

$1 \# 2$	$2 \# 1$

$$q = \frac{8}{9}$$

13.

$q^2 + q^4 + q^6$	$q + q^3 + q^5$

Column A	Column B

The product of three consecutive *odd* integers is 15 times their sum.

14.

The average (arithmetic mean) of the three integers	9

For all positive numbers c,

$$\langle\langle c \rangle\rangle = \frac{c}{2} + \frac{1}{2} \quad \text{if } c \ge 3$$

$$\langle\langle c \rangle\rangle = c + 1 \quad \text{if } c < 3$$

15.

$\langle\langle 6 - 2 \rangle\rangle$	$\langle\langle 6 \rangle\rangle - \langle\langle 2 \rangle\rangle$

Directions: *For questions 16–30, solve each problem, and circle the appropriate answer choice, A–E.*

16. If y is an unknown and $10{,}105 + y = 12{,}125$, then what is the value of $10{,}105 - 5y$?

    (A)   5
    (B)   2020
    (C)   8085
    (D)   10,100
    (E)   20,205

17. If u, v, w, and x are odd integers between 5 and 11 inclusive, and $u < v < w < x$, which of the following is an odd integer?

    (A) $\dfrac{(u+v+w+x)}{4}$
    (B) $(u)\,(v)\,(w)\,(x)$
    (C) $(v-u)\,(x-w)$
    (D) $(u-v)\,(w-x)$
    (E) $\dfrac{(u+v)}{2} + \dfrac{(w+x)}{2}$

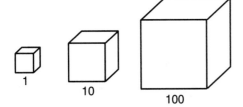

Note: Figure not drawn to scale.

18. What is the sum of the total surface areas of the three cubes shown above if the given dimensions represent the length of each edge of the cube?

    (A)   666
    (B)   10,101
    (C)   60,066
    (D)   60,606
    (E)   1,001,001

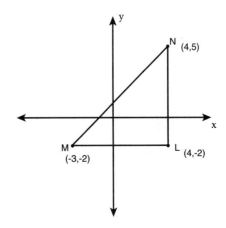

19. In the figure above, what is the length of MN?

    (A) $\sqrt{10}$
    (B) $\sqrt{98}$
    (C)   14
    (D) $\dfrac{49}{2}$
    (E)   98

20. If the diameter of a planet's circular orbit is about 1.28×10^4 meters, what is the approximate area, in square meters, of the circle enclosed by the orbit?

    (A) 0.4×10^4
    (B) 1.4×10^4
    (C) 0.4×10^6
    (D) 0.4×10^8
    (E) 1.4×10^8

Questions 21–25 are based on the following figure.

```
              Students in Jefferson High Schoo''s
                        Class of 1996
                  Total number of students: 872

Males                                            Females
(468)                                            (404)
_____

                        Ethnicity
219                    Anglo-Saxon                187
 86                    Asian                        63
 97                    Black                       107
 59                    Hispanic                     44
  2                    Native American               0
  5                    Other                         3


                   Number of Awards Won
 48                        4                         58
127                        3                        154
189                        2                        122
 92                        1                         68
 12                        0                          4


                  Post-High School Plans
234                   College-bound               287
149                   Work-bound                   83
 85                   Undecided                    34
```

NOTE: The following categories are listed by the approximate <u>percent</u> of students participating in each activity by gender. Percentage figures don't necessarily add up to 100.

```
                   Sports Participation
13                     Football                     0
 7                     Soccer                        4
20                     Track & Field               20
20                     Swimming                      5
 8                     Tennis                        7


                    Club Participation
 9                     Science Club                  6
17                     Languages                    18
 3                     Glee Club                     7
23                     Drama Club                   21
 6                     Math Club                     3
 8                     Debate Team                   8
```

21. How many students are undecided about their post-high school plans?
    - (A) 34
    - (B) 51
    - (C) 85
    - (D) 119
    - (E) 129

22. Approximately how many students participate in swimming?
    - (A) 20
    - (B) 25
    - (C) 94
    - (D) 114
    - (E) 218

23. If all of the Hispanic students in the school participate in track & field, approximately how many non-Hispanic students participate in track & field?
    - (A) 35
    - (B) 37
    - (C) 72
    - (D) 103
    - (E) 175

24. What is the average number of awards won by female students?
    - (A) Between 0 and 1
    - (B) Between 1 and 2
    - (C) Between 2 and 3
    - (D) Between 3 and 4
    - (E) Cannot be determined

25. Which of the following statements can be inferred from the data given?

 I. The percent of male students who are undecided about their post-high school plans is less than the percent of work-bound female students.

 II. More than 50 percent of the students in Jefferson High School's Class of 1996 are males.

 III. An equal number of male and female students participate in the debate team.

 (A) I only
 (B) II only
 (C) III only
 (D) I and II
 (E) I, II, and III

26. The sum of 12 numbers is 276. If 4 numbers are removed, the average (arithmetic mean) of the remaining numbers is 26. What is the average of the four numbers removed?

 (A) 17
 (B) 26
 (C) 43
 (D) 68
 (E) 104

27. The tick marks in the figure above are equally spaced.

 If line segment AB is 30% longer than line segment PB, which of the following could be the value of A?

 (A) 12
 (B) 52
 (C) 62
 (D) 92
 (E) 102

28. Two trains travel without stopping from station A to station B, a distance of 480 miles. The first train travels at 40 miles per hour, and the second train travels at 120 miles per hour. If the first train leaves station A at 11:00 a.m., at what time must the second train leave station A in order to arrive at station B at the exact time that the first train arrives?

 (A) 2:00 p.m.
 (B) 3:00 p.m.
 (C) 7:00 p.m.
 (D) 8:00 p.m.
 (E) 11:00 p.m.

29. A trip from town W to town Z must go through towns X and Y. If the distance between towns W and X is $\frac{1}{4}$ larger than the average distance of the three trip segments, and the distance between towns W and Y is $\frac{5}{6}$ of the total distance between towns W and Z, what is the ratio of the distance between X and Y to the distance between Y and Z?

 (A) 1:2
 (B) 3:2
 (C) 5:2
 (D) 5:72
 (E) 10:7

30. A certain hockey player scored 1 goal per game in the first two games. In every other game in which he played, he scored *at least* four goals per game. If his overall average (arithmetic mean) is exactly three goals per game, what is the *most* number of games he could have played?

 (A) 4
 (B) 5
 (C) 6
 (D) 7
 (E) Cannot be determined from the information given.

Quick Answer Guide

Test 2, Section 1: Math

1. C	9. B	17. B	25. B
2. B	10. C	18. D	26. A
3. C	11. A	19. B	27. D
4. C	12. D	20. D	28. C
5. A	13. B	21. D	29. C
6. D	14. B	22. D	30. C
7. C	15. A	23. C	
8. B	16. A	24. C	

For explanations of these questions, see Day 23.

Test 2, Section 2: Verbal

Questions and Answers

Assignment for Today:

Take a sample GRE Verbal Test under actual test conditions. Allow yourself exactly 30 minutes to complete the 38 questions in this test.

Directions: *For questions 1–7, one or more words have been left out of each sentence. Circle the answer, A–E, which contains the word or words that best fit the meaning of the entire sentence.*

---

1. Because the cyberware industry was just beginning to boom, Olivia's small technology company grew rapidly and quickly became ____.

   (A) obsequious

   (B) indigent

   (C) lucrative

   (D) voluble

   (E) exotic

2. Even though Brian was unattractive and ____, whenever he talked on the phone, he acted as though he were the most ____ and outgoing man in the world.

   (A) retiring..handsome

   (B) dull..frivolous

   (C) depraved..diligent

   (D) poor..disagreeable

   (E) suave..bereft

3. The newborn's incessant wailing convinced the young mother that it was impossible to ____ her ____ infant.

   (A) dominate..unruly

   (B) placate..discontented

   (C) satisfy..empathetic

   (D) delude..colicky

   (E) enthrall..indolent

4. The meaning of the original Egyptian "picture writing" remains a mystery to modern civilizations long after these ancient hieroglyphics have been ____.

   (A) defaced

   (B) decanted

   (C) deciphered

   (D) debunked

   (E) debriefed

5. Every night the artist would lock herself in her
   ____ and work ____ to finish all her paintings in
   time for her exhibition.
   - (A) studio..sporadically
   - (B) chateau..somberly
   - (C) retreat..perilously
   - (D) bedroom..industriously
   - (E) atelier..assiduously

6. A(n) ____ essay, Marcel Mauss' *The Gift*, is
   acknowledged by many as having created the field
   of economic anthropology.
   - (A) parochial
   - (B) apocryphal
   - (C) jejune
   - (D) seminal
   - (E) eponymous

7. While many think of advertisements as being uni-
   formly ____ and ____ , some of the most shocking
   and disturbing pictures in the media may be found
   in ads.
   - (A) anodyne..idyllic
   - (B) subliminal..erotic
   - (C) misleading..manipulative
   - (D) contrived..unimaginative
   - (E) innovative..inspiring

*Directions: For questions 8–16, determine the
relationship between the two words given in capital
letters. Then, from the choices listed A–E, select the
one pair that has a relationship most similar to that
of the capitalized pair. Circle the letter of that pair.*

8. SMOKE:CONFLAGRATION::
   - (A) breathing:exercise
   - (B) exhaust:pipe
   - (C) moisture:precipitation
   - (D) gravity:attraction
   - (E) light:reflection

9. BULWARK:PRIVACY::
   - (A) mailbox:communication
   - (B) jail:sanctuary
   - (C) village:activity
   - (D) spy:danger
   - (E) jacket:warmth

10. GRAVITY:MIRTH::
    - (A) levity:laughter
    - (B) fealty:oath
    - (C) energy:force
    - (D) inertia:fatigue
    - (E) sincerity:guile

11. GARRULOUS:LACONIC::
    - (A) succulent:juicy
    - (B) weighty:pithy
    - (C) placid:proud
    - (D) bombastic:demure
    - (E) onerous:noisome

12. FLATTERY:SYCOPHANCY::
    - (A) modesty:arrogance
    - (B) spleen:generosity
    - (C) invective:honesty
    - (D) malice:animosity
    - (E) clarity:obscurity

13. CAR:BRAKE::
    - (A) war:treaty
    - (B) ship:sailor
    - (C) flu:inoculation
    - (D) mileage:transmission
    - (E) conception:birth

14. PARLAY:TRANSFORM::
    - (A) recount:redound
    - (B) overwhelm:surrender
    - (C) disabuse:mistake
    - (D) discern:confuse
    - (E) eclipse:surpass

15. PLIANT:OBDURATE::
    (A) insensible:ingenious
    (B) malleable:flaccid
    (C) silent:nocturnal
    (D) predatory:carnivorous
    (E) glowing:flaming

16. TINY:HOMUNCULUS::
    (A) dead:corpse
    (B) still:lake
    (C) immense:shoe
    (D) dangerous:animal
    (E) teenage:girl

Directions: Read each passage and answer the questions that follow. Base your answers only on what is stated or implied in the passage.

Questions 17–20 are based on the following passage.

The pearl, so highly valued for its chaste beauty, is but a secretion of animal matter, resulting from the efforts of some uneasy mollusk, annoyed by a foreign substance, which has found its way
(5) into his habitation, to make the best of an unavoidable evil by enclosing it in a soft, smooth covering. Let us imitate the oyster; when annoyed or afflicted, by meekness and patience strive to turn our vexations and troubles into
(10) "pearls of great price," valuable products of beauty and wonder.

It is on the northwest coast of the island of Ceylon, in the Indian Ocean, that the pearl oyster most abounds, and there it is that the pearl
(15) fishery is conducted in the most extensive, systematic, and successful manner. A single oyster will sometimes contain several pearls, which are generally embedded in the body of the animal, but are sometimes fixed to the shell. It is re-
(20) corded of one rich oyster that there were found in his possession no less than 150 precious jewels. He must have been a miser, or perhaps he had taken them in pledge from his less provident neighbors.

(25) From the earliest times, pearls have been considered to be valuable ornaments, and are often alluded to by Greek and Roman writers. Various attempts have been made to imitate them, and one mode of producing them, practiced, it is
(30) said, more than a thousand years ago, is still carried on in China. In the shells of pearl oysters, holes are bored, into which pieces of iron are introduced; these wounding and irritating the animal, cause it to deposit coat upon coat of
(35) pearly matter over the wounded part, and so the pearl is formed. Artificial pearls are made of hollow glass globules or little gloves, covered on the inside with a liquid called pearl-essence, and filled up with white wax. Historians speak of an
(40) ancient traffic in native pearls carried on in Great Britain. Generally, artificially produced pearls are inferior in the two requisites of color and size.

Native divers who subsist on their finding these "gems" expose themselves to danger from
(45) voracious sharks, which hover about the fishing grounds, and make a dash at their victim, heedless of the written charms with which the shark-charmer has provided him previous to his descent. The diver, upon retrieving a day's worth
(50) of work, places the fruits of his labor in heaps, where they are allowed to remain until they become putrid, at which time they undergo a very elaborate process of washing and separating from the shells, which are carefully examined
(55) and deprived from their pearly treasures. The stench arising from the decomposed animal matter is described as horrible, and the whole process is filthy and loathsome. Yet out of the slime and mud and disgusting effluvia come
(60) gems of inestimable value, calculated to adorn the brow of beauty and form ornaments the most pure and delicate that can be imagined.

17. The main purpose of the passage is to
    (A) teach the reader how to find natural pearls and create artificial ones
    (B) explain why pearls are valuable
    (C) compare artificial pearls with natural pearls
    (D) argue that pearls are among the most interesting gems found in nature
    (E) explain bits of the history, hunting, and production of pearls

18. In comparing artificial and natural pearls, the author of the passage implies that
    (A) Ceylon produces most of the world's artificial pearls
    (B) artificial pearls result from irritants, while natural pearls do not
    (C) natural pearls are larger and more beautiful than artificial pearls
    (D) artificial pearls will survive longer than natural ones
    (E) natural pearls were in great demand in China

19. In describing how artificial pearls are made, the passage indicates all of the following steps EXCEPT
    (A) fill the globule with white wax
    (B) use a liquid called pearl-essence
    (C) start with hollow glass globules
    (D) introduce an iron pellet
    (E) fill a "little glove" with liquid

20. One can infer from the passage that an irony of a pearl's beauty is that
    (A) people can make pearls just as beautiful
    (B) pearls have not been in big demand recently
    (C) collecting pearls is a stinky business
    (D) some oysters contain no pearls at all
    (E) something natural can cost so much

Questions 21–27 are based on the following passage.

The word "kitchenette" seems admirably descriptive, for it really tells you what it is, a little kitchen; whereas, a suffragette is not a little suffrage, nor Hamlet a little ham. One warms up to
(5) kitchenette, the word, before one is warmed up by kitchenette, the thing.

The idea of a tiny place where you can handily reach everything you need in the preparation and serving of food is truly fascinating. On your
(10) right is the refrigerator, on your left the sink, just above are pots and pans. Open a drawer and lo, you have your forks and spoons and other table utilities—all actually without moving. It is almost beyond belief how convenient it is. The
(15) water runs hot or cold, and the microwave is right at eye level for speed cooking. It is all a miracle of condensation and comfort. After a careful calculation—this is a most conservative estimate—I am ready to declare that in the use
(20) of a kitchenette, you save in steps no less than three miles a day over an ordinary good-sized kitchen.

A notable asset of the kitchenette is the superb way in which you become by means of it
(25) independent of help. A mere individual with any knack at all for boiling an egg and making a cup of coffee can, with the assistance of that urban lifesaver, the delicatessen, have a breakfast a king could not outdo. When you stop to think of it,
(30) what could or would any sovereign have for his matutinal meal more than you, kitchenetted and fearless, can provide? Fruit, cereal, fresh cream, the egg done to a turn (this does not seem quite the correct idiom, but let it pass), coffee that
(35) smokes its fragrant way to heaven, and crisp rolls with their dab of dainty butter; yes, and, be it whispered, sugar enough not to make the berry brown and beloved a mockery; what more could any mortal, be one queen or king, desire
(40) here below? Merely to enumerate the items of such a breakfast makes me hungry. And this delectable result is easy to manage because the kitchenette has come in these latter days to simplify, to soothe, and to sanctify these homely,
(45) necessary details of daily living.

But we have hardly more than begun to cata-
logue the virtues of our kitchenette. If it has been
implied that breakfast is the only meal to be got
in the kitchenette, an injustice has been done to
(50) ourselves, and the subject. Not so. Even the un-
skilled hand can evoke dishes that are not only
suitable for lunch but welcome at dinner. There
is something so intimate and homelike and
sweet about the sight of a gracious host moving
(55) in and out of the room, not banging doors and
disappearing to another part of the house, to
leave you lonesome and skeptical until return,
but just stepping out of vision for a mere moment, able to keep up the conversation, and back
(60) almost before you notice your companion
is gone. And all the while the food is being
set upon the shining board, and you, albeit a
visitor, feel as if you were a participant in the
preparations, even as you fondly hope to be an
(65) accessory to the deed of consumption.

Never was the kitchenette so touchingly utili-
tarian as now, when a professional chef is about
the rarest thing in modern civilization. It is the
way out for the cook of the house, his or her Dec-
(70) laration of Independence. No longer need one
fear the tyranny of the ruler of the kitchen—a
phrase fraught with ominous meanings to all
who have learned its full implications. With the
kitchenette, one can enter into a freedom not
(75) dreamed of before. One can raise a family by the
kitchenette, and it will enjoy life more than it
ever did in the kitchen days of old. No more
haggard haggling over wages or haughty laying
down of rules. The cook can now say, with one
(80) eye on the kitchenette and the other on the smil-
ing, contented faces of well-fed homebodies,
"Very well, leave if you prefer; I can get along
fine without your help."

21. The passage can be best described as which of the
following?
(A) an attempt to prove the utility of kitchenettes
(B) a whimsical argument in favor of kitchenettes
(C) a comparison between full-sized kitchens
and kitchenettes

(D) a listing of modern time-saving devices in
domestic life
(E) an impassioned argument for the liberation
of those who cook

22. By claiming that a kitchenette will save three miles
of walking a day, the author intends to
(A) use hyperbole for comic effect
(B) quantify the benefits of kitchenettes
(C) show how modern inventions simplify our
lives
(D) exaggerate the size of ordinary kitchens
(E) praise the amount of work typical cooks
perform

23. In asserting that kitchenettes improve people's
lifestyles, the author
(A) says that breakfast is the most important
meal of the day
(B) cites how comfortable one feels as a visitor
in kitchenette homes
(C) claims cooks will no longer want help in the
kitchen
(D) outlines how kitchenette users save money
(E) compares people with kitchenettes to
royalty

24. The tone of the passage can best be described as
(A) defensive
(B) melodramatic
(C) progressive
(D) pompous
(E) austere

25. The author emphasizes that breakfast
(A) is not the only meal that is ably prepared in
a kitchenette
(B) is the most appropriate meal for a kitchenette
(C) has menu options that tend to make people
hungry
(D) uses each part of the kitchenette to a
roughly equal degree
(E) demonstrates the superior utility of the
kitchenette

26. The passage implies that hosts with full-sized kitchens tend to
    (A) sanctify the homely details of daily living
    (B) neglect their guests
    (C) prepare meals that are far too elaborate
    (D) move graciously in and out of view
    (E) burden their guests with food preparation

27. The passage uses the word "consumption" in line 65 to mean
    (A) cleaning up
    (B) thanking a host with proper dignity
    (C) wasting away of the body
    (D) eating
    (E) tuberculosis

Directions: For questions 28–38, circle the lettered choice most nearly oppposite in meaning to the word given in CAPITAL letters.

---

28. TRANSIENT:
    (A) municipal
    (B) premature
    (C) perpetual
    (D) prescient
    (E) intransigent

29. OBSTINATE:
    (A) obstreperous
    (B) pertinacious
    (C) headstrong
    (D) fortunate
    (E) pliable

30. JUDICIOUS:
    (A) imprudent
    (B) prejudiced
    (C) jaundiced
    (D) entrapped
    (E) officious

31. FOIBLE:
    (A) infirmity
    (B) heathen
    (C) hypocrite
    (D) virtue
    (E) idiosyncrasy

32. INVIOLATE:
    (A) inundated
    (B) fragmented
    (C) ventilated
    (D) invalidated
    (E) indoctrinated

33. EXTENUATE:
    (A) extricate
    (B) annihilate
    (C) buttress
    (D) alleviate
    (E) enervate

34. PRISTINE:
    (A) primordial
    (B) sullied
    (C) antebellum
    (D) antithetical
    (E) prodigious

35. SENESCENCE:
    (A) adolescence
    (B) candescence
    (C) obsolescence
    (D) acquiescence
    (E) incandescence

36. TREPIDANT:
    (A) tremulous
    (B) incisive
    (C) lateral
    (D) dauntless
    (E) languorous

37. OSTENSIBLE:

    (A) indiscernible

    (B) specious

    (C) egregious

    (D) indigenous

    (E) reprehensible

38. MARTINET:

    (A) dilettante

    (B) teetotaler

    (C) laggard

    (D) contrary

    (E) disciplinarian

Quick Answer Guide

Test 2, Section 2: Verbal

1. C	11. D	21. B	31. D
2. A	12. D	22. A	32. B
3. B	13. A	23. E	33. C
4. C	14. E	24. B	34. B
5. E	15. E	25. A	35. A
6. D	16. A	26. B	36. D
7. A	17. E	27. D	37. A
8. C	18. C	28. C	38. C
9. E	19. D	29. E	
10. E	20. C	30. A	

For explanations to these questions, see Day 23.

Day 23

Test 2, Section 1: Math, and Section 2: Verbal
Explanations and Strategies

Assignment for Today:

Review the explanations for the Math Test that you took on Day 21 and for the Verbal Test that you took on Day 22.

SECTION 1: MATH

1. Correct choice (C)

We can simplify the ratio by cross-multiplying:

$$\frac{12x}{5} = \frac{3}{y}$$

$$12xy = 15$$

Dividing both sides of the equation above by 3 yields

$$4xy = 5$$

Thus, we see that Column A equals Column B.

2. Correct choice (B)

We want to know which side of the triangle is larger, MN or NL. To solve, we look at the angles opposite these sides. The side that has the larger angle opposite it will be longer. First, let's see what angle L is. We know that

(angle M) + (angle L) + (angle N) = 180

So, $\qquad$ 46 + (angle L) + 89 = 180

Or, $\qquad$ angle L = 180 − 46 − 89

Then, $\qquad$ angle L = 45°

We see that angle M is larger than angle L. So, side NL (opposite angle M) will be greater than side MN (opposite angle L). So, Column B is larger.

3. Correct choice (C)

Notice that $x = y$. We can determine this by the following steps:

$$x^5 - y^5 = 0$$

$$x^5 = y^5$$

And, if we take the fifth root on both sides, we get:

$$x = y$$

Therefore, for Column A, we have:

$$\frac{x^2}{y^4} = \frac{x^2}{x^4} = \frac{1}{x^2}$$

For Column B, we have:

$$\frac{1}{xy} = \frac{1}{xx} = \frac{1}{x^2}$$

So, Column A and Column B are equal.

4. Correct choice (C)

We can compute the quantity in Column A by following the pattern of the $\langle u \,|\, v \,|\, w \rangle$ operation:

151

$$\langle u|v|w\rangle = \frac{u}{v} + \frac{v}{w} \longrightarrow \langle 4|-2|-1\rangle = \frac{4}{-2} + \frac{-2}{-1}$$

This problem could be tricky because of the mixture of positive and negative numbers. To get the right answer, it's important for us to deal with the signs correctly. A positive number divided (or multiplied) by a negative number is negative, so $\frac{4}{-2} = -2$, and a negative number divided (or multiplied) by a negative number is positive, so $\frac{-2}{-1} = 2$.

So $\langle 4|-2|-1\rangle = -2 + 2 = 0$, and the two quantities are equal.

5. Correct choice (A)

We're told that y is less than 4, but equal to or greater than –7.

Let's try Column A. We're looking for the greatest value of $-8y$. For a quantity to be "greatest," we'd like it to be positive. For $-8y$ to be positive, we'd like y to be negative so that the two negatives give a positive value. The greatest possible value of $-8y$ occurs when y is at its most negative value, –7. Then, the greatest possible value of $-8y$ is $-8 \times -7 = 56$.

Let's look at Column B. We want the greatest value of $14y$. Here, y should be positive so that $14y$ becomes positive. Then, the highest value y can take is just a little less than 4. It cannot take the value of 4, because we're told "$y < 4$," not "$y \le 4$." Notice that if y were 4, $14y$ would be 56. But, because y has to be less than 4, $14y$ will always be less than 56.

So, Column A is 56 and Column B is less than 56 and the correct answer is choice (A).

6. Correct choice (D)

There is no possible way to determine whether KN or NL is the longer segment.

7. Correct choice (C)

We know that Clyde's bicycle wheel has a radius of 8 inches. Then, for one revolution of the wheel, Clyde's bicycle travels one circumference = $2\pi r = 2\pi \times 8 = 16\pi$ inches. In one minute the wheel turns 60 times. So, the distance traveled by the bicycle every minute is equal to 60 circumferences = $60 \times 16\pi = 960\pi$.

Donna's bicycle has a radius of 16 inches. Then, for one revolution of the wheel, Donna's bicycle travels $2\pi r = 2\pi \times 16 = 32\pi$ inches. In one minute, Donna's wheels make 30 revolutions. So, the distance traveled by Donna's bicycle every minute is equal to 30 circumferences = $30 \times 32\pi = 960\pi$ inches.

So, both columns are equal and the correct answer is choice (C).

8. Correct choice (B)

The price of the sweater before December was $100. If it was marked down by 20% in December, the cost of the sweater in December was 80% of 100 = $80. The price was further reduced by half in April. So, the final price of the sweater was $40. If there was a 6% sales tax, the tax was 6% of $40 (note, it's not 6% of $100). So, the tax was $.06 \times 40 = \$2.40$, which means the total price of the sweater was 40 + 2.40 = $42.40.

Then, Column A = $42.40 and Column B = $46, which means Column B is greater than Column A.

9. Correct choice (B)

First, let's square the expressions in the parentheses.

Then,   Column A $= 7^2 \left(\dfrac{x^2}{y^2}\right) + 2^2 \left(\dfrac{x^2}{y^2}\right)$

and   Column B $= 9^2 \left(\dfrac{x^2}{y^2}\right)$

Notice that $\dfrac{x^2}{y^2}$ is common to both columns. We can cancel it. Normally, this is a risky thing to do because if $\dfrac{x}{y}$ is a negative quantity, or say zero, a term that looks greater may turn out to be a greater negative, or both sides may be zero. But here we know that $\dfrac{x^2}{y^2}$ is a positive quantity.

So, if we cancel the $\dfrac{x^2}{y^2}$ terms from each column, we're left with $7^2 + 2^2$ in Column A and 9^2 in Column B.

Then, Column A = 49 + 4 = 53 and Column B = 81. So, Column B is greater than Column A.

10. Correct choice (C)

Let's list all possible values of g and h. We know that g is an even integer between 16 and 20 inclusive.

So, g can be 16, 18, or 20.

We also know that h is an odd integer between 5 and 15 inclusive.

So, h can be 5, 7, 9, 11, 13, or 15.

Finally, we know that g is twice h. Let's go down the list of possible g's:

If $g = 16$, $h = 8$ (not possible, because h should be odd).

If $g = 18$, $h = 9$ (possible).

If $g = 20$, $h = 10$ (not possible).

So, $g = 18$ and $h = 9$.

Column A = $g + h = 18 + 9 = 27$. Column B = 27. The two are equal, and so the correct answer is choice (C).

11. Correct choice (A)

Let's plug in values for k. k has to be a negative integer, so let's try −1. Then, Column A equals $\frac{1}{-1-1} = -\frac{1}{2}$. And, Column B is equal to $-\frac{1}{1} = -1$. In this case, Column A is greater. Now, let's see what happens when $k = -2$. Then, Column A = $\frac{1}{-32-8} = -\frac{1}{40}$ and Column B becomes $-\frac{1}{32}$. Again, Column A is greater.

For all negative values of k, the denominator (the number at the bottom) of Column A will be smaller than the denominator of Column B. This means that Column A will be more than Column B.

12. Correct choice (D)

We can tell that the quantity in Column A is −1 times the quantity in Column B, but we don't know exactly what either quantity is. The quantity in Column A could be positive, in which case Column B would be negative and Column A would be greater. Or, Column A could be negative, in which case Column B would be positive and Column B would be greater.

Also, Column A could be zero, in which case Column B would be zero and the two quantities would be equal. Without further information, we cannot determine which column is greater.

13. Correct choice (B)

We can rewrite column A as: $q^2 + q^4 + q^6 = q \times (q + q^3 + q^5)$. Now look at both columns. We have :
Column A: $q \times (q + q^3 + q^5)$ and Column B: $q + q^3 + q^5$.

Now imagine canceling the entire term $(q + q^3 + q^5)$ from both columns so that we're left with q in Column A and 1 in Column B.

(NOTE: Sometimes, it's risky to cancel unknowns from both sides, especially if the unknowns can be negative numbers or zeros. But here, we're told that q is $\frac{8}{9}$, which means we can cancel freely.)

If we substitute the value of q, we're comparing $\frac{8}{9}$ in Column A with 1 in Column B. So, Column B is greater than Column A.

14. Correct choice (B)

Column A is the average of three consecutive odd integers. But, the average of three consecutive odd integers is always the middle integer. For example, if the three integers are 1, 3, and 5, their sum is 9, and their average is $9 \div 3 = 3$.

So we need to compare the middle integer (Column A) with 9 (Column B). Let's suppose that this middle integer *is* 9. Then, the smallest of the three integers must be 7 and the largest must be 11. So, the three consecutive odd integers are 7, 9, and 11.

Then, their product is $7 \times 9 \times 11 = 63 \times 11 = 693$. And their sum is $7 + 9 + 11 = 27$. The product, 693, is supposed to be 15 times the sum. Is this true? 15 times 27 is 405, not 693. Actually, 693 is about 30 times 27 (because $30 \times 20 = 600$). This tells us that 9 cannot be the middle integer.

If we choose 11 as the middle integer, watch what happens. The three integers must be 9, 11, and 13, which means their sum is 33 and their product is $9 \times 11 \times 13 = 1287$. And now the product is close to 40 times the sum (because 30×40 is 1200). As you can see, when we choose larger integers, the product gets larger and larger. So, we should choose smaller integers.

We found that the product was too high when 9 was the middle integer. What happens if 7 is the middle integer? Then the three integers are 5, 7, and 9. Their sum is 21 and their product is $5 \times 7 \times 9 = 315$. Is 315 equal to 15 times 21? Yes, $15 \times 21 = 315$. So, the middle integer, which is also the average of the three integers, is 7.

In other words, Column A is 7 and Column B is 9, and so the right answer is choice (B).

15. Correct choice (A)

Since the "6 − 2" in Column A is inside one set of << >> operators, let's subtract first, before applying the << >> rule. Then, the quantity in Column A is <<4>>. Since 4 is greater than 3, we apply the first rule:

$$<<4>> = \frac{4}{2} + \frac{1}{2} = \frac{5}{2}$$

To find the value of the quantity in Column B, let's apply the << >> rule to each number:
6 is more than 3, so we apply the first rule:

$$<<6>> = \frac{6}{2} + \frac{1}{2} = \frac{7}{2}$$

2 is less than 3, so we apply the second rule:
$$<<2>> = 2 + 1 = 3$$

$$\text{So,} <<6>> - <<2>> = \frac{7}{2} - 3 = \frac{1}{2}$$

We're left with $\frac{5}{2}$ in Column A and $\frac{1}{2}$ in Column B, and so Column A is greater.

16. Correct choice (A) 5

Let's first find the value of y. We are given:
$$10,105 + y = 12,125$$
Then, $y = 12,125 - 10,105$
Or, $y = 2,020$
Now, let's find the value of $-5y$. Let's multiply both sides of the equation by -5.
Then $-5y = 2,020 \times (-5)$
Or, $-5y = -10,100$
Now, let's add 10,105 to both sides of the equation. Then, we get:
$$-5y + 10,105 = -10,100 + 10,105$$
Or, $-5y + 10,105 = 5$, which is choice (A).

17. Correct choice (B) $(u)(v)(w)(x)$

We are told that the four terms u, v, w, and x are odd integers between 5 and 11 and that $u < v < w < x$. Then, the values for the four terms are: $u = 5$, $v = 7$, $w = 9$, and $x = 11$. Now, let's look at the choices. Choice (A), you will notice, is the average of the four numbers, which is the number in the middle between 5 and 11, which is 8. It is an even number. Choice (B) is the product of $5 \times 7 \times 9 \times 11$. Before you actually do the multiplying for all four terms, take two at a time: 5×7 is 35 and 9×11 is 99. Now if you multiply 35×99, you will notice that the last term of the product will end in a 5 (because the 5 of 35 times the 9 of 99 will end in a 5). So the product will be an odd number. This has to be the answer.

18. Correct choice (D) 60,606

To find the surface area of a cube we have to find the area of one surface and then multiply it by 6. So, the area of one surface of the smallest cube is $1 \times 1 = 1$. Then, its total surface area $= 1 \times 6 = 6$.

Speed note: At this point you can tell that the right answer cannot be choices (B) and (E). You know why? Because the right answer has to end in a "6." You'll soon see why.

The area of one surface of the mid-sized cube $= 10 \times 10 = 100$. Then, its total surface area $= 100 \times 6 = 600$. So far, the sum of the surface areas of the two cubes is: $6 + 600 = 606$. Now check your answers. Only one answer ends in a "606," choice (D). So, you know that choice (D) has to be the right answer. But let's keep going.

The area of one surface of the largest cube $= 100 \times 100 = 10,000$. So, its total surface area $= 10,000 \times 6 = 60,000$.

So, total surface area of three cubes $= 60,000 + 606 = 60,606$, choice (D).

19. Correct choice (B) $\sqrt{98}$

To solve this problem, we first need to find the length of NL. To do this, we simply calculate the distance between the two points along the y-axis. This distance is, from N, 5 down to the x-axis plus 2 more to L. So $NL = 7$.

Now we need to find the length of *LM*. To do this, we simply calculate the distance between the two points along the x-axis. From *L*, it is 4 to the y-axis and then 3 more to *M*. So, *LM* = 7.

Notice that *MNL* forms a right triangle with *MN* as the hypotenuse. Then,

(length of *MN*)^2 = (7)^2 + (7)^2

(length of *MN*)^2 = 98

length of *MN* = $\sqrt{98}$

20. Correct choice (D) $0.4 \times 10^8 \pi$

We're told that the diameter is 1.28×10^4 meters. Then, the radius is half this amount, which is 0.64×10^4. (Notice that when we take half of 1.28×10^4, we take half only of 1.28. We don't take half of 10^4.) The area of a circle is πr^2. So let's plug in the value of the radius.

Then, Area = $\pi(0.64 \times 10^4)^2$

$= \pi \times 0.64^2 \times (10^4)^2$

$= \pi \times 0.4 \times 10^8$ (because 0.64^2 is about 0.4)

$= 0.4 \times 10^8\ \pi.$

21. Correct choice (D) 119

Under the heading "Post-High School Plans," we see that 85 male students and 34 female students are undecided. Thus, a total of 119 students are undecided.

22. Correct choice (D) 114

Under the heading "Sports Participation," we see that 5 percent of female students and 20 percent of male students participate in swimming. Also, we know that there are 404 female students and 468 male students.

So, the number of female students who participate in swimming is 5% of 404. Note that 10% would've been 40.4, which means that 5% is half of that, or 20.

The number of male students who participate in swimming is 20% of 468. Ten percent of 468 is 46.8, which means that 20% is twice that amount, or about 93 male students.

So the total number of swimmers, both male and female, is 20 + 93, which is 113. The closest answer is choice (D) 114.

23. Correct choice (C) 72

Under the heading "Ethnicity," we see that 59 male students and 44 female students are Hispanic. Therefore, 103 students are Hispanic.

Under the heading "Sports Participation," we see that 20% of the males and 20% of the females participate in track & field. There are 468 males, which means that the number of males who participate in track & field is

20% of 468 = $.20 \times 468$ = 94

Similarly, there are 404 females, which means that the number of females who participate in track & field is

20% of 404 = $.20 \times 404$ = 81

Then, in total, the number of students participating in track & field is: 81 + 94 = 175. Of these, we know that 103 are Hispanic students (because the problem says that all Hispanic students participate). This means that the number of non-Hispanic students participating in track & field is

175 − 103 = 72.

24. Correct choice (C) Between 2 and 3

To answer this question, we first need to find the total number of awards won by female students. Then, we divide this number by the total number of female students in the school to get our answer.

From the heading "Number of Awards Won," we see that 58 females won 4 awards each, 154 won 3 awards each, 122 won 2 awards each, 68 won 1 award each, and 4 did not win any. So, the total number of awards won is

$58 \times 4 = 232$

$154 \times 3 = 462$

$22 \times 2 = 244$

$68 \times 1 = 68$

$0 \times 1\ = 0$

Total   = 1006

We know that there are 404 female students. So the average number of awards won by female students is:

$$\text{Average number} = \frac{\text{Total Awards}}{\text{No. of females}}$$

$$= \frac{1006}{404}$$

Notice that this is approximately 1,000 divided by about 400. The answer is going to be slightly more than 2, but less than 3, which means the best answer is choice (C).

25. Correct choice (B) II only

Let's take the first option. The percent of male students who are undecided about their post-high school plans is 85 out of a total of 468. Notice that 10% of 468 would've been 46.8 and 20% would've been about 94. So, 85 is slightly less than 20%. In other words, percent of male students who are undecided is slightly less than 20%.

There are 83 work-bound female students out of a total of 404 female students. Notice that 10% of 404 is 40.4, which means that 20% is 80.8. This means that 83 is slightly greater than 20%.

So, for the first option, the percent of male students who are undecided is less than 20% and the percent of female students who are work-bound is greater than 20%. Clearly, the first option is false. At this point, we can knock out choices (A), (D), and (E) because they all contain option I. We're now left only with choices (B) and (C).

Let's look at the second option. We know that there are 872 students in Jefferson High. Half of this (50%) is 436, and the number of male students is 468. This means that more than 50% of the students are males, and so the second option is true. Now we know that the right answer has to have option II in it. From the remaining choices, we can knock out choice (C), and we're left with only one answer choice, choice (B). Notice that, by eliminating the incorrect answer choices, we didn't even have to look at the third option.

26. Correct choice (A) 17

In problems dealing with averages, it's easier to work with sums. The sum of the numbers is always equal to the average times however many numbers

there are. For example, if the average of three numbers is 6, their sum is $6 \times 3 = 18$.

In this problem, the sum of 12 numbers = 276. If four numbers are removed, there are eight numbers.

The average of these eight numbers $= 26$.

So, the sum of the eight numbers $= 26 \times 8 = 208$

Then, the sum of the numbers removed $= 276 - 208 = 68$

So, if the sum of the 4 numbers removed is 68, their average $= 68 \div 4 = 17$.

27. Correct choice (D) 92

There are five tick marks between 0 and 50, and so each tick mark is 10 units long. Point B is four tick marks from P. So $PB = 40$.

We know that AB is 30% more than PB. In other words, AB is 130% of PB (because 30% *more* means we should add 30% to 100%).

If $PB = 40$, then $AB = 1.3 \times PB$

(Note: AB is *not* $0.3 \times PB$.)

So, $AB = 1.3 \times 40 = 52$

If $AB = 52$, then PA, which gives us the value of A, is $52 + 40 = 92$.

28. Correct choice (C) 7:00 p.m.

The first train travels 40 miles every hour and the distance it has to travel is 480 miles. So, to get to station B, it will take $480 \div 40 = 12$ hours. So, if it leaves the station A at 11 a.m., it will arrive at station B at 11:00 p.m.

The second train travels 120 miles every hour. So, it will take $480 \div 120 =$ four hours to get to station B. If it has to get to station B by 11:00 p.m. (the time that the first train gets there), it should leave four hours before 11:00 p.m., or at 7:00 p.m.

29. Correct choice (C) 5:2

We have three important unknowns in this problem: the distance between town W and town X (let's call it a), the distance between town X and town Y (let's call it b), and the distance between Y and Z (and let's call this distance c). It may be helpful to us to draw a diagram:

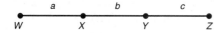

The question asks for the ratio of the distance from X to Y to the distance from Y to Z, or b:c.

Note that we don't know how far it is from any town to any other town—whether it's one mile or 100 miles or a million miles—and it doesn't matter. What's important in this problem is the relative distances between the towns. Let's assume that the total distance from W to Z is 1 (one mile? one carrot? It doesn't matter).

Then the average segment is $\frac{1}{3}$. The distance from W to X is $\frac{1}{4}$ larger than $\frac{1}{3}$, so we write $a =$ $\frac{1}{3} + \left(\frac{1}{3} \times \frac{1}{4}\right) = \frac{5}{12}$. The distance between W and Y, that is $a + b$, is $\frac{5}{6}$, so we know $b = \frac{5}{6} - \frac{5}{12} = \frac{5}{12}$. Finally, since we know that a, b, and c must add up to 1, $c = 1 - \frac{5}{12} - \frac{5}{12} = \frac{2}{12}$. And so b:$c = \frac{5}{12} : \frac{2}{12}$, or 5:2.

30. Correct choice (C) 6

This looks like a very difficult problem. It is—if we don't start from the answers. If we plug in choices, it's not too bad. Let's start from the answers. Because we're looking for the *most* number of games, let's start from the highest end, choice (D) 7.

If the player played in seven games and his overall average was three goals per game, the total number of goals he scored must be $7 \times 3 = 21$. Let's see if this works.

In the first two games, the player scored two goals, which means in the next five games he must have scored $21 - 2 = 19$ goals. Does this give us an average of *at least* four goals per game? No. Because if the average over five games was *at least* four goals, the total number of goals should be at least 20. Choice (D) doesn't work. Zap it.

Let's try choice (C) 6. If he played in six games, and his overall average was three goals per game, the total number of goals he scored must be $3 \times 6 =$

18. We know he scored two goals in the first two games. So, in the next four games, he must have scored $18 - 2 = 16$ goals. Does this give us an average of *at least* four goals? Yes, because $16 \div 4 = 4$. This works and so choice (C) is the right answer.

SECTION 2: VERBAL

1. Correct choice (C) lucrative

Use clues from the sentence to anticipate what kind of word best fits in the blank. Because Olivia's company grew rapidly, you would expect it to make a lot of money. A word like "profitable" will likely be the correct answer. Choice (C) fits just right: Her company became *lucrative*, which is to say, profitable.

Because the cyberware industry was just beginning to boom, Olivia's small technology company grew rapidly and quickly became *lucrative*.

2. Correct choice (A) retiring..handsome

Notice that this sentence gives you two words that describe Brian in reality: *unattractive* and ____. Then you have two words that describe Brian over the phone: _____ and *outgoing*. The flag words "even though" signal that these pairs should contrast with each other. And they do. Choice (A) gives you the logical pairing: Brian changes from *unattractive* to *handsome* and from *retiring* to *outgoing*. *Retiring* means shy.

Even though Brian was unattractive and *retiring*, whenever he talked on the phone, he acted as though he were the most *handsome* and outgoing man in the world.

3. Correct choice (B) placate..discontented

Using clues in the sentence, you should be able to see that the first blank needs a word that means something like "please" or "satisfy," while the second blank should have a word that means something like "cranky." Choice (B) fits best. To *placate* means to satisfy. *Discontented* means unhappy.

The newborn's incessant wailing convinced the young mother that it was impossible to *placate* her *discontented* infant.

4.   Correct choice (C) deciphered

The meaning of the Egyptian hieroglyphics is *still* ("remains") a mystery to us, long after something happened. What could have occurred for them to *keep* being a mystery? Perhaps the best strategy is to read in each choice to see which one works. Choice (C), *deciphered*, means decoded: The hieroglyphics are still a mystery even after they've been decoded. So we know what the pictures represent, but we still don't know their meaning. This sentence makes sense.

The meaning of the original Egyptian "picture writing" remains a mystery to modern civilizations long after these ancient hieroglyphics have been *deciphered*.

5.   Correct choice (E) atelier..assiduously

This sentence provides plenty of clues to let you know which words will work in the blanks. The artist has a habit of working hard every night in some workspace. Of all the choices, (E) works best. An *atelier* is an artist's workroom. *Assiduously* means diligently. These words make the best sense.

Every night the artist would lock herself in her *atelier* and work *assiduously* to finish all her paintings in time for her exhibition.

6.   Correct choice(D) seminal

This sentence is giving us a definition and asking us to supply the missing word. A foundational essay is a *seminal* essay; *seminal* means original and influential.

7.   Correct choice (A) anodyne..idyllic

The flag word "while" indicates that the two missing words are opposite to the words "shocking" and "disturbing." All the choices describe what people may think about advertisements, but only one choice contrasts with "shocking" and "disturbing." *Anodyne* refers to something that relieves pain or distress. And *idyllic* means ideal, soothing. So while many think that ads sell ideas and commodities by presenting pleasurable, attractive, and soothing images, some ads try to shock or disturb in order to reach their audience. Even if you don't know the meaning of *anodyne* and *idyllic*, if you noticed the flag word "while," you could still eliminate those choices that are not opposite to "shocking" and "disturbing."

While many think of advertisements as being uniformly *anodyne* and *idyllic*, some of the most shocking and disturbing pictures in the media may be found in ads.

8. Correct choice (C) moisture:precipitation

smoke—a substance that comes from fire.
conflagration—fire.
    Smoke is a sign of *conflagration*.
    Is *moisture* a sign of *precipitation*? Yes. Therefore, *smoke* is to *conflagration* as *moisture* is to *precipitation*.

9. Correct choice (E) jacket:warmth

bulwark—a barrier that obstructs passage.
privacy—a quality of being alone.
    A *bulwark* provides *privacy*.
    Is a *jacket* something that provides *warmth*? Yes.

10. Correct choice (E) sincerity:guile

gravity—a dignity or sobriety of bearing, seriousness.
mirth—hilarity, laughter, glee.
    Gravity is the absence of *mirth*.
    Is *sincerity* the absence of *guile*? Yes. *Sincerity* describes activity that is honest. *Guile* has to do with trickery and dishonesty.

11. Correct choice (D) bombastic:demure

garrulous—to be excessively talkative.
laconic—to be extremely terse and concise.
    Garrulous is the opposite of *laconic*.
    Is *bombastic* the opposite of *demure*? Yes. To be *bombastic* is to be showy or pompous, while to be *demure* is to be shy and timid.

12. Correct choice (D) malice:animosity

flattery—insincere or excessive praise.
sycophancy—self-seeking, obsequious flattery.
    Flattery is a sign of *sycophancy*.
    Is *malice* a sign of *animosity*? Yes. *Malice* means ill will, and *animosity* means hatred.

13. Correct choice (A) war:treaty

car—a vehicle moving on wheels.
brake—something used to slow down or stop movement.

Brake is a device for slowing down or stopping the motion of a *car*.

A *treaty* is a device (an agreement made by negotiation) that helps slow down and/or stop a war in progress, just as a brake helps slow down or stop a car in motion.

14. Correct choice (E) eclipse:surpass

parlay—to increase or otherwise transform in value.
transform—to change the composition, appearance or structure of something.

Parlay means to *transform*.
Does *eclipse* mean to *surpass*? Yes.

15. Correct choice (E) glowing:flaming

pliant—bending easily, flexible, easily influenced.
obdurate—unmoved, unyielding, or stubborn.

Pliant is opposite in meaning to *obdurate*.

Is *glowing* opposite in meaning to *flaming*? Yes, if you think very hard. *Glowing* implies bright light without flame. *Flaming* implies bright light with a flame.

16. Correct choice (A) dead:corpse

tiny—extremely small.
homunculus—a person who is extremely small, a midget.

Tiny is the defining characteristic of a *homunculus*.

Is *dead* the defining characteristic of a *corpse*? You bet, because if something isn't *dead*, it can't be a *corpse*.

17. Correct choice (E)

This passage does many things in a very short space. It talks a little about the history of pearls; it describes how pearls are made, both natural and artificial; and it describes how pearls are hunted and harvested. Because the passage is so short, none of the topics receives a lot of attention. This passage is simply an overview—an introduction of sorts.

18. Correct choice (C)

At the end of paragraph three, the passage explicitly states that artificial pearls are not as large or colorful as natural pearls. You probably could have guessed this, right?

19. Correct choice (D)

Toward the end of the third paragraph, the author gives a simple list of how to make pearls. The iron pellet idea is not mentioned. An iron pellet was used to stimulate a real oyster to make real pearls. Therefore, this step is not part of the process for making artificial pearls.

20. Correct choice (C)

The passage specifically states that collecting pearls from the ocean is a stinky business. The irony is that from all the stench comes an object of great beauty and value. We can infer that those who wear the pearls would probably never be the ones who would be willing to harvest them from the sea.

21. Correct choice (B)

No matter how you look at it, the passage is an argument—it outlines the reasons why kitchenettes are so great. However, the argument is not totally serious. The author has a lot of fun in describing the virtues of kitchenettes—so much fun we may well call it whimsical.

22. Correct choice (A)

This line is funny, isn't it? Of course, no cook is going to walk around the kitchen for more than three miles each day. That's crazy. Therefore, we can conclude that the author is exaggerating (or using hyperbole—a gross overstatement) to be funny.

23. Correct choice (E)

The point of paragraph three is to show how kitchenettes increase a person's standard of living. The author compares people with kitchenettes to kings and queens, saying that kitchenettes create royal luxuries, such as free time and delicious food.

24. Correct choice (B)

The passage is humorous because it exaggerates, making a big deal out of little things. We can call this melodrama. Note how much emotion goes into describing the kinds of food kitchenette owners can eat and what kind of freedom they will enjoy. The language is unnecessarily grandiose; the author uses big, silly words when small ones would work fine. This passage is a performance of sorts.

25. Correct choice (A)

The first part of paragraph four states that breakfast is not the only meal that can be prepared in a kitchenette. The author then describes how the kitchenette works well in other settings: for lunch, dinner, and entertaining.

26. Correct choice (B)

The end of the fourth paragraph makes the point that people with kitchenettes can be more attentive hosts. On the other side of the coin, people with full-sized kitchens tend to spend too much time away in the kitchen, leaving their guests "lonesome and skeptical."

27. Correct choice (D)

"Consumption" can have a wide variety of meanings, but the best meaning in this context is "eating." That's pretty straightforward, especially since the passage is all about food preparation.

28. Correct choice (C) perpetual

Transient means short in duration.
Perpetual means going on forever. Is *perpetual* the opposite of *transient?* Yes.

29. Correct choice (E) pliable

Obstinate means stubborn.
Pliable means yielding readily. Is *pliable* the opposite of *obstinate?* Yes, a stubborn person is not *pliable.*

30. Correct choice (A) imprudent

Judicious means prudent, sensible.
Imprudent means unwise. Is *imprudent* the opposite of *judicious?* Yes, unwise is the opposite of sensible.

31. Correct choice (D) virtue

Foible means defect or peculiarity.
Virtue means without defect. Is *virtue* the opposite of *foible?* Yes—without a defect is the opposite of defective.

32. Correct choice (B) fragmented

Inviolate means unbroken, undivided.
Fragmented means broken, incomplete. Is *fragmented* the opposite of *inviolate?* Yes, these words demonstrate broken versus unbroken.

33. Correct choice (C) buttress

Extenuate means to lessen.
Buttress means to support or strengthen. Is *buttress* the opposite of *extenuate?* Yes, to strengthen is the opposite of to lessen.

34. Correct choice (B) sullied

Pristine means in newest state, untouched.
Sullied means spoiled, dirtied. Is *sullied* the opposite of *pristine?* Yes—it's a case of dirty versus clean.

35. Correct choice (A) adolescence

Senescence means seniority, old age.
Adolescence means the process of growing up. Is *adolescence* the opposite of *senescence?* Yes, youth and old age are opposites.

36. Correct choice (D) dauntless

Trepidant means timid, trembling.
Dauntless means fearless. Is *dauntless* the opposite of *trepidant?* Yes, someone fearless would not be timid.

37. Correct choice (A) indiscernible

Ostensible means apparent.
Indiscernible means not distinct. Is *indiscernible* the opposite of *ostensible?* Yes, not distinct is the opposite of distinct or apparent.

38. Correct choice (C) laggard

Martinet means a strict disciplinarian.
Laggard means one who procrastinates, who does not have the discipline to finish tasks. Is *laggard* the opposite of *martinet?* These are close to being opposites, and the best of the five choices.

Test 2, Section 3: Analytical

Questions and Answers

Assignment for Today:

Take a sample GRE Analytical Test under actual test conditions. Allow yourself exactly 30 minutes to complete the 25 questions in this test.

Directions: *The following questions are based either on a brief passage or on a number of conditions. For each question, circle the best answer among the choices given. You may wish to draw diagrams to help you answer some of the questions.*

Questions 1–6 are based on the following.

At the fashion show, ten new outfits—four blue, two green, two red, one purple and one white—are to be modeled, in pairs and in five time slots, based on these rules:

> One of the outfits to be modeled in the last time slot is white.
>
> Blue and green outfits cannot be modeled together.
>
> Two blue outfits will be modeled together in the middle time slot. The remaining blue outfits cannot be modeled together.
>
> The two green outfits cannot be modeled together in one time slot.
>
> No more than one red outfit can be modeled in one time slot.

1. Suppose no blue outfit is modeled in either the first or the last time slot. Which of the following must be true?

    (A) The first time slot will have a purple outfit.

    (B) The second time slot will have a green outfit.

    (C) The second time slot will have a red outfit.

    (D) The fourth time slot will have a red outfit.

    (E) The fifth time slot will have a green outfit.

2. It is possible to have which outfits modeled first?

    (A) One red outfit and one purple outfit

    (B) One blue outfit and one green outfit

    (C) One purple outfit and one white outfit

    (D) One white outfit and one yellow outfit

    (E) Two green outfits

3. Which of the following outfits must be modeled at the designated time if the first and second time slots are to have green outfits?

   (A) A blue outfit; time slot 4

   (B) A red outfit; time slot 5

   (C) A red outfit; time slot 4

   (D) A red outfit; time slot 1

   (E) A purple outfit; time slot 4

4. All of the following outfits can be modeled together EXCEPT

   (A) blue and red

   (B) blue and purple

   (C) green and red

   (D) green and purple

   (E) blue and green

5. If one red outfit is modeled in a time slot immediately after the other red outfit is modeled, then it must be true that

   (A) The first and second time slots will have green outfits.

   (B) The first and second time slots will have red outfits.

   (C) The second and third time slots will have green outfits.

   (D) The fourth and fifth time slots will have green outfits.

   (E) The fourth and fifth time slots will have red outfits.

6. Suppose a green outfit and a purple outfit are to be modeled together. Then what must be true?

   (A) The fourth time slot will have a green outfit.

   (B) The fifth time slot will have a red outfit.

   (C) The second time slot will have a purple outfit.

   (D) Blue and red outfits will be modeled together.

   (E) Green and red outfits will be modeled together.

Questions 7–10 are based on the following.

Purchasing agents Amy, Beth, and Cindy (women) and Harry, Ian, Jim, Kevin, and Leo (men) divide into four groups for store visits:

> Two groups contain three agents apiece, and each group visits one of two clothing stores.
>
> A single agent visits a health store.
>
> A single agent visits a shoe store.
>
> Each group visiting a clothing store must contain at least one woman.
>
> Amy or Beth, but not both, visit a health store.
>
> Leo must be in the same group with Jim.
>
> Each agent visits only one store.

7. If Beth visits a clothing store and Jim is not with her, which of the following must be true?

   (A) Beth is in the same group as Kevin.

   (B) Cindy is in the same group as Leo.

   (C) Harry is in the same group as Ian.

   (D) Kevin is in a different group than Harry.

   (E) Ian is in a different group than Harry.

8. If Harry and Cindy are in the same group, all the following can be true EXCEPT

   (A) Amy and Ian are in the same group.

   (B) Beth and Jim are in the same group.

   (C) Cindy and Kevin are in the same group.

   (D) Ian is going to the shoe store.

   (E) Harry and Ian are in the same group.

9. Who of the following may comprise a group visiting a clothing store?

   (A) Amy, Kevin, Leo

   (B) Beth, Ian, Kevin

   (C) Beth, Cindy, Harry

   (D) Cindy, Harry, Jim

   (E) Harry, Jim, Leo

10. The shoe store could be visited by which of the following agents?

(A) Amy

(B) Beth

(C) Cindy

(D) Jim

(E) Kevin

11. The locals in Alpine, Wyoming, have been known to use firearms to keep would-be poachers away from their prized huckleberry crops. Although the berries grow on public lands, access to these areas requires crossing private property. Because the locals make nearly one-half their income selling huckleberry pies and preserves, providing public access roads to the public lands would seriously harm the economy of the area.

Which of the following, if true, provides evidence to support the claim that public access roads would hurt the economy of Alpine, Wyoming?

(A) Neighboring towns that created access roads saw an increase in tourism.

(B) Because locals and nonlocals pay taxes, public lands should be accessible to all.

(C) Locals have begun to grow huckleberries hydroponically.

(D) The contractor that builds public access roads would come from Cheyenne, Wyoming, but Alpine would supply the workers.

(E) The near monopoly on huckleberries makes them a prized and expensive ingredient.

12. Because Professor Chadwick won a Pulitzer Prize for his news reporting, it would be a great opportunity to study news writing under him. He is sure to be a great teacher.

The passage above is based on the assumption that

(A) The university hired Professor Chadwick because of his teaching abilities.

(B) News writing is an important skill for students to have.

(C) People who are excellent at what they do are also excellent at teaching that skill.

(D) Teachers who can span the generation gap tend to be much more effective than those who don't.

(E) All else being equal, Pulitzer Prize winners will attract the brightest students.

13. Most people never realize how complex popcorn really is. Popcorn will pop as a result of two conditions: either because of the rate of temperature increase or because of the absolute kernel temperature. Whenever the temperature inside a popcorn kernel increases by more than 5 degrees per second, the increased pressure inside the kernel will cause it to explode. Alternatively, whenever the temperature inside a kernel reaches 322 degrees, it will explode. However, if a kernel is slowly heated to just under 322 degrees and then returned to room temperature, it will never pop and becomes what's known as an *old maid*.

Which of the following statements, if true, can be inferred from the passage above?

(A) When using a heating unit with an upper limit of 300 degrees, one must heat the popcorn quickly to initiate popping.

(B) When *old maids* are reheated at more than 5 degrees per second, they will eventually explode.

(C) Different varieties of popcorn pop at different temperatures.

(D) Popcorn popped by the mechanism of temperature-rate increase results in a larger end product.

(E) A batch of partially popped kernels indicates that the temperature must have increased too slowly.

Questions 14–18 are based on the following.
A spy network consists of five spies—Acme, Baker, Cash, Donut, and Eagle. Each spy can receive orders only from certain other spies, as follows:

> Orders can be passed directly from one spy to another spy.
>
> A spy can serve as an intermediate, passing an order from a sender spy to a receiver spy.
>
> There may be more than one intermediate in the passing of orders.
>
> Baker can directly receive orders only from Acme or Donut.
>
> Eagle can directly receive orders only from Acme or Donut.
>
> Acme can directly receive orders only from Baker or Cash.
>
> Cash can directly receive orders only from Eagle.

14. Which of the following pairs are the spies who can receive orders from Donut through only one intermediate?
    - (A) Acme, Baker
    - (B) Acme, Cash
    - (C) Baker, Cash
    - (D) Cash, Eagle
    - (E) Baker, Eagle

15. If Acme is captured and out of commission, an order can still be originally sent and finally received by which pair?
    - (A) Baker (receiver); Eagle (sender)
    - (B) Cash (receiver); Baker (sender)
    - (C) Cash (receiver); Donut (sender)
    - (D) Donut (receiver); Baker (sender)
    - (E) Eagle (receiver); Cash (sender)

16. If Baker is captured and out of commission, which of the following pairs of final receiver and original sender will require more than two intermediates?
    - (A) Acme (receiver); from Donut (sender)
    - (B) Acme (receiver); from Cash (sender)
    - (C) Acme (receiver); from Eagle (sender)

    - (D) Cash (receiver); from Donut (sender)
    - (E) Eagle (receiver); from Donut (sender)

17. All of the following spies receive orders EXCEPT
    - (A) Acme
    - (B) Baker
    - (C) Cash
    - (D) Donut
    - (E) Eagle

18. Which of the following orders must go through the most intermediates?
    - (A) Baker (sender); Acme (receiver)
    - (B) Cash (sender); Baker (receiver)
    - (C) Eagle (sender); Baker (receiver)
    - (D) Acme (sender); Cash (receiver)
    - (E) Donut (sender); Cash (receiver)

Questions 19–22 are based on the following.
An amusement park plans its weekly employment schedule as follows:

> Each staffer works only five days per week.
>
> A staffer must work either Saturday or Sunday, but not both.
>
> If a staffer works Thursday, he or she must also work on Wednesday.
>
> If a staffer works Tuesday, he or she does not work on Saturday.

19. If a staffer does not work on Sunday, which of the following is her other day off?
    - (A) Monday
    - (B) Tuesday
    - (C) Wednesday
    - (D) Saturday
    - (E) Friday

20. If a staffer works on Tuesday, then she must also work on
    (A) Monday
    (B) Saturday
    (C) Friday
    (D) Thursday
    (E) Sunday

21. A staffer cannot take her days off on Monday, Tuesday, or Friday. This staffer must work on
    (A) Wednesday and Saturday
    (B) Wednesday and Thursday
    (C) Wednesday and Sunday
    (D) Saturday and Thursday
    (E) Thursday and Sunday

22. A staffer is allowed to take which two days off?
    (A) Saturday and Sunday
    (B) Wednesday and Saturday
    (C) Tuesday and Saturday
    (D) Monday and Sunday
    (E) Monday and Tuesday

23. In 1919, 35% of the U.S. population drank alcoholic beverages just before the 18th Amendment to the U.S. Constitution was passed to prohibit its sale, manufacture, and consumption. One year later, nearly 45% of the population drank alcoholic beverages.

    Which of the following, if true, would help to account for the phenomenon described above?
    (A) After prohibition, alcoholic beverages were available only through illegal sources.
    (B) The younger generation was most likely to violate the new amendment.
    (C) The prohibition highlighted the dangers of drinking alcoholic beverages.
    (D) Gangs in Chicago committed notoriously reckless acts of violence during the Prohibition period.
    (E) The prohibition of alcohol consumption somehow turned drinking into a fashionable activity.

24. A seismology lab studying the behavior of animals noted that animals display certain behaviors prior to any earthquake that measures over 3.75 on the Richter scale. In dogs, this behavior consists of rhythmic barking and head shaking, which the lab has named the *carpoid response*. Because records from the past five years show that the laboratory dogs displayed the carpoid response immediately before 92 percent of earthquakes, the chief scientist concluded that using the carpoid response as a cue could predict earthquakes with 92 percent accuracy.

    The head scientist's claim would be most seriously weakened if it were shown that
    (A) Cats have no analogous behavior to the carpoid response.
    (B) The carpoid response was often recorded when no earthquake occurred.
    (C) Most seismologists have studied the psychology of animal behavior.
    (D) Of the three types of earthquake waves, only the long waves cause damage at the earth's surface.
    (E) Mayan rulers are known to have maintained zoological preserves in order to predict earthquakes.

25. The Armstrong Foundation has established a fish farming program in the Peruvian highlands that allows three types of fish to be grown in the same tank: magills, freshurs, and peshaws. Corn is the optimal food for peshaws and freshurs, but it is deadly for magills. Only freshurs eat rice. Magills feed on bean curd only when peshaws are feeding in the same tank. Quinoa is an excellent food for peshaws and magills, but only when both fish are not in the same tank.

    If the fish farmers have only corn and bean curd to feed all three kinds of fish, which of the following must be true?
    (A) No tank contains both magills and peshaws.
    (B) Some magills will die since they must eat corn.
    (C) The fish farmers cannot raise peshaws.
    (D) Each tank has only one type of fish.
    (E) At least one tank contains two types of fish.

Quick Answer Guide

Test 2, Section 3: Analytical

1. E	8. A	15. C	22. C
2. A	9. B	16. A	23. E
3. A	10. E	17. D	24. B
4. E	11. E	18. C	25. E
5. B	12. C	19. B	
6. D	13. A	20. E	
7. B	14. B	21. C	

For explanations to these questions, see Day 26.

Test 2, Section 4: Math

Questions and Answers

Assignment for Today:

Take a sample GRE Math test under actual test conditions. Allow yourself exactly 30 minutes to complete the 30 questions on this test.

Directions: *For questions 1–15, each question contains two quantities—one on the left (Column A), and one on the right (Column B). Compare the quantities and answer*

(A) if Column A is greater than Column B

(B) if Column B is greater than Column A

(C) if the two columns are equal

(D) if you cannot determine a definite relationship from the information given

Never answer E

In some questions, information appears centered between the two columns. Centered information concerns each of the columns for that question only. Any symbol in one column represents the same value if it appears in the other column.

Column A	Column B

$$11 + \frac{10}{3} = \frac{4}{3} + x$$

1. x	$15\frac{2}{3}$

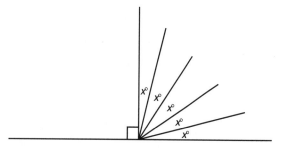

2. x	16

Column A	Column B

3. $(5.998)^3$ | 216

Stadium A seats x number of people. Stadium B seats y fewer people than Stadium A, where y is a positive number.

4. The average (arithmetic mean) number of people that can be seated in the two stadiums. | $x - \left(\dfrac{1}{2}\right)y$

a is an integer

5. 7^a | $2(7)^a$

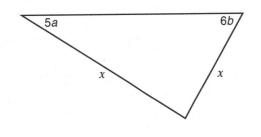

6. a | b

Column A	Column B

S is the sum of the series (3, 6, 9, ... 24)
T is the sum of the series (9, 18, 27, ...72)

7. $\dfrac{S}{T}$ | $\dfrac{1}{3}$

F = temperature in Fairbanks = –10 degrees
A = temperature in Anchorage
J = temperature in Juneau
F > A > J

8. $(A)(J)$ | $(AJ)^2$

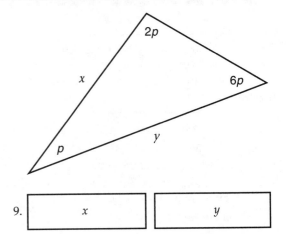

9. x | y

10. $235(63)$ | $63(230) + 63(5)$

Column A	Column B

x ounces of Type A milk contain *y* calories

11.
The number of calories in *c* ounces of Type A milk	The number of calories in *d* ounces of Type A milk

The area of a circle is 25π.

12.
The ratio of the radius to the area	$(5\pi)^{-1}$

$xy > 0$

13.
$\dfrac{1}{x}+\dfrac{1}{y}$	$\dfrac{xy}{x+y}$

14.
$a + b$	90

Column A	Column B

A right triangle has perpendicular sides of lengths *x* and *y* and a hypotenuse of length *z*. Both *x* and *y* are less than 1.

15.
z^2	$x + y$

Directions: For questions 16–30, solve each problem, and circle the appropriate answer choice, A–E.

16. What is the value of $10\pi + \dfrac{10\pi}{2} + \dfrac{10\pi}{200} + \dfrac{10\pi}{2000}$?
 (A) 5.055π
 (B) 5.55π
 (C) 10.055π
 (D) 15.055π
 (E) 15.55π

17. Which of the following is the largest integer smaller than $-\dfrac{7}{3}$?
 (A) -3
 (B) -2.4
 (C) -2
 (D) -1
 (E) 2

18. What is the value of $(p - q)$, if
 $r = 3$
 $s = 5$
 $p = r - s$
 $q = s - r$
 (A) -4
 (B) -10
 (C) 0
 (D) 4
 (E) 10

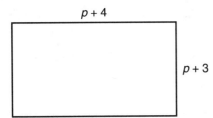

$p + 4$

$p + 3$

19. If the area of the rectangle is 42, what is a possible value of p?

(A) –3

(B) 3

(C) $\sqrt{30}$

(D) 7

(E) $17\dfrac{1}{2}$

20. One gallon of water can water 2 trees or 10 house plants. How many gallons are needed to water 25 house plants and 5 trees?

(A) $2\dfrac{1}{2}$

(B) 4

(C) 5

(D) 6

(E) 13

Questions 21–25 are based on the given figure.

1995 Earnings of Company X and Company Y, Percent by Month

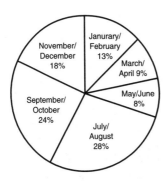

COMPANY X
Total Earnings: $300,000

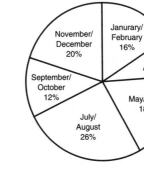

COMPANY Y
Total Earnings: $400,000

21. How much more money did Company X earn during the July/August period than during the November/December period?

(A) $3000

(B) $24,000

(C) $30,000

(D) $54,000

(E) $84,000

22. During how many two-month periods shown did Company X earn less than Company Y in the same period?

(A) 1

(B) 2

(C) 3

(D) 4

(E) 5

23. For the September/October period, Company X earned how much more than Company Y?

    (A) $14,000

    (B) $24,000

    (C) $36,000

    (D) $48,000

    (E) $72,000

24. Among the six two-month periods shown, the ratio of Company X's largest two-month earnings to Company Y's smallest two-month earnings is approximately

    (A) 0.23

    (B) 0.38

    (C) 2.6

    (D) 3.5

    (E) 4.3

25. In 1996, Company X's total earnings remained the same from the previous year's total earnings, but its earnings in the January/February period increased by 7% from its earnings in the same period in 1995. Company X's earnings in January/February 1996 were approximately what percent of its total earnings for 1996?

    (A) 7

    (B) 14

    (C) 17

    (D) 20

    (E) 22

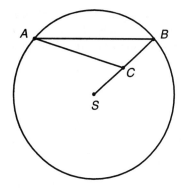

26. In the figure above, S is the center of the circle and arc AB is one quarter of the circle's circumference. If the radius of the circle is 6, and BC is one half of the radius, what is the area of $\triangle ABC$?

    (A) 6

    (B) 9

    (C) $\dfrac{9}{2}\sqrt{5}$

    (D) 18

    (E) 9π

27. A company distributes 10 percent of its profits to its shareholders and invests the rest. If the total amount invested by the company as a result of profits was $100, what was the company's profit in dollars?

    (A) $\dfrac{100}{9}$

    (B) 90

    (C) $\dfrac{1000}{9}$

    (D) 110

    (E) 190

28. A child has one penny, one nickel, one dime, one quarter, and one half-dollar. How many different amounts of money can she make by using only *two* of her coins?

    (A) 5

    (B) 10

    (C) 15

    (D) 20

    (E) 25

29. If w, r, and t are positive integers and $w + r + t = 16$, which of the following is the *least* possible value of $w(r + t)$?

    (A) 0

    (B) 15

    (C) 16

    (D) 28

    (E) 39

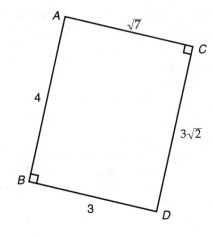

30. What is the area of the quadrilateral *ABCD*?

    (A) $3\sqrt{14}$

    (B) $6 + \dfrac{3}{2}\sqrt{14}$

    (C) 12

    (D) $18\sqrt{14}$

    (E) $12 + 3\sqrt{14}$

Quick Answer Guide

Test 2, Section 4: Math

1. B	9. A	17. A	25. B
2. A	10. C	18. A	26. B
3. B	11. D	19. B	27. C
4. C	12. C	20. C	28. B
5. B	13. D	21. C	29. B
6. A	14. C	22. E	30. B
7. C	15. B	23. B	
8. B	16. D	24. C	

For explanations to these questions, see Day 26.

Test 2, Section 3: Analytical, and Section 4: Math
Explanations and Strategies

Assignment for Today:

Review the explanations for the Analytical Test you took on Day 24 and for the Math Test you took on Day 25.

SECTION 3: ANALYTICAL

Questions 1–6

From the facts, we have

$$3 \; - - \; B \; B, \; \text{otherwise } \cancel{B \; B}$$
$$5 \; - - \; W \; -$$
$$\cancel{G \; G} \quad \cancel{R \; R} \quad \cancel{B \; G}$$

1. Correct choice (E)

In this question, we have

Time slot	Colors
1	— —
2	B —
3	B B
4	B —
5	W —

Since blue and green outfits cannot be modeled together, the green outfit has to be in either the first or the fifth time slot. In fact, since the two green outfits cannot be modeled together, one green outfit must be modeled in the first slot and the other in the fifth slot. In other words, one of the outfits in the fifth slot must be green.

2. Correct choice (A)

To get the answer, we should eliminate all answer choices that are incorrect or violate the rules in some way. Only choice (A) does not violate any rules.

3. Correct choice (A)

For this question, we have

Time slot	Colors
1	G __
2	G __
3	B B
4	__ __
5	W __

Since blue and green outfits cannot be modeled together, and there are two blue outfits other than the ones in time slot 3, one blue outfit must be modeled during time slot 4.

4. Correct choice (E)

There are four blue outfits, two of which are modeled in the third slot. Since, in other time slots, the blue outfits cannot be modeled together, the four blue outfits must be modeled over three time slots: definitely in slot 3, and then in two others: 1, 2, 4, or 5. Also, we know that the blue and green outfits cannot be modeled together and that there are two green outfits. This means that slots 1, 2, 4, and 5 must have either a blue or a green outfit, but none can have both. Hence, blue and green outfits cannot be modeled together.

5. Correct choice (B)

We know that the two green outfits cannot be modeled during the same time slot, and the four blue outfits must be modeled during three different time slots (including slot 3). Since blue and green outfits cannot be modeled together, each of the time slots other than 3 must have exactly one outfit that is blue or green.

Thus, we have

Time slot	Colors
1	B/G __
2	B/G __
3	B B
4	B/G __
5	B/G W

Thus, the consecutive slots open are slots 1 and 2, which is where the two red outfits must be modeled.

6. Correct choice (D)

We know that the two green outfits cannot be modeled during the same time slot, and the four blue outfits must be modeled during three different time slots (including slot 3). Since blue and green outfits cannot be modeled together, each of the time slots other than 3 must have exactly one outfit that is blue or green.

Thus, we have

Time slot	Colors
1	B/G __
2	B/G __
3	B B
4	B/G __
5	B/G W

If a green and a purple outfit are to be modeled together, let's say in the first slot, then the two red outfits will have to be in slots 2 and 4. One of these two slots will have a green and the other will have a blue outfit. Either way, a red outfit has to be modeled with a blue outfit.

Questions 7–10:

From the facts, we have

Clothing	Clothing	Shoe	Health	
W __ __	W __ __	__ __	A/B	JL

7. Correct choice (B)

If Beth is in a group of three, then Amy must go to the health store. If Jim is in a different group than Beth, then one group going to the clothing store must include Cindy, Jim, and Leo. Thus, Cindy and Leo must be in the same group.

8. Correct choice (A)

For this question, we also have HC. This means one group going to the clothing store will include Jim, Leo, and either Amy or Beth, and the other group will have Harry and Cindy. This leaves Ian and Kevin either going with Harry and Cindy or going to the shoe store. Thus, Ian cannot be in the same group as Amy.

9. Correct choice (B)

The best way to arrive at this answer is to apply the facts and eliminate each of the incorrect choices. Exactly one woman will be in each group going to the clothing store. For this choice, we could have the following arrangement:

Clothing	Clothing	Shoe	Health
C J L	B I K	H	A

10. Correct choice (E)

The person going to the shoe store must be a man because the three women must go to two clothing stores and the health store. The man cannot be Jim because he must be in the same group as Leo. However, the man can be Kevin.

11. Correct choice (E)

This question asks you to find a statement supporting the claim that public access roads to the huckleberries would hurt the local economy. Your best bet is to read each choice and ask yourself if the new idea would support the conclusion of the passage. When you do this, you should see that only choice (E) works. Choice (E) says that because huckleberries are controlled in a near monopoly, they are valuable. With public access roads, the monopoly would be threatened as poachers would be more likely to get to the huckleberries, which in turn would likely reduce their value.

12. Correct choice (C)

This question asks you to identify an assumption that the passage relies on to reach the conclusion that Chadwick is a great teacher. The only thing we really know about Chadwick is that he won a Pulitzer Prize. The missing assumption will somehow connect winning a prize with being a great teacher, which is exactly what choice (C) does: "people who are excellent at what they do are also excellent at teaching that skill." If prize winners are also great teachers, as choice (C) states, then the conclusion holds. If the assumption doesn't hold (i.e., prize winners aren't necessarily great teachers), then you can't safely draw the conclusion stated in the passage.

13. Correct choice (A)

This question asks you to draw a logical inference based on the facts given in the passage. The most supported answer is (A). This choice says that if you have a stove that reaches only 300 degrees, you must use the rate of temperature increase method to pop the kernels because you will never reach the 322 degree popping threshold. Therefore, you must heat the kernels rapidly in order for them to pop.

Questions 14–18:
From the facts, we have the following network (arrows indicate the direction the orders will go):

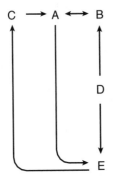

14. Correct choice (B)

D can pass orders to E and B. B can pass orders only to A, and E can pass orders only to C. Thus, A and C are the only spies that can receive orders from D through exactly one intermediate.

15. Correct choice (C)

We arrive at this answer by eliminating all the other choices. C can still receive orders from D through E.

16. Correct choice (A)

Now that B is out of commission, A must receive orders from D through E and C. Thus, this request must go through at least two other spies.

17. Correct choice (D)

D cannot receive orders from anybody.

18. Correct choice (C)

B must receive orders from E through A and C. A can receive orders from B directly, and all the remaining choices must go through exactly one other intermediate. Thus, this choice is the one which goes through the most intermediates.

Questions 19–22:
From the facts, we have

Sat or Sun

Thurs → Wed

Tues → ~~Sat~~

19. Correct choice (B)

If a staffer has Sunday off, then she works on Saturday. This means that she does not work on Tuesday because, from the facts, if the staffer works Tuesday, then she *also* doesn't work Saturday.

20. Correct choice (E)

If she works on Tuesday, then she cannot work on Saturday. This means she has to work on Sunday, because, from the facts, we know that staffers must work either on Saturday or on Sunday.

21. Correct choice (C)

For this question, we know that Monday, Tuesday, and Friday are work days. This means that Saturday cannot be a work day, and so Sunday must be a work day. The fifth work day cannot be Thursday because Thursday requires that Wednesday also be a work day. This leaves Wednesday as the fifth day. This was a tough question.

22. Correct choice (C)

The best way to find the correct answer is to work from the facts, eliminating the choices that violate any one of them. For choice (C), Tuesday and Sunday are days taken off. So Thursday is worked and so is Wednesday, which agree with Fact 2. Saturday is worked but Sunday is not, which agree with Fact 1, and Tuesday is not worked, so Fact 3 can be ignored.

23. Correct choice (E)

The task here is to find the statement that explains why drinking levels increased after alcohol became illegal. Only (E) is a logical explanation. Once alcohol was prohibited, people wanted it even more. If it became fashionable to break the law, then we would be able to explain the increased level of drinking. The more fashionable something is, the more people are inclined to do it.

24. Correct choice (B)

Your goal in this question is to find a statement that *weakens* the seismologist's claim that she can predict earthquakes by using her dogs. Your best bet is to read through the choices and eliminate those that are irrelevant or that strengthen the claim. You should be able to eliminate all of the choices except (B). Another method is to read through the choices and find the one that displays the silliness of the scientist's logic. Again, choice (B) is the right one here.

Choice (B) says that the dogs barked and wagged their heads a lot, not just before earthquakes. It just so happened that the dogs were barking before 92% of the earthquakes. But if the dogs barked a lot of the time (not just before earthquakes), then it's impossible to know how much of their barking had to do with sensing an earthquake. Therefore, the chief scientist would not be able to predict earthquakes accurately using the dogs' *carpoid response*.

25.   Correct choice (E)

The question asks you to find a statement that must be true, given the facts in the paragraph. Your best strategy is to read each choice and see if it *must* be true, not just if it is possibly true. You'll find that the only choice that must be true is (E): at least one tank contains two types of fish. The reason is straightforward: Since magills die from corn and they don't eat rice, they can be fed only with bean curd. But, according to the passage, "Magills only feed on bean curd when peshaws are feeding in the same tank."

SECTION 4: MATH

1.   Correct choice (B)

The equation is $11 + \dfrac{10}{3} = \dfrac{4}{3} + x$

Subtract $\dfrac{4}{3}$: $11 + \dfrac{10}{3} - \dfrac{4}{3} = x$

$11 + \dfrac{6}{3} = x$

$11 + 2 = x$

$x = 13$

So, Column A = 13 and Column B = $15\dfrac{2}{3}$, which means Column B is greater than Column A.

2.   Correct choice (A)

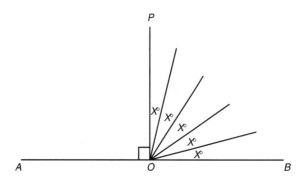

In the figure, $\angle AOP = 90$ degrees, which means that $\angle POB$ is also 90 degrees (because $\angle AOB$ is a straight line). This 90-degree angle is divided into 5 equal angles, each x degrees. So, the measure of each of these small angles is $90 \div 5 = 18$ degrees.

Hence, Column A is greater than Column B.

3.   Correct choice (B)

Don't even attempt to find the third power of 5.998. There's something else going on here. 5.998 is a little smaller than 6 and $6^3 = 216$, so 5.998^3 must be less than 216.

4.   Correct choice (C)

Instead of working with x and y, let's plug in our own values. Just to make things simple, let's say that $x = 10$ and $y = 2$ (this is a pretty pathetic stadium if it seats only 10 people, right? But who cares!)

So, Stadium A can seat 10 people, and Stadium B can seat $10 - 2 = 8$ people. The average then is

$\dfrac{(10+8)}{2} = 9$. So, Column A = 9.

Column B = $x - \left(\dfrac{1}{2}\right)y = 10 - \left(\dfrac{1}{2}\right)2 =$

$10 - 1 = 9$.

So, Column A = Column B.

5. Correct choice (B)

Let's see what happens if a is 1.

| Then, | Column A $= 7^1 = 7$ |
| And | Column B $= 2(7)^1 = 14$. |

Here, Column B is greater. Or, if $a = 0$,

| Then, | Column A $= 7^0 = 1$ |
| And | Column B is $2(7)^0 = 2 \times 1 = 2$. |

(Don't forget that any number raised to a power of 0 is equal to 1.)

And, what happens if a is a negative number, say, -1?

| Then, | Column A $= 7^{-1} = \dfrac{1}{7}$ |
| And | Column B $= 2(7)^{-1} = \dfrac{2}{7}$. |

Notice that, because 7 is a positive number, 7^a will always be a positive number, too, and Column B will always be twice as large as Column A. Hence, the right answer is choice (B).

6. Correct choice (A)

We see that the two sides of the given triangle are equal to x. This means that the triangle is an isosceles triangle. In an isosceles triangle, the two angles opposite, or facing, the equal-length sides are equal. In other words, angles $5a$ and $6b$ are equal. So, we can write: $5a = 6b$.

Dividing both sides of the equation by 5, we get

$$a = \frac{6}{5}b$$

In other words, a is greater than b (because a is actually 1.2 times b), and the right answer is choice (A).

7. Correct choice (C)

Notice that the second series is identical to the first series, except that every term in it is 3 times the corresponding term in the first series. In other words, the first term, 9, is 3 times the first term, 3. The second term, 18, is 3 times the second term, 6, and so on, up to the last term.

This tells us that the sum of all numbers, T, in the first series is going to be 3 times the sum of all numbers, S, in the second series. In other words, we can write the following equation:

$$T = 3S$$

Dividing both sides by T, we get:

$$1 = \frac{3S}{T}$$

Dividing by 3, we get:

$$\frac{1}{3} = \frac{S}{T}.$$

In other words, Column A is equal to Column B.

8. Correct choice (B)

Let's suppose that the temperature in Anchorage, A, is 1 degree lower than the temperature in Fairbanks. Then, $A = -11$.

Also, let's assume, just to make things simple, that the temperature in Juneau, J, is 1 degree lower than the temperature in Anchorage. So, $J = -12$.

Then, Column A $= (A)(J) = (-11)(-12)$. Notice that this will be a positive number (because a negative times a negative is positive).

And, Column B $= (AJ)^2 = (-11)(-12) \times (-11)(-12)$. So, we can set up the comparison as follows:

Column A $= (-11)(-12)$

Column B $= (-11)(-12) \times (-11)(-12)$

We can divide out the common terms $(-11)(-12)$ from both sides and we're left with 1 in Column A and $(-11)(-12)$ in Column B. Notice that Column B is positive and much larger than 1, which means Column B is greater than Column A.

9. Correct choice (A)

The key here is to know that, in a triangle, the largest side is always opposite the largest angle, the smallest side is always opposite the smallest angle, and so on.

In the given figure, y is opposite angle $2p$, and x is opposite the largest angle, $6p$. So, x is the largest side, which means x is greater than y.

10. Correct choice (C)

Let's look at Column A, 235(63). What if we break 235 down into $230 + 5$? Then we get $(230 + 5)63$. Now if we multiply each term within the parentheses by 63, we get $(230)63 + (5)63$, which is exactly what we see in Column B, so the two columns are equal.

11. Correct choice (D)

Just to make things easier, let's suppose that x is 1 and y is 1. Then, we know that 1 ounce of milk contains 1 calorie.

Column A: How many calories in c ounces? c calories.

Column B: How many calories in d ounces? d calories.

Now, which is greater? We have no way of knowing. What if c were 1 and d were 10 million? Then, Column B would be greater. And, if c were 1 and d were 1, the two columns would be equal. So, without knowing the relationship between c and d, we have no way of knowing which column is greater.

12. Correct choice (C)

We know that the area of a circle is: $A = \pi r^2$, where r is the radius. We're given that the area of the circle is 25π. Then we can write:

$$25\pi = \pi r^2$$

Or,

$$25 = r^2$$

This means that the radius of the circle, r, is 5. Now, Column A wants us to find the ratio of the radius to the area. This is

$$\frac{radius}{area} = \frac{5}{25\pi} = \frac{1}{5\pi}$$

But, another way of $\frac{1}{5\pi}$ writing is $(5\pi)^{-1}$.

So, the two columns are equal.

13. Correct choice (D)

To solve this problem, let's plug in our own numbers. We know that $xy > 0$. This simply means that neither x nor y is zero. So what happens if $x = 1$ and $y = 10$, just for fun?

Then, Column A $= \dfrac{1}{x} + \dfrac{1}{y} = \dfrac{1}{1} + \dfrac{1}{10} = 1 + .1 = 1.1,$

And Column B $= \dfrac{xy}{x + y} + \dfrac{1 \times 10}{1 + 10} = \dfrac{10}{11}$

This means that Column A is greater than Column B. Now what happens if, say $x = -1$ and $y = -10$ (notice that xy is still greater than 0).

Then, Column A $= \dfrac{1}{x} + \dfrac{1}{y} = \dfrac{1}{-1} + \dfrac{1}{-10} = -1 + (-.1) = -1.1$

And Column B $= \dfrac{xy}{x + y} + \dfrac{(-1)(-10)}{(-1) + (-10)} = \dfrac{10}{-11} = -\dfrac{10}{11}$

So here Column A is negative 1.1, and Column B is negative $\frac{10}{11}$. Notice that $\frac{10}{11}$ is less than 1.1, which means that negative $\frac{10}{11}$ is actually more than negative 1.1. So, in this example, Column B is actually greater than Column A.

As soon as we get two different results, we know that the right answer has to be choice (D).

14. Correct choice (C)

First, let's mark the given diagram, as shown here.

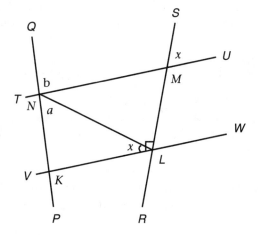

We know that $\angle SMU = \angle NML$ (they are called vertical angles, and vertical angles are equal). This means that $\angle NML$ is also x. Notice that $\angle KLM$ is given to be 90 degrees and $\angle KLN$ is x. So then, $\angle NLM$ must be $90 - x$.

Then, in triangle NLM, one angle is x, another is $90 - x$, and the third angle is $\angle MNL$. We know that the three angles in a triangle must sum to 180 degrees.

So, $x + (90 - x) + \angle MNL = 180$

$90 + \angle MNL = 180$

$\angle MNL = 90$

Now look at the straight line QNP.
We know that $a + \angle MNL + b = 180$. But, $\angle MNL = 90$.
So we have: $a + 90 + b = 180$.

Or $a + b = 90$.

In other words, Column A is equal to Column B.

15.   Correct choice (B)

From the geometry of a right triangle, we know that
$z^2 = x^2 + y^2$.

   Since x and y are both less than 1, $x^2 < x$ and
$y^2 < y$. (If you don't see why this is so, consider what
would happen if $x = .5$. Then, $x^2 = .25$, which is less
than x.) Thus, $z^2 = x^2 + y^2 < x + y$.

   Or, another way to solve this problem is to plug
in values for x and y. Suppose $x = .5$ and $y = .5$. Then,
$x^2 = y^2 = .25$. And, we know that $z^2 = x^2 + y^2 = .25 +$
$.25 = .5$. Further, $x + y = .5 + .5 = 1$. So, $z^2 = .25$ and
$x + y = 1$.

16.   Correct choice (D) 15.055π

Let's scan the answers. All choices are in terms of π.
So, there's no need to convert π to its numerical
value.

   The first two terms of the problem, $10\pi + \frac{10\pi}{2}$,
tell us that the answer has to be more than 15π
because $\frac{10\pi}{2}$ equals 5π and $10\pi + 5\pi = 15\pi$. Zap
choices (A), (B), and (C).

   Now, let's look at the third term, $\frac{10\pi}{200}$. This
equals $\frac{\pi}{20}$, which is $.05\pi$ because $\frac{1}{20} = .05$. When we
add this term to 15π, we get 15.05π. At this point, we
know the answer has to be choice (D), because
choice (E) is too high. The addition of the last term
$\frac{10\pi}{2000}$ is much too small for choice (E) to be correct.
(Because the last term, $\frac{\pi}{200}$ is only $.005\pi$.)

17.   Correct choice (A) –3

In order to solve this problem, it's necessary to know
that integers include negative numbers, zero, and
positive numbers (without a fractional component).
The number $-\frac{7}{3}$ can be simplified to $-2\frac{1}{3}$. We need
the next smaller integer, which means we want the
quantity to be "more negative."

   In other words, we want a bigger whole number
with a negative sign. The next number that is less
than $-2\frac{1}{3}$ is -3, which is choice (A). Note that the
correct answer is not -2 or -1 because these numbers
are greater than $-2\frac{1}{3}$.

18.   Correct choice (A) – 4

Let's plug in values of r and s in the given equations.
We're told that $r = 3$ and $s = 5$.

Then, $p = r - s = 3 - 5 = -2$

                        $q = s - r = 5 - 3 = 2$

Then $p - q = -2 - 2 = -4$, which is choice (A).

19.   Correct choice (B) 3

We are given that the area of the rectangle, which is
the product of the length and width, is 42. Then, we
can write

   $(p + 4) (p + 3) = 42$

To get the answer, we can expand the two parentheses in the equation and solve for p. (Yeah, right!) We
have a better way, don't we? We plug in values from
the answer choices.

   We could start with choice (C)—if we were
Einstein. We don't want to get anywhere close to that
choice. Let's start with choice (D) and plug in the
value of 7 for p.

Then, $(7 + 4) (7 + 3) = 42$

Or $11 \times 10 = 42$.

No, it doesn't work. And we see that the value of p
is too high. At this point, we can zap choices (D) and
(E). Let's go backwards and try choice (B), 3 (notice,
we're still avoiding the ugly radical sign; hey, that's
not illegal). Plugging in the value of 3, we get $(3 + 4)$
$(3 + 3) = 42$

Or, $7 \times 6 = 42$.

It works, and so choice (B) is the right answer.

20. Correct choice (C) 5

Let's break this down into trees and plants and take them separately.

Trees: One gallon waters 2 trees. So, for 5 trees, we'll need

$$\frac{5}{2} = 2\frac{1}{2} \text{ gallons.}$$

Plants: One gallon waters 10 plants. So, for 25 plants, we'll need

$$\frac{25}{10} = 2\frac{1}{2} \text{ gallons.}$$

So, the total amount of water needed is

$$2\frac{1}{2} + 2\frac{1}{2} = 5 \text{ gallons.}$$

21. Correct choice (C) $30,000

From the given chart, we see that Company X earned 28% in July/August and 18% in November/December. So, the earnings in July/August exceeded the earnings in November/December by 28% – 18% = 10%.

We know that $300,000 is the total earnings. So, 10% of this amount is .10 × 300,000 = $30,000.

22. Correct choice (E) 5

January/February: Without calculating the actual amount, we can tell that Company X earned less than Company Y (because the percent amount is less and the total earnings are less for Company X than for Company Y).
March/April: For Company X, 9% of $300,000 is $27,000, and for Company Y, 8% of $400,000 is $32,000. So this period also counts toward our answer.
May/June: Again, without calculating the actual amount, we can see that Company X earned less than Company Y (because the percent amount is less and the total earnings are less for Company X than for Company Y). This period also counts.
July/August: Company X's earnings are 28% of $300,000 = $84,000, and Company Y's earnings are 26% of $400,000 = $104,000. This period should also be counted. (So far, we have four periods; let's keep going.)
September/October: Company X's earnings are 24% of $300,000 = $72,000, and Company Y's earnings are 12% of $400,000 = $48,000. So, this period does not count.

November/December: Company X's earnings are 18% of $300,000 = $54,000, and Company Y's earnings are 20% of $400,000 = $80,000. This period also counts.

Hence, we see that, of the six two-month periods, only the September/October period does not count. In other words there are five two-month periods when Company X's earnings were less than Company Y's earnings for the same period.

23. Correct choice (B) $24,000

First, we want to find the amount earned by Company X during the September/October period. Then, we want to find the amount earned by Company Y during the same period. From this, we can determine how much more Company X earned than Company Y.

During September/October, Company X earned 24% of $300,000, which is .24 × 300,000 = $72,000.

In the same period, Company Y earned 12% of $400,000, which is .12 × 400,000 = $48,000.

So, Company X's earnings exceeded Company Y's earnings by $72,000 – $48,000 = $24,000.

24. Correct choice (C) 2.6

Company X's largest earnings occurred during the July/August period, which was 28%. The dollar amount is 28% of $300,000 = .28 × 300,000 = $84,000. Company Y's smallest earnings occurred during the March/April period, which was 8%. So, the dollar amount is 8% of $400,000 = .08 × 400,000 = $32,000.

Then the required ratio is $\frac{84,000}{32,000} = \frac{84}{32} = \frac{21}{8}$, which is greater than 2 and slightly less than 3. In other words, our answer should be greater than 2, but less than 3. We can see that choice (C) 2.6 is the closest.

25. Correct choice (B) 14

In 1995, Company X's earnings during the January/February period were 13%. In dollars, this is .13 × 300,000 = $39,000. We know that, in the following year, earnings during the same period increased by 7%. So, to find the dollar amount, let's first find 7% of $39,000. It is

.07 × 39,000 = $2,730.

So, the earnings for January/February 1996 are $39,000 + $2,730 = $41,730. We can approximate this to $42,000.

We know that the total earnings did not change in 1996. In other words, Company X's total earnings were still $300,000.

Now we need to know what percent of $300,000 is $42,000. This is given by the ratio

$$\frac{42,000}{300,000} \times 100\% = \frac{42}{300} \times 100\% = \frac{42}{3} = 14\%$$

So the correct answer is 14%.

26.   Correct choice (B) 9

We're told that arc AB is one quarter of the circumference. This means that angle ASB is 90 degrees (because 90 degrees is one quarter of the total number of degrees in a circle, which is 360). So, let's draw this 90-degree angle by connecting A and S.

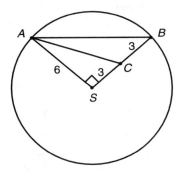

Then, AS is also 6 because it's another radius. We're told that BC is half the radius. In other words, $BC = SC = 3$. We need to find the area of triangle ABC. We can take BC to be the base. We now need the height. To find the height, we need a 90-degree angle from the base to the opposite corner of the triangle. If we extend BC to S, we see that the height of the triangle = AS = 6. Remember, height is simply a perpendicular line from the base to the opposite corner. It's not necessary for SC to be part of the triangle. So now we know the height and the base. Then, the area is

$$A = \frac{1}{2}bh,$$

So, $A = \frac{1}{2} \times 3 \times 6 = 9$

27.   Correct choice (C) $\frac{1000}{9}$

Let's work from the answers and plug values back into the problem. As usual, we start with choice (C) $\frac{1000}{9}$. This is supposed to be the company's profit. Well, if this is the profit, then we know that 90% of this amount should equal $100. Why? Because we're told that 10% is given back to the shareholders and the rest (which is 90%) is invested. We're also told that the total amount invested is $100.

In other words, 90% of $\frac{1000}{9}$ should be equal to 100.

That is, $.90 \times \frac{1000}{9} = 100.$

Or, $\frac{90}{100} \times \frac{1000}{9} = 100.$

This equation is true, so choice (C) is the answer. Notice how easy it was once we started from the answers. Always look for this shortcut.

28.   Correct choice (B) 10

Each of the five coins can combine with the four others. So $5 \times 4 = 20$ combinations.

penny + nickel	PENNY COMBINATIONS
penny + dime	
penny + quarter	
penny + half-dollar	
nickel + penny	NICKEL COMBINATIONS
nickel + dime	
nickel + quarter	
nickel + half-dollar	
dime + penny	DIME COMBINATIONS
dime + nickel	
dime + quarter	
dime + half-dollar	

quarter + penny　　　QUARTER
　　　　　　　　　　　COMBINATIONS

quarter + nickel

quarter + dime

quarter + half-dollar

half-dollar + penny　HALF-DOLLAR
　　　　　　　　　　　COMBINATIONS

half-dollar + nickel

half-dollar + dime

half-dollar + quarter

But notice that each of the combinations is counted twice in this operation. (For example, *penny + half-dollar* is the same amount as *half-dollar + penny*; both equal 51 cents!) So half of these combinations are repeats! So half of 20 = 10 *different* amounts.

29.　Correct choice (B) 15

We are looking for the *least* possible value of $w(r + t)$. We should start from the lowest end of the answer choices, which is choice (A) 0. Is it possible for $w(r + t)$ to be 0 if w, r, and t are all positive integers?

$w(r + t) = 0$ only if $w = 0$ (which is not allowed because w is a positive integer) or if $r = -t$ (which is also not allowed because both r and t have to be positive). So, (A) 0 is not possible.

Let's see if choice (B) 15 is possible. To get the least value for $w(r + t)$, we should let w be the smallest of the three because it is being multiplied by both r and t. Choose w to be the smallest positive integer, 1.

Then, if $w = 1$, $r + t$ has to equal 15 so that $w + r + t = 16$. Now, $w(r + t) = 1(15) = 15$. This is the answer.

30.　Correct choice (B) $6 + \frac{3}{2}\sqrt{14}$

We cannot simply multiply the length and the width of the quadrilateral because it's not a rectangle (although it looks like one). It has two different lengths and two different widths. But notice that we're given two right angles. Yes, we can construct two right triangles if we draw a diagonal from B to D.

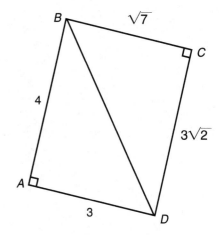

Then, the area of the right triangle *ABD* is

$$A_{\triangle ABD} = \frac{1}{2} \times AD \times AB$$

$$= \frac{1}{2} \times 3 \times 4$$

$$= 6$$

And the area of the right triangle *BCD* is

$$A_{\triangle BCD} = \frac{1}{2}bh$$

$$= \frac{1}{2}BC \times CD$$

$$= \frac{1}{2} \times \sqrt{7} \times 3\sqrt{2}$$

$$= \frac{3}{2}\sqrt{14}$$

Now, we simply add these two values together to find the entire area of *ABCD*.

$$A_{\triangle ABCD} = 6 + \frac{3}{2}\sqrt{14}$$

Test 2 Section 5: Verbal

Questions and Answers

Assignment for Today:

Take a sample GRE Verbal Test under actual timed conditions. Allow yourself exactly 30 minutes to complete the 38 questions in this test.

Directions: For questions 1–7, one or more words have been left out of each sentence. Circle the answer, A–E, which contains the word or words that best fit the meaning of the entire sentence.

---

1. Working hard to _____ the requirements of his current position, Clarence became the next person in line for a promotion.

   (A) scorn

   (B) assert

   (C) misjudge

   (D) fulfill

   (E) amplify

2. Our city's extensive and versatile public transit network offers the nation's most _____ means of travel, from trains and cable cars to the many electric and diesel busses.

   (A) expensive

   (B) varied

   (C) questionable

   (D) exciting

   (E) private

3. When the DNA sample from the _____ murderer did not match the sample from the murder weapon, the suspect was _____ in the public's mind.

   (A) convicted..blamed

   (B) alleged..released

   (C) famous..incriminated

   (D) accused..exonerated

   (E) transient..exculpated

4. When the Andersons' infant cried all night, it severely _____ the young couple's volatile relationship; furthermore, the _____ task of caring for a new baby required more energy than the new parents had to give.

   (A) exacerbated..relentless

   (B) enhanced..simple

   (C) aggravated..pleasing

   (D) mitigated..arduous

   (E) solidified..tedious

5. Dress styles among female White House staff have abruptly switched from Kappa Gamma Kappa to ____, including everything from long, flowing skirts and suede vests to threadbare jeans.

   (A) Neolithic

   (B) eclectic

   (C) indelicate

   (D) demure

   (E) comfortable

6. It was within the ____ of the queen to ____ her husband's unpopular decree.

   (A) domain..chastise

   (B) puissance..instigate

   (C) purview..rescind

   (D) temerity..delineate

   (E) disparagement..repeal

7. The widespread fascination with the novel is generated by the ____ of possible interpretations that resist reduction to a single voice.

   (A) plethora

   (B) anathema

   (C) quorum

   (D) enigma

   (E) regalia

Directions: *For questions 8–16, determine the relationship between the two words given in capital letters. Then, from the choices listed A–E, select the one pair that has a relationship most similar to that of the capitalized pair. Circle the letter of that pair.*

---

8. COBWEBS:DISUSE::

   (A) mirage:condensation

   (B) telephone:isolation

   (C) treaty:agreement

   (D) road:industrialization

   (E) rust:paint

9. WANE:DIMINISH::

   (A) curse:praise

   (B) recover:discover

   (C) exhort:exile

   (D) pawn:buy

   (E) inter:bury

10. CLEVER:OBTUSE::

    (A) graceful:maladroit

    (B) trite:obsequious

    (C) rustic:homely

    (D) precocious:sagacious

    (E) abstruse:universal

11. SPEECH:BLURTING::

    (A) wind:gusting

    (B) muscle:releasing

    (C) rain:misting

    (D) vision:sparkling

    (E) hearing:amplifying

12. SOLILOQUY:MONOLOGUE::

    (A) tire:car

    (B) script:play

    (C) solo:duo

    (D) human:mammal

    (E) silence:noise

13. REGALE:AMUSEMENT::

    (A) marry:engagement

    (B) relish:delight

    (C) endorse:approval

    (D) rule:authority

    (E) renege:agreement

14. POIGNANT:BANAL::

    (A) wet:frigid

    (B) frozen:thawed

    (C) fatuous:trite

    (D) moldy:mildewed

    (E) eternal:forever

15. DIPLOMAT:CONCILIATORY::

    (A) demagogue:unemotional

    (B) iconoclast:unconventional

    (C) seer:uninspired

    (D) dogmatist:unassertive

    (E) pundit:uninformed

16. ABROGATE:VOID::

    (A) debilitate:healthy

    (B) derogate:admired

    (C) endorse:valid

    (D) encumber:possible

    (E) endanger:protected

Directions: *For questions 17–27, read each passage and answer the questions that follow. Base your answers only on what is stated or implied in the passage.*

Questions 17–20 are based on the following passage.

France at the end of the Fifteenth Century had fully recovered from the effects of the English wars. The devastated fields were again cultivated; civilization had returned to the districts
(5) from which foreign invasion and civil war had banished it. Observers speak of the country as flourishing throughout its length and breadth; the population was increasing, and commerce showed an unprecedented volume and activity.
(10) The great towns, large and self-governed, were centers of industrial life, and were the chief provincial capitals. Probably no country in Europe possessed such inherent power for resistance or attack. England had hardly yet recovered from
(15) the War of the Roses, and the Tudors did not feel themselves quite secure upon the throne. Italy was richer and more civilized, but so disunited as to be helpless. Neither the Empire nor Spain possessed such a strong or popular monarchy as
(20) France.

The European world generally was passing through a very critical stage in its perpetual transformation. Vast changes in the very constitution of European society had come in the last
(25) two centuries; the materials for further unsuspected revolutions in politics and religion were accumulated on every side. The medieval conception of things was almost dead, and though the institutions that had been generated by that
(30) conception still presented an imposing appearance, they were seriously threatened—all the more seriously because they did not suspect the coming attack. The shock which the Church had received by the so-called Babylonian Captivity,
(35) the Great Schism, and the Great Councils of the Fifteenth Century had shaken the very foundations of its power, both secular and spiritual, though the external traces of the blows had been very nearly smoothed away. The mind of Europe,
(40) no longer satisfied with the old ideas, was feeling after new ideas and new guides and was developing new and unsuspected energies.

Printing had come on the heels of the New Learning. Columbus had found land beyond the
(45) Atlantic waters, and this and other geographical discoveries gave an incalculable impetus to people's thoughts and imaginations. However, it was not only the explorers who were ready to push away from the old landmarks into un-
(50) known waters. Italy was the first country that was affected by these new ideas, which soon passed from Italy to France and were eagerly welcomed there. The effects were far-reaching.

17. The major purpose of this passage is to

    (A) describe the rejuvenation of Europe after the demise of religious institutions

    (B) recognize the role France played in being the primary source of ideas that transformed post-Fifteenth Century Europe

    (C) demonstrate how technological discoveries such as printing and Columbus' geographical discoveries provoked the imagination

    (D) analyze the impact of a popular monarchy upon a country's overall dynamic or static tendencies

    (E) describe the conditions that made France a fertile environment for accepting revolutionary thought

18. The author uses Columbus' discovery of land beyond the Atlantic as an example of

    (A) a technological breakthrough born of the ferment in newly stirred imaginations

    (B) how people were willing to explore unknown waters and go abroad

    (C) a changing reality that inspired people to break the bonds of parochial thought

    (D) an historical event that had immeasurable impact on modern civilizations

    (E) the superior ability of European nations to extend their geographical boundaries

19. The passage implies that

    (A) dissatisfaction with the monarchy prevented people in most European nations from being receptive to new ideas

    (B) France flourished because its population increased during post-war peace and harmony

    (C) France's quick recovery from the English wars had its roots in agricultural rebirth

    (D) most medieval institutions were weakened by their failure to recognize the changing climate of thought and ideas

    (E) France eagerly welcomed new ideas because they originated in Italy

20. The critical stage in the transformation of Fifteenth-Century Europe was characterized by all of the following EXCEPT

    (A) stability in the belief of traditional concepts and values

    (B) a general dissatisfaction with old ideas in the minds of most European countries

    (C) institutions conceived in medieval times being undermined

    (D) an accumulation of new thoughts and ideas in politics and religion

    (E) weakening of the Church's power in matters both secular and spiritual

Questions 21–27 are based on the following passage.

A diligent searcher along any beach or coastline will be sure sometimes to light upon curious and valuable specimens, especially after violent storms may such be sought for with the greatest (5) chance of success, for the agitation of the waters will then have loosened them from their natural beds and dwelling places and cast them on the shore. Very frequently, however, they will be so beaten about and defaced that they will be com- (10) paratively valueless; if enveloped in tangled masses of seaweed, they are likely to be preserved from injury, and such heaps of uprooted marine vegetation will often afford a rich harvest to the young conchologist, who should always (15) carefully examine them. Many of the shells are so minute as scarcely to be seen with the naked eye; therefore, this search can scarcely be properly effected without the assistance of a pocket lens, the cost of which is but trifling. The under- (20) sides of pieces of stranded timber, the bottoms of boats lately returned from a fishing voyage, the fisherman's dredge or net, the cable, and the deep-sea line; all these may prove productive, and should be looked to whenever opportunity (25) offers. Nor should the search for land and fresh-water shells be neglected, for many of these are very curious, as well as beautiful, and no conchological collection is complete without them. For these, the best hunting grounds are the (30) ditch-side and the riverbed, the mossy bank and the hedgerow, amid the twining, serpentine roots of the old thorn and elder trees, the crevices of the garden wall, the undersides of stones, and all sorts of out-of-the-way holes, nooks, and corners, (35) where may be found the Striped Zebra, and other prettily marked snail shells, and many other kinds worthy of a place in a collection.

When live shells—those that have the living fish in them—are obtained, the best plan is to (40) place them in spirits or wine. This at once deprives the inhabitants of life, without injuring the shell, which should then be placed in hot water for a time. The body of the mollusk is thus rendered firm, and may be removed by means (45) of some pointed instrument. Care should be taken to leave no portion of animal matter within, or after a while it will become putrid and give out a stain, which will show through and injure the delicate markings of the shell. The sur- (50) est, most expeditious, and least troublesome

mode of cleansing a shell is to place it in an ant heap for a day or two; the busy little insects will penetrate into its inmost cavities, and remove hence all offending matter. There will be no dif-
(55) ficulty in this respect with the multivalve and bivalve kinds, which are only kept closed by means of a set of muscles which can be tightened or relaxed at the pleasure of the animal within, and become powerless to keep the shell closed
(60) as soon as that is dead. Great care must be taken to preserve unbroken the smaller parts of these shells, such as the hinges or teeth. The beard, also, as it is called, and silky threads, must not be removed, as these have much to do in deter-
(65) mining the particular species.

River and land shells are generally very thin and brittle, and must be carefully handled. Their colors are not usually so brilliant as those of the marine species, but they form links in the
(70) testaceous chain, which are necessary to a proper study and elucidation of conchology.

The most glowing and gorgeous of all shells are those brought from the tropical seas, and, excepting a few rare instances, specimens of most
(75) of these can be obtained at little cost from any dealer, or from friends returning from a voyage. If it is necessary to send those any distance, or to pack them away, the best plan is to wrap them separately in soft paper, place them in a box,
(80) and then pour in sawdust, bran, or fine sand, very dry, until all the open spaces are completely filled up.

21. The primary purpose of the passage is to
   (A) demonstrate that seashell collecting can be interesting and rewarding
   (B) explain the primary difference between ocean shells and river shells
   (C) instruct shell collectors on the basic means of finding, preparing, and transporting shells
   (D) describe the best kinds of seashells to have in a collection
   (E) motivate readers to begin shell collecting as a hobby

22. Who is the primary audience for this passage?
   (A) professional conchologists
   (B) budding conchologists
   (C) recreational beachcombers
   (D) travelers
   (E) novices

23. With which of the following statements would the author most likely DISAGREE?
   (A) A good time to collect shells is after storms.
   (B) Shells were once houses for sea animals.
   (C) A good collection should have all types of shells.
   (D) A good conchologist will handle shells carefully.
   (E) Sometimes collectors forget to search for land shells.

24. With which of the following would the author DISAGREE?
   (A) Nature exists for our enjoyment and use.
   (B) Readers will have access to natural environments.
   (C) Conchology is a worthwhile pursuit.
   (D) Preserving sea life is more important than preserving shells.
   (E) Sea shells can be injured.

25. In comparing ocean shells with river shells, the author of the passage implies that
   (A) river shells are more valuable
   (B) ocean shells are more brittle
   (C) river shells are less beautiful
   (D) river shells should have a higher priority in a collection
   (E) river shells are more dangerous to collect

26. The passage states that the problem with leaving animal matter inside a shell that is part of a collection is that
    (A) the value of the shell decreases
    (B) the shell will discolor
    (C) ants will invade the collection
    (D) animals deserve to be set free
    (E) the shell will soon break

27. In paragraph two, the author advises the reader to leave the beard and teeth of a shell intact because
    (A) they show that shells have features like humans
    (B) they injure the delicate markings of the shell
    (C) they can be used to extract the body of the mollusk
    (D) they attract ants that help clean the shell
    (E) they help identify the species

Directions: For questions 28–38, circle the lettered choice most nearly opposite in meaning to the word given in CAPITAL letters.

28. LACONIC:
    (A) pithy
    (B) verbose
    (C) ostensible
    (D) disorganized
    (E) holographic

29. ACUTE:
    (A) homely
    (B) attractive
    (C) obtuse
    (D) jocund
    (E) discredited

30. TRIBUTE:
    (A) panegyric
    (B) cenotaph
    (C) entropy
    (D) sodality
    (E) censure

31. TANTAMOUNT:
    (A) salubrious
    (B) identical
    (C) paramount
    (D) contradistinctive
    (E) incomparable

32. APROPOS:
    (A) inapposite
    (B) germane
    (C) de rigueur
    (D) ludic
    (E) manic

33. SEDITION:
    (A) credulity
    (B) fealty
    (C) treason
    (D) erosion
    (E) derision

34. VEX:
    (A) abrade
    (B) hex
    (C) mollify
    (D) jinx
    (E) modulate

35. PERSPICACIOUS:
    (A) injudicious
    (B) prescient
    (C) orotund
    (D) juridical
    (E) sagacious

36. COETANEOUS:

   (A) subcutaneous

   (B) execrative

   (C) phlegmatic

   (D) primeval

   (E) contemporary

37. PROTEAN:

   (A) impuissant

   (B) antediluvian

   (C) antidromic

   (D) mutable

   (E) abiding

38. ELUTRIATE:

   (A) extricate

   (B) vitiate

   (C) adulterate

   (D) objurgate

   (E) ensorcell

Quick Answer Guide

Test 2, Section 5: Verbal

1. D	11. A	21. C	31. D
2. B	12. D	22. B	32. A
3. D	13. C	23. C	33. B
4. A	14. B	24. D	34. C
5. B	15. B	25. C	35. A
6. C	16. C	26. B	36. D
7. A	17. E	27. E	37. E
8. C	18. C	28. B	38. C
9. E	19. D	29. C	
10. A	20. A	30. E	

For explanations to these questions, see Day 29.

Day 28

Test 2, Section 6: Analytical

Questions and Answers

Assignment for Today:

Take a sample GRE Analytical Test under actual timed conditions. Allow yourself exactly 30 minutes to complete the 25 questions in this test.

Directions: The following questions are based either on a brief passage or on a number of conditions. For each question, circle the best answer among the choices given. You may wish to draw diagrams to help you answer some of the questions.

Questions 1–6 are based on the following.

Seven coins (chosen from pennies, nickels, dimes, quarters, half-dollars, and silver dollars) are placed on a checkerboard, each on a different square. The coins are placed on the seven squares—let's call the squares A, B, C, D, E, F, and G—such that only two squares that share a side hold different coins. We know that:

Square D shares a side with square G.

Square F shares a side with square A and square B.

Square C shares a side with square A, square B, square D, and square E.

Square G shares sides only with square D and square E.

Square E and square G each hold quarters.

1. Square C cannot have the same coin as any of the following squares EXCEPT

   (A) A
   (B) B
   (C) D
   (D) G
   (E) F

2. Squares E and Q both have quarters. Which of the following squares can also have the same coin (not necessarily quarters)?

   (A) C, D
   (B) C, E
   (C) C, B
   (D) A, B
   (E) D, E

3. All of the following pairs of squares can hold the same coins EXCEPT

   (A) A, D
   (B) B, D
   (C) B, F
   (D) D, F
   (E) E, F

4. Which of the following must be true if squares D and F each hold a dime?

   (A) The coin placed on square E is different from all the other coins.

   (B) The coin placed on square D is different from all the other coins.

   (C) The coin placed on square B is different from all the other coins.

   (D) The coin placed on square A is different from all the other coins.

   (E) The coin placed on square C is different from all the other coins.

5. If the squares hold coins of the most number of different denominations (values), how many different denominations will there be?

   (A) 2

   (B) 3

   (C) 4

   (D) 5

   (E) 6

6. If the squares hold coins of the least number of different denominations (values), and four squares hold quarters, which square will hold a coin different from the other squares?

   (A) C

   (B) F

   (C) A or B

   (D) C or D

   (E) C, E, or F

7. The "Peter Principle" claims that people rise to their level of incompetence. In other words, people who do well at work get promoted until they reach a position for which they are not well suited. They then remain at that position, frustrated with themselves and aggravating others. Less frequently, they are fired. Personnel managers should realize that demotions may be a good solution.

Which of the following is best supported by the information above?

   (A) Most successful employees are in entry-level positions.

   (B) People with excellent job performance should never be promoted.

   (C) Incompetent employees rarely get promoted beyond entry level.

   (D) Demotions may alleviate frustration and aggravation.

   (E) People who move up the corporate ladder are those who know how to play office politics.

8. The Worldwide Wrestling Federation is in the semifinals of its annual tournament, leaving two more rounds for the four top wrestlers: Abe, Bruno, Cateye, and Danger. Abe always beats Bruno. Cateye always beats Abe. Cateye always beats Bruno. Bruno always beats Danger. Danger always beats Cateye. Each match consists of a wrestler going head to head against one other wrestler.

If, in the first match, Danger is disqualified from the tournament, which of the following must be true?

   (A) Bruno has a good chance to reach the finals.

   (B) Abe will meet Bruno in the finals.

   (C) Bruno will finish fourth.

   (D) Abe cannot win the tournament.

   (E) Abe will never again wrestle Bruno.

9. In order to promote world unity, all inhabitants of the Earth should speak one common language in addition to their native language. Even though this would involve a great deal of time and resources, all governments should make it a law for their people to learn the language "Earthese."

The argument above assumes that

(A) Without a common language, people of different countries would be unable to interact with each other.

(B) Earthese is superior to all languages in terms of self-expression and ease of learning.

(C) The small costs of learning the Earthese language is offset by the vast benefits the world will gain from international harmony and understanding.

(D) The reason that undeveloped third-world countries currently exist is that Earthese is not being spoken by all people.

(E) The learning of Earthese by all citizens of the world should be voluntary and not mandated by government officials.

Questions 10–14 are based on the following.
Seven players, Al, Bob, Carl, Don, Ed, Frank, and Gene, are teammates on a basketball team. The coach must choose five players, based on the following, to play at any given time:

Frank must play if Bob is playing.

If Carl plays, Ed also plays.

Al can play only if Ed is not playing.

If a player is not playing, he is sitting on the bench.

10. If Carl is playing, which of the following must be true?
(A) Bob is playing.
(B) Don is playing.
(C) Gene is playing.
(D) Al is not playing.
(E) Frank is not playing.

11. Which of the following two players can be the two sitting on the bench at the same time, NOT playing in the game?
(A) Carl and Gene
(B) Don and Ed
(C) Bob and Carl
(D) Al and Gene
(E) Al and Ed

12. Which of the following changes by the coach is possible?
(A) Al can substitute for Carl.
(B) Bob can substitute for Frank.
(C) Carl can substitute for Ed.
(D) Don can substitute for Gene.
(E) Gene can substitute for Ed.

13. Suppose Gene is not in the game. Who of the following must also be on the bench?
(A) Al
(B) Bob
(C) Carl
(D) Don
(E) Ed

14. If Al is playing, who of the following must be sitting on the bench?
(A) Bob
(B) Carl
(C) Don
(D) Frank
(E) Gene

Questions 15–21 are based on the following.
Checkout lines one and two are the only lines open at the grocery store. At this time, there are eight shoppers—A, B, C, D, E, F, G, and H—who are in line, as follows:

Each line has at least two shoppers.

A is next to E in line.

B is in a different line from D.

D is not the first person in line one.

F is not next to A.

G is first or last in a line.

15. If D is the first shopper in line two, who cannot be in line two?
    (A) A
    (B) B
    (C) C
    (D) E
    (E) F

16. Suppose the only three shoppers in line one are B, C, and H. The shoppers in line two, respectively, can be
    (A) G, A, E, F, and D
    (B) G, E, F, D, and A
    (C) D, A, F, E, and G
    (D) A, E, F, G, and D
    (E) E, A, F, D, and G

17. If F is the second of four shoppers in line one, what is a possible order of the shoppers in line one?
    (A) H F G C
    (B) H F D G
    (C) A F C H
    (D) D F B H
    (E) H F A B

18. The shoppers in line one and line two can be
    (A) Line one: A, E, D, G
        Line two: B, F, C, H
    (B) Line one: G, F, A, E
        Line two: D, B, C, H
    (C) Line one: B, F, C
        Line two: E, A, H, G, D
    (D) Line one: C, F, E, H
        Line two: A, B, G, D
    (E) Line one: D, A, G
        Line two: H, F, E, B, C

19. If B, C, H, and G are the only shoppers in line one and E is the first shopper in line two, it must also be true that
    (A) A is the last person in line two.
    (B) F is the last person in line two.
    (C) F is the third person in line two.
    (D) A is the third person in line two.
    (E) D is the second person in line two.

20. Which of the following must be true if A, F, G, and H are included in line one?
    (A) Line two has exactly three shoppers.
    (B) Line one has exactly six shoppers.
    (C) Shopper B is in line one.
    (D) Shopper D is in line two.
    (E) Shopper C is first in line two.

21. If in line two, H and E are the first and second shoppers, respectively, and D is the last of five shoppers, it must also be true that
    (A) B is in line two.
    (B) C is in line two.
    (C) F is first in line one.
    (D) G is last in line one.
    (E) A is in line one.

22. Mr. Smackle, the CEO of a huge retail company, personally chooses the locations for his new stores by flying in a plane over the outskirts of a city to select the right property. Because all of Mr. Smackle's chosen locations have quickly become new hubs of commercial development, he obviously has an innate gift for predicting where new growth will occur.

    Which of the following, if true, would most seriously weaken the claim that Mr. Smackle has an innate gift to predict areas of new growth?

    (A) Mr. Smackle was a poor student, excelling only in athletics.

    (B) Commercial developers tend to follow Mr. Smackle's lead.

    (C) Innate gifts often persist into old age.

    (D) Location is the most important factor for success in retail business.

    (E) Mr. Smackle is highly successful in the stock market.

23. Malaria, a disease typically spread by mosquitoes, has been nonexistent in the United States since the 1950s; however, several cases have recently emerged in Texas, and disease-carrying mosquitoes have been suspected. These new cases could be due to the lack of resources to manage stagnant bodies of water, places where mosquitoes breed. To stop malaria from being a significant problem, Texas authorities need to reduce mosquito populations.

    Which of the following statements, if true, most weakens the conclusion of the passage above?

    (A) The life expectancy for a mosquito is only two weeks.

    (B) Dengue fever is also carried by mosquitoes and is more serious than malaria.

    (C) Keeping people indoors during evening hours has no effect on the incidence of malaria.

    (D) Humans can easily transmit malaria to other humans.

    (E) Texas has maintained the best malaria task force in the nation.

24. Research in psychophysiology has shown that when people are afraid, their heart rate increases and their skin conductance level increases. When people are angry, their heart rate increases, but their skin conductance level decreases.

    After being exposed to a film clip on euthanasia, an individual showed a decrease in skin conductance level. The researchers concluded this subject got angry.

    Which of the following statements, if true, weakens the conclusion of the researchers?

    (A) Emotions other than anger can induce a decrease in skin conductance level.

    (B) Euthanasia is a highly controversial topic that would likely evoke an emotional response in most subjects.

    (C) Psychophysiology researchers can pinpoint emotions by measuring physiological responses.

    (D) Surprise and fear are too similar to be differentiated accurately.

    (E) Angry people always show a decrease in skin conductance level.

25. Studies have shown that university graduates just beginning a new career get most of their training on the job and not from their college education. Therefore, it is not necessary for people to make such a large investment of both time and money on higher education, but instead, they should go directly into the job market after high school.

    Which of the following statements, if true, is a valid objection to the conclusion drawn above?

    (A) A university education does not provide the essential training a person needs in order to succeed in the job market.

    (B) College life provides many networking opportunities to meet people who may be able to enrich a graduate's social life.

    (C) Community colleges offer courses that are more practical than state and private institutions, which aim to provide a broader, liberal arts education.

    (D) A college education is an important phase in a young adult's maturation process since it provides the opportunity to interact with a wide variety of people in different situations.

    (E) Job recruiters seek candidates who can think critically and consider a broader perspective of different situations, qualities that are enhanced by a college education.

Quick Answer Guide

Test 2, Section 6: Analytical

1. E	8. D	15. B	22. B
2. D	9. C	16. A	23. D
3. C	10. C	17. B	24. A
4. E	11. D	18. A	25. E
5. E	12. D	19. B	
6. D	13. A	20. B	
7. D	14. B	21. B	

For explanations to these questions, see Day 29.

Day 29

Test 2, Section 5: Verbal, and Section 6: Analytical
Explanations and Strategies

Assignment for Today:

Review the explanations for the Verbal Test you took on Day 27 and the Analytical Test you took on Day 28.

SECTION 5: VERBAL

1. Correct choice (D) fulfill

Reading the sentence, you should understand that Clarence is a hard worker and ready to get a promotion. This means he must have followed the requirements of his current job. With this in mind, you can look for a positive word. The two positive words are *fulfill* and *amplify*. *Fulfill* sounds right; *amplify* doesn't, since it means to enlarge, to heighten, to increase. One would not increase the requirements for a job in order to get a promotion.

Working hard to *fulfill* the requirements of his current position, Clarence became the next person in line for a promotion.

2. Correct choice (B) varied

This sentence tells us that the public transportation system in our city is "extensive and versatile," which indicates that the system is large and can do lots of different things. "Trains and cable cars. . . many electric and diesel buses" tells us that there are a lot of choices. All these elements together indicate that the

network offers various, or *varied*, means of travel. Trying each of the choices in the sentence may have helped you find the correct choice.

Our city's extensive and versatile public transit network offers the nation's most *varied* means of travel, from trains and cable cars to the many electric and diesel buses.

3. Correct choice (D) accused..exonerated

The sentence should give you adequate clues to come up with your own words to fill in the blanks. You probably won't think of the exact words given in the choices, but you can find synonyms. The context indicates that an investigation is under way, and the murderer is merely a suspected murderer, not a convicted one. *Accused* works well. Not finding a DNA match should make the accusation less believable, so *exonerated*, which means freed from blame, works well.

When the DNA sample from the *accused* murderer did not match the sample from the murder weapon, the suspect was *exonerated* in the public's mind.

4. Correct choice (A) exacerbated.. relentless

From the clues in the sentence, you should be able to guess the kinds of words that will adequately fill the blanks. The verb in the first blank should mean something like "made worse." *Exacerbated* is the right word here. The second blank should describe tasks of caring for a new baby. Actually, many words might work here—depending what you think of caring for babies—but the word *relentless* works with the rest of the sentence. *Relentless* means neverending, which certainly would add stress to a marriage.

When the Anderson's infant cried all night, it severely *exacerbated* the young couple's volatile relationship; furthermore, the *relentless* task of caring for a new baby required more energy than the new parents had to give.

5. Correct choice (B) eclectic

This is a tough one, because the clues are located after the blank. There are no obvious flags, so perhaps the best way to work this question is to plug in choices and eliminate the ones that don't fit.

We know that the dress preference has switched to now include a wide range of clothing. And *eclectic* means "selecting or borrowing from a wide variety." If you know the definition of *eclectic*, you'll get it right. If you don't recognize the word, don't panic. See if you can eliminate at least some of the other choices.

Dress styles among female White House staff have abruptly switched from Kappa Gamma Kappa to *eclectic*, including everything from long, flowing skirts and suede vests to threadbare jeans.

6. Correct choice (C) purview..rescind

The best way to find the right choice is to read the choices and eliminate those that don't make sense. The only stem pair that works together and with the logic of the sentence is (C). *Purview* means range of authority. To *rescind* means to make something invalid.

It was within the *purview* of the queen to *rescind* her husband's unpopular decree.

7. Correct choice (A) plethora

This is a vocabulary-based question. The context of the sentence tells us that we are looking for a word meaning multitude or collection: "the multitude of possible interpretations that resist reduction to a single voice." The correct choice is (A), *plethora*, which means an excess or overabundance.

These are tough words, some of which you might not have known. But had you known the meanings of some (*quorum*, for example, is the necessary number for a meeting to take place), you could have eliminated several choices and taken a better guess.

The widespread fascination with the novel is generated by the *plethora* of possible interpretations that resist reduction to a single voice.

8. Correct choice (C) treaty:agreement

cobweb—a web spun by a spider.
disuse—not being used.

Cobwebs are a sign of disuse.

Is a *treaty* a sign of *agreement*? Yes. A *treaty* is a signed document indicating that some *agreement* between parties has been reached.

9. Correct choice (E) inter:bury

wane—to decrease or diminish.
diminish—to decrease.

To *wane* means the same thing as to *diminish*.

Does to *inter* mean the same thing as to *bury*? Yes. Therefore, *wane* relates to *diminish* in the same way that *inter* relates to *bury*.

10. Correct choice (A) graceful:maladroit

clever—smart and witty.
obtuse—slow, dull, and stupid.

Clever is nearly the opposite of *obtuse*.

The stem words, CLEVER:OBTUSE, should tell you that the correct choice will be a pair of opposites. Of course, you had to know that *obtuse* means dull or stupid. And the problem here is also knowing the definition of the words in the choices. Most of them were toughies.

Is *graceful* nearly the opposite of *maladroit*? You probably know what *graceful* means: pleasing or attractive in movement. But what does *maladroit* mean? *Maladroit* means lacking adroitness, or awkward. (You might have gotten a clue from the prefix, *mal-*, which means bad or poorly.) So *graceful* and *maladroit* are near opposites in the same way that *clever* and *obtuse* are near opposites.

11. Correct choice (A) wind:gusting

speech—manner or act of speaking.
blurting—speaking suddenly.

Blurting is when *speech* erupts suddenly.

Is *gusting* when *wind* erupts suddenly? Yes. Therefore, *speech* is to *blurt* as *wind* is to *gust*.

12. Correct choice (D) human:mammal

soliloquy—a speech by a person talking to himself/herself, often used to disclose innermost thoughts.
monologue—a speech or discourse uttered by a single speaker.

A *soliloquy* is a special kind of *monologue*.

Is a *human* a special kind of *mammal*? Yes.

13. Correct choice (C) endorse:approval

regale—to give amusement to, to delight.
amusement—delight, pleasure, entertainment.

To *regale* someone is to give them *amusement*.

Does to *endorse* someone give them *approval*? To *endorse* a person or a project means to give one's *approval*, to support that project.

14. Correct choice (B) frozen:thawed

poignant—extremely touching, deeply affecting the feelings.
banal—trite, common or ordinary.

Poignant means the opposite of *banal*.

Does *frozen* mean the opposite of *thawed*? Yes. *Thawed* means melted.

15. Correct choice (B) iconoclast:unconventional

diplomat—a person who makes relationships better.
conciliatory—making things more friendly, less severe.

A diplomat is conciliatory.

Is an *iconoclast unconventional*? Yes. An *iconoclast* is someone who fights against tradition. Therefore, *diplomat* is to *conciliatory* as *iconoclast* is to *unconventional*.

16. Correct choice (C) endorse:valid

abrogate—to make something void.
void—without force or value.

To *abrogate* is to make something *void*, the opposite of making something healthy or stronger.

Is to *endorse* to make something *valid*? Yes. For example, when you endorse a check, you make it valid.

17. Correct choice (E)

Each paragraph must contribute to the main idea. So, for each paragraph, ask, "What's your point?"

Here, the first paragraph says, "France was flourishing like no other country." The second paragraph says, "Old European ideas were changing." The third paragraph says, "All sorts of people welcomed new, expansive ideas, especially the French."

The three points taken together suggest that France was a flourishing, united, strong, and fertile nation where people were willing to accept new ideas and put them into practice.

That's more or less what choice (E) says.

18. Correct choice (C)

People had no idea there was land beyond the Atlantic. Columbus' discovery changed reality. You don't need to know that, though.

The passage specifically states "this and other geographical discoveries gave an incalculable impetus to people's thoughts and imaginations." This means it inspired people to think beyond usual limits. That's choice (C).

Sometimes you can locate the exact information in the passage.

19. Correct choice (D)

The passage specifically states "the institutions. . . were seriously threatened. . .because they did not suspect the coming attack [of unsuspected revolutions in religion and politics]."

Which means people were inspired to think beyond usual limits. That's choice (D).

Try to locate the exact information in the passage.

20. Correct choice (A)

The passage specifically states that "the mind of Europe was no longer satisfied with the old ideas," and was "feeling after new ones."

21. Correct choice (C)

This passage is written as an instructive passage for those who are at least a little interested in shell collecting. The various parts of the passage explain how to find, prepare, and transport shells.

22. Correct choice (B)

This passage is addressed to those already interested in shell collecting, but the passage is too basic for professional conchologists—they already know this information. However, the budding conchologist would probably be eager to learn some of the tricks of the trade.

23. Correct choice (C)

The author implies at the end of the first paragraph that certain kinds of shells are better for a shell collection. Some shells—drab shells, broken shells, common shells—the author would likely banish from a collection.

24. Correct choice (D)

The only statement that the author would disagree with is choice (D)—preserving sea life is more important than preserving shells. In fact, the author seems not to care at all about the sea creatures who have made the shells their homes. The passage provides the reader with a quick way to dispose of the animals so the shell can be collected and preserved.

25. Correct choice (C)

Paragraph three makes the point that river and land shells are usually less brilliant than shells from the ocean. We can safely assume that the author uses brilliance as a measure of beauty.

26. Correct choice (B)

The middle of paragraph two says that dead animal matter left inside the shell will stain the shell. "Get those creatures out!" the author says, in so many words.

27. Correct choice (E)

At the end of paragraph two, the author warns the reader not to remove the beard and teeth "as these have much to do in determining the particular species."

28. Correct choice (B) verbose

Laconic means succinct, concise.
Verbose means wordy. Is *verbose* the opposite of *laconic*? Yes—*verbose* means using a lot of words whereas *laconic* means using a few well-chosen words.

29. Correct choice (C) obtuse

Acute means sharp, severe.
Obtuse means blunt, not sharp. Is *obtuse* the opposite of *acute*? Yes, blunt is the opposite of sharp.

30. Correct choice (E) censure

Tribute means praise.
Censure means criticism. Is *censure* the opposite of *tribute*? Yes, criticism is the opposite of praise.

31. Correct choice (D) contradistinctive

Tantamount means same, uniform.
Contradistinctive means different by contrast. Is *contradistinctive* the opposite of *tantamount*? Yes.

32. Correct choice (A) inapposite

Apropos means appropriate.
Inapposite means not relevant. Is *inapposite* the opposite of *apropos*? Yes.

33. Correct choice (B) fealty

Sedition means resistance to lawful authority.
Fealty means fidelity, allegiance. Is *fealty* the opposite of *sedition*? Yes—*sedition* is lack of allegiance or *fealty*.

34. Correct choice (C) mollify

Vex means bother.
Mollify means appease. Is *mollify* the opposite of *vex*? Yes, to appease is the opposite of to bother.

35. Correct choice (A) injudicious

Perspicacious means shrewd.
Injudicious means unwise. Is *injudicious* the opposite of *perspicacious*? Yes, unwise is not shrewd or wise.

36. Correct choice (D) primeval

Coetaneous means contemporary.
Primeval means ancient, primitive. Is *primeval* the opposite of *coetaneous*? Yes, ancient is the opposite of contemporary.

37. Correct choice (E) abiding

Protean means changeable, variable.
Abiding means unchanging. Is *abiding* the opposite of *protean*? Yes, one means not changing, the other changing.

38. Correct choice (C) adulterate

Elutriate means to purify by washing.
Adulterate means to corrupt or make impure. Is *adulterate* the opposite of *elutriate*? Yes, it's a case of purity versus impurity.

SECTION 6: ANALYTICAL

Questions 1–6:
From the facts, we can draw a rough diagram:

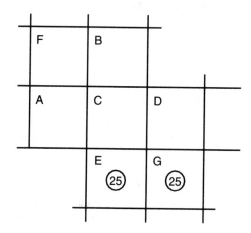

1. Correct choice (E)

Since C shares sides with A, B, D, and E, its coin must be different from the coins in those four other squares. However, C's coin does not have to be different from F's.

2. Correct choice (D)

Nothing in the chart above prevents A and B from having the same coin.

3. Correct choice (C)

B and F share a side and cannot have the same coin.

4. Correct choice (E)

Let's add the new information to the diagram:

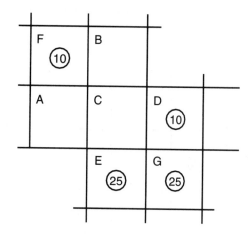

Since C shares sides with A, B, D, and E, C's coin must be different from those in each of those other squares. If D and F each have the same coin (a dime), then F must also be different from C. Thus, C's coin is different from that of every other square.

5. Correct choice (E)

Let's put in as many different types of coins as possible. For example:

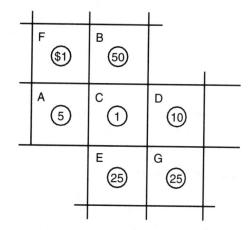

Except for the two quarters, one of each of the different coins can be placed on the squares, for a total of six different kinds of coins.

6. Correct choice (D)

Start with quarters. A and B must also hold quarters to bring the number of squares with quarters up to 4. So add the new information to the diagram:

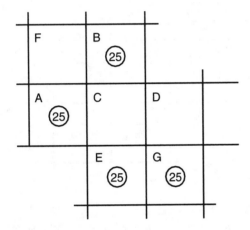

C and F, or D and F, can each hold the same coin (let's say dimes), which leaves either square D or square C to hold a third type of coin, different from all the other squares.

7. Correct choice (D)

This question asks you to decide which choice is most supported by the passage. On reading each choice, you'll find that choices (B) and (D) have some support. However, the support for (B) is far too broad; in contrast, the evidence for (D) is clear and direct. The paragraph states that because people rise to their level of incompetence, the result is frustration and aggravation. This implies that demotions to positions of people's level of skill may well alleviate frustration and aggravation.

8. Correct choice (D)

This question asks you to find a response that must be true, not just one that may be possible. The passage gives you all the clues you need to sketch

out the tournament and see who will win. Then you should go through the choices and eliminate those choices that do not have to be true. When you sketch out the tournament, you'll find there are only three possible matches: A versus B; A versus C; and B versus C. Because Cateye always beats both Abe and Bruno, Cateye must win. Thus Abe cannot win the tournament.

9. Correct choice (C)

This justifies the teaching of Earthese by assuming that Earthese will result in international harmony and understanding, and that these elements of "world unity" vastly outweigh the short-term costs of time and resources involved with learning another language.

Questions 10–14:
From the facts, we have:

> if B, then F
> if C, then E
> if A, then ~~E~~

10. Correct choice (D)

If we know that C is playing, then from the rules E must also be playing. Thus, we know that A cannot be playing because if A is playing, then E must not be playing.

11. Correct choice (D)

For this choice, B is playing, so F is also playing. C is playing, so E is also playing. Since A is not playing, E can be playing.

12. Correct choice (D)

Since none of the rules involve either D or G, the coach can always substitute D for G if G is in the game and D is not.

13. Correct choice (A)

If G is not in the game, then there must only be one more player who cannot be playing. That player must be A because E cannot play if A is playing, but E must play since C is playing (because only one player other than G will sit out).

14. Correct choice (B)

When A is in the game, E cannot be playing in the game. However, if C is in the game, E must also be playing in the game. Thus, if A is in the game, C cannot be in the game.

Questions 15–21:
From the facts,

1. ~~D~~ __ __ B/D

2. __ __ __ D/B

AE or EA

~~FA~~, ~~AF~~

G is first or last

15. Correct choice (B)

Since D is in line 2, the fact which states that B and D cannot be in the same line implies that B must be in line 1.

16. Correct choice (A)

In this question, we have
Line 1: B, C, H
Thus, line 2 must have A, D, E, F, and G. In this choice, G is first in line, A and E are adjacent to each other, and A and F are not adjacent to each other.

17. Correct choice (B)

Solve this question by eliminating answer choices. Eliminate (D) because D can't be first in line. Eliminate (C) and (E) because F and A cannot be next to each other. Eliminate (A) because G must be first or last. That leaves (B) as the correct answer.

18. Correct choice (A)

Take a fact and apply it to the choices, knocking out those choices that violate that fact. Then take the next fact, do the same and so on until the one correct choice remains.

For this choice, A and E are adjacent to each other in the same line; G is last in line 1; B and D are not in the same line; D is not first in line; F and A are not in the same line; and there are at least two shoppers in each line.

19. Correct choice (B)

In this question, we know
Line 1: B, C, H, G
This means line 2 has A, E, F, and D. Since line 2 begins with E, A must be second in line because A must be adjacent to E. Since F cannot be adjacent to A, F cannot be third in line. Thus, F must be last in line.

20. Correct choice (B)

In this question, we know
Line 1: A, F, G, H ..
Since A is in line 1, E must also be in line 1. In addition, B and D cannot both be in line 2. This means that exactly one of the two must be in line 1. Thus, there have to be at least six shoppers in line 1. Since there are only eight shoppers total, and at least two of them must be in line 2, there can be at most six shoppers in line 1. Thus, there are exactly six shoppers in line 1.

21. Correct choice (B)

In this question, we know
Line 2: E A _ _ D
Since E is first in line 2, A must be second in line 2 since they must be adjacent to each other in the same line. F cannot be third in line 2 because F and A cannot be adjacent to each other in the same line. G cannot be third in line 2 because G must either be first in a line or last in a line. B cannot be in line 2 because B and D cannot be in the same line. Thus, the only possible shopper to be third in line 2 is C.

22. Correct choice (B)

Your task here is to find a statement that suggests Mr. Smackle's gift may not be such a personal talent after all. The best way to answer this question about Mr. Smackle's innate gift is to read each answer and decide if it weakens the claim for this remarkable ability. By doing this, you should see that only choice (B) works: If other developers follow Smackle's lead, then he is not *predicting* the future; he is *determining* the future. Even if Smackle picked a lousy location, other developers would likely follow, causing new growth.

23. Correct choice (D)

Your task here is to find a statement that weakens the idea in the last sentence of the paragraph: Texas officials need to reduce the number of mosquitoes in order to end problems with malaria. The most efficient way to do this is to read each choice and eliminate those that do not weaken this argument. While a few choices have some merit, the most powerful rebuttal to the conclusion is choice (D): humans can transmit malaria to each other. If this is true, then malaria may continue to be a problem, regardless of a reduced level of mosquitoes.

24. Correct choice (A)

The logical problem with the researchers' conclusion is that many causes may produce a similar result. In this case, other emotions—such as happiness or disgust—might cause a decrease in skin conductance level. Therefore, choice (A) seriously challenges the researchers' conclusion. Anger is not the only emotion that decreases skin conductance level. The subject could have been happy.

25. Correct choice (E)

The passage takes a very practical point of view of getting a university education by suggesting that none of the skills learned in college directly relate to the job itself. The argument does not take into account that often, the skills and experiences encountered during the college years are intangible but extremely valuable. Job recruiters realize this and do not discount the value of higher education, especially when considering potential personnel.

Day 30

Final Review

Assignment for Today:

Review the strategies in Days 1–8. Look over the sample tests and explanations.

If you have followed this 30-Day Program, you should now be in great shape to take the GRE. By now you have taken two complete tests—12 sections in all—and you have gone over the questions and explanations. Remember that doing well on the GRE requires not only good verbal, math, and analytical skills, but also "test smarts."

In this book, you have been introduced to lots of strategies and shortcuts designed to save you time and make you test-smart. We recommend that you use whatever time you have left before your test to go back and review the test-taking, verbal, math, and analytical strategies. Then you should look over the sample tests and explanations and make sure you understand how to tackle each question type.

GOOD LUCK!